HARROW

— SNAKE DOCTOR —

COUNTY

™

HARROW

◆ SNAKE DOCTOR ◆

COUNTY

Script
CULLEN BUNN

Art, chapter 1
CARLA SPEED McNEIL

Colors, chapter 1
JENN MANLEY LEE

Art, chapters 2–3
TYLER CROOK

Art and letters, chapter 4
HANNAH CHRISTENSON

Cover art, chapter breaks, and letters
TYLER CROOK

DARK HORSE BOOKS

President and Publisher
MIKE RICHARDSON

Editor
DANIEL CHABON

Assistant Editor
CARDNER CLARK

Designer
KEITH WOOD

Digital Art Technician
CHRISTIANNE GOUDREAU

NEIL HANKERSON Executive Vice President · TOM WEDDLE Chief Financial Officer · RANDY STRADLEY Vice President of Publishing
MICHAEL MARTENS Vice President of Book Trade Sales · MATT PARKINSON Vice President of Marketing · DAVID SCROGGY Vice President
of Product Development · DALE LAFOUNTAIN Vice President of Information Technology · CARA NIECE Vice President of Production and Scheduling
NICK McWHORTER Vice President of Media Licensing · KEN LIZZI General Counsel · DAVE MARSHALL Editor in Chief · DAVEY ESTRADA
Editorial Director · SCOTT ALLIE Executive Senior Editor · CHRIS WARNER Senior Books Editor · CARY GRAZZINI Director of Specialty Projects
LIA RIBACCHI Art Director · VANESSA TODD Director of Print Purchasing · MATT DRYER Director of Digital Art and Prepress · MARK BERNARDI
Director of Digital Publishing · SARAH ROBERTSON Director of Product Sales · MICHAEL GOMBOS Director of International Publishing and Licensing

Published by Dark Horse Books
A division of Dark Horse Comics, Inc.
10956 SE Main Street
Milwaukie, OR 97222

First edition: September 2016
ISBN 978-1-50670-071-7

International Licensing: (503) 905-2377 · Comic Shop Locator Service: (888) 266-4226

Harrow County Volume 3: Snake Doctor

This volume collects *Harrow County* #9–#12.

10 9 8 7 6 5 4 3
Printed in China

DarkHorse.com

Library of Congress Cataloging-in-Publication Data

Names: Bunn, Cullen, author. | McNeil, Carla Speed, illustrator. | Lee, Jenn Manley, illustrator. |
Crook, Tyler, illustrator. | Christenson, Hannah, illustrator.
Title: Harrow County. Volume 3, Snake doctor / script, Cullen Bunn ; art,
chapter 1, Carla Speed McNeil ; colors, chapter 1, Jenn Manley Lee ; art,
chapters 2-3, Tyler Crook ; art, chapter 4, Hannah Christenson ; letters,
Tyler Crook ; cover art and chapter breaks by Tyler Crook.
Other titles: Snake doctor
Description: First edition. | Milwaukie, OR : Dark Horse Books, 2016. | "This volume collects
issues #9-#12 of the southern-gothic fairy tale Harrow County."
Identifiers: LCCN 2016013548 | ISBN 9781506700717 (paperback)
Subjects: LCSH: Witches--Comic books, strips, etc. | Southern States--Comic books, strips, etc. |
Horror--comic books, strips, etc. | BISAC: COMICS & GRAPHIC NOVELS / Horror.
Classification: LCC PN6727.B845 H37 2016 | DDC 741.5/973--dc23
LC record available at https://lccn.loc.gov/2016013548

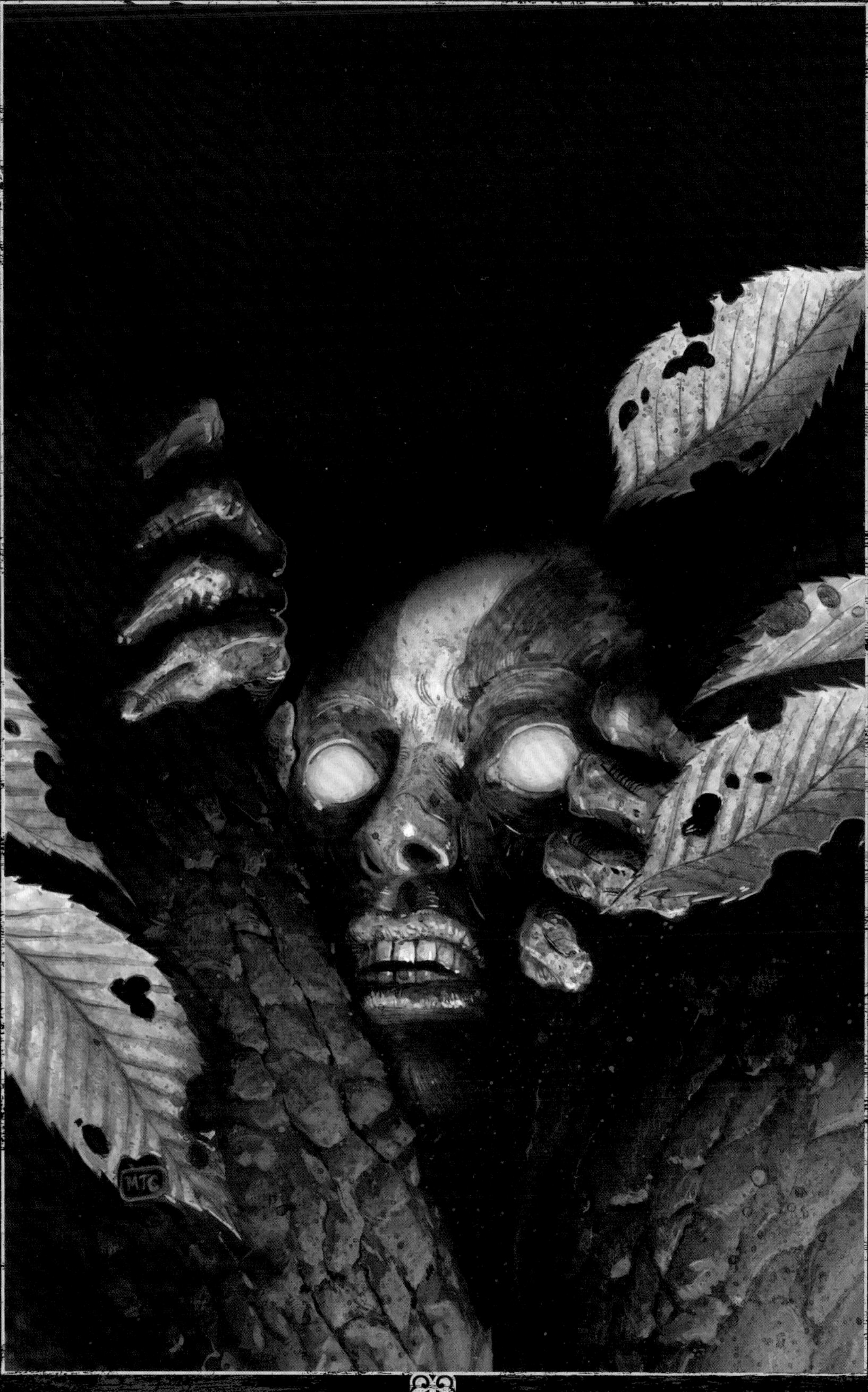

ONE

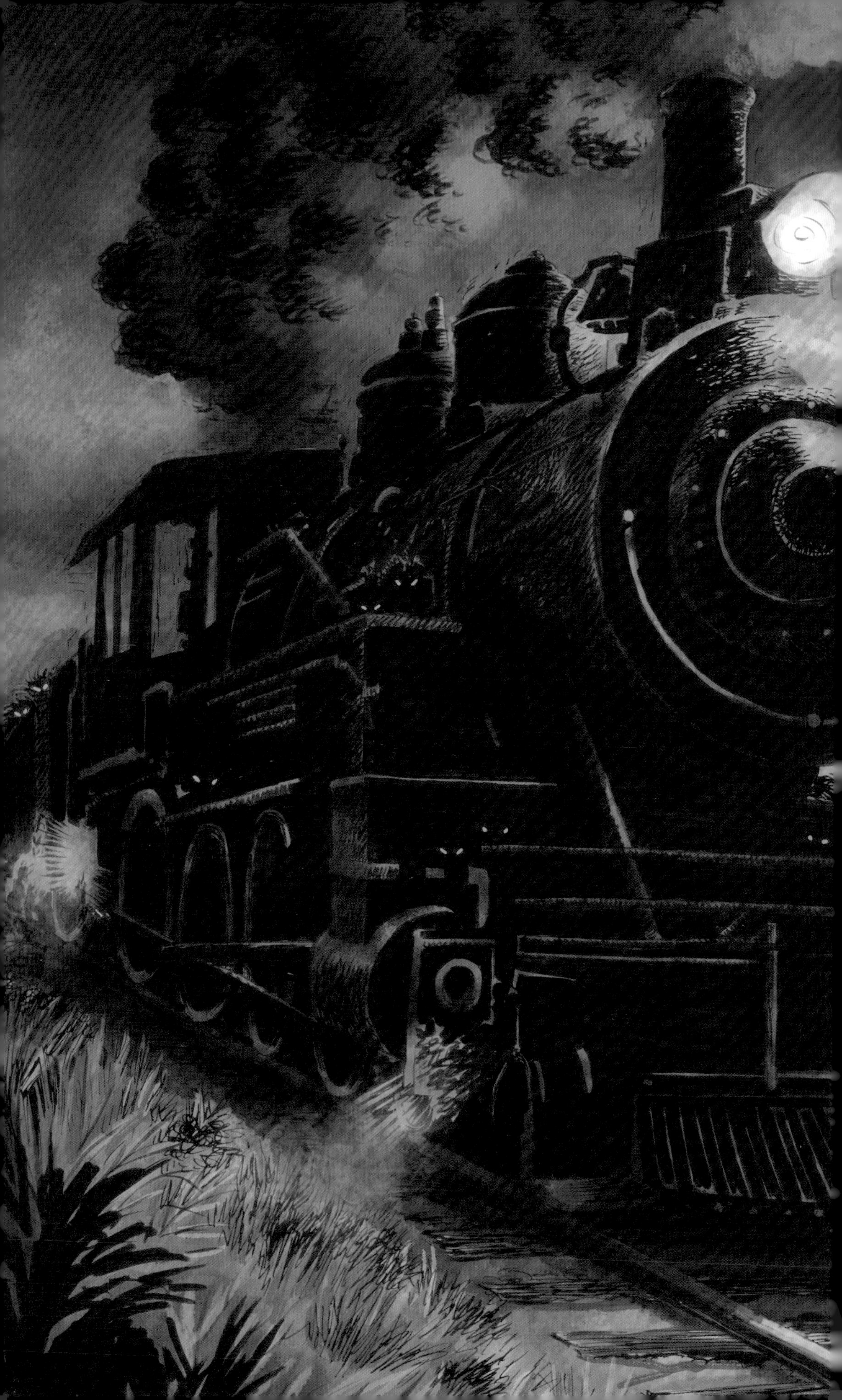

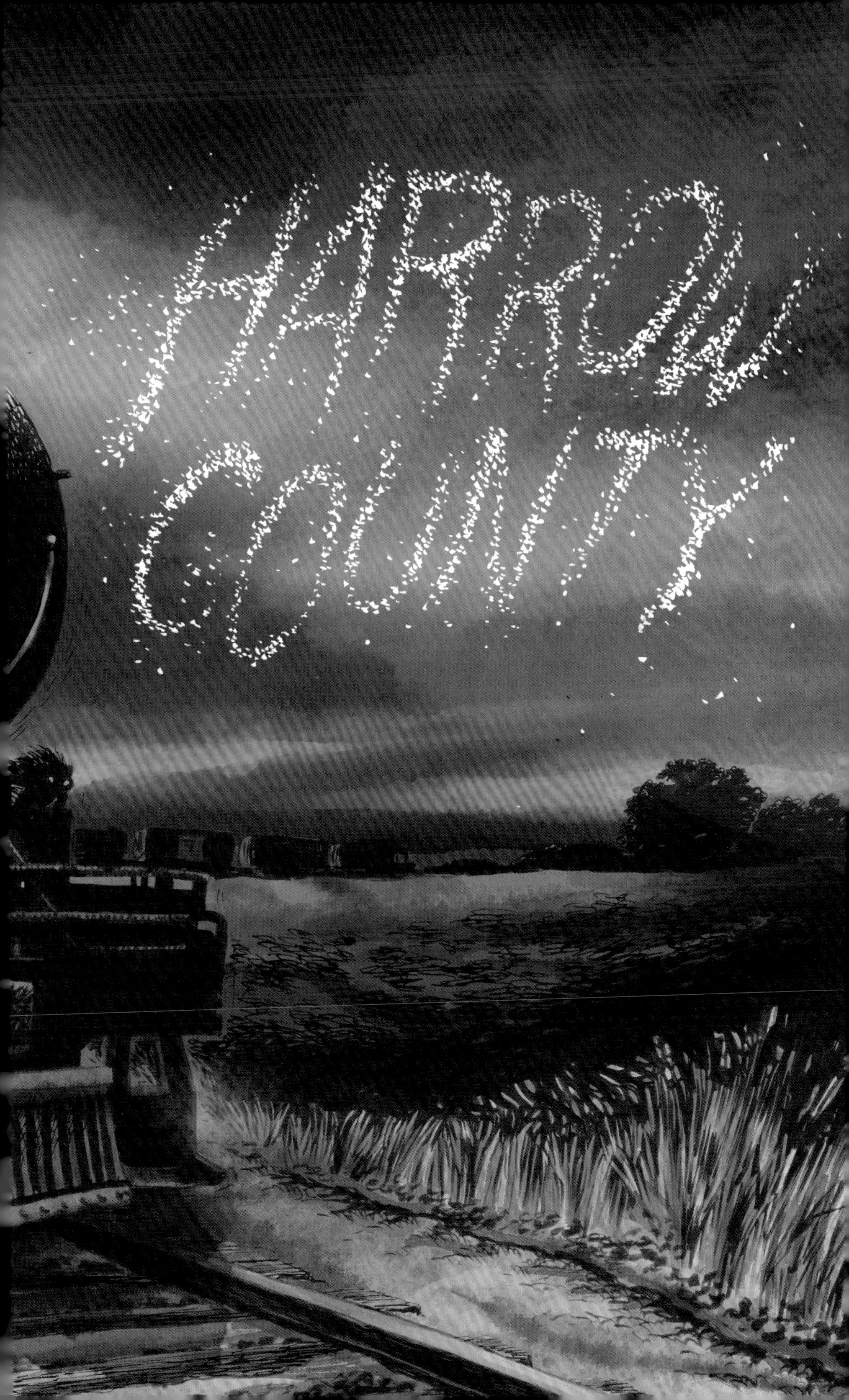
HARROW
COUNTY

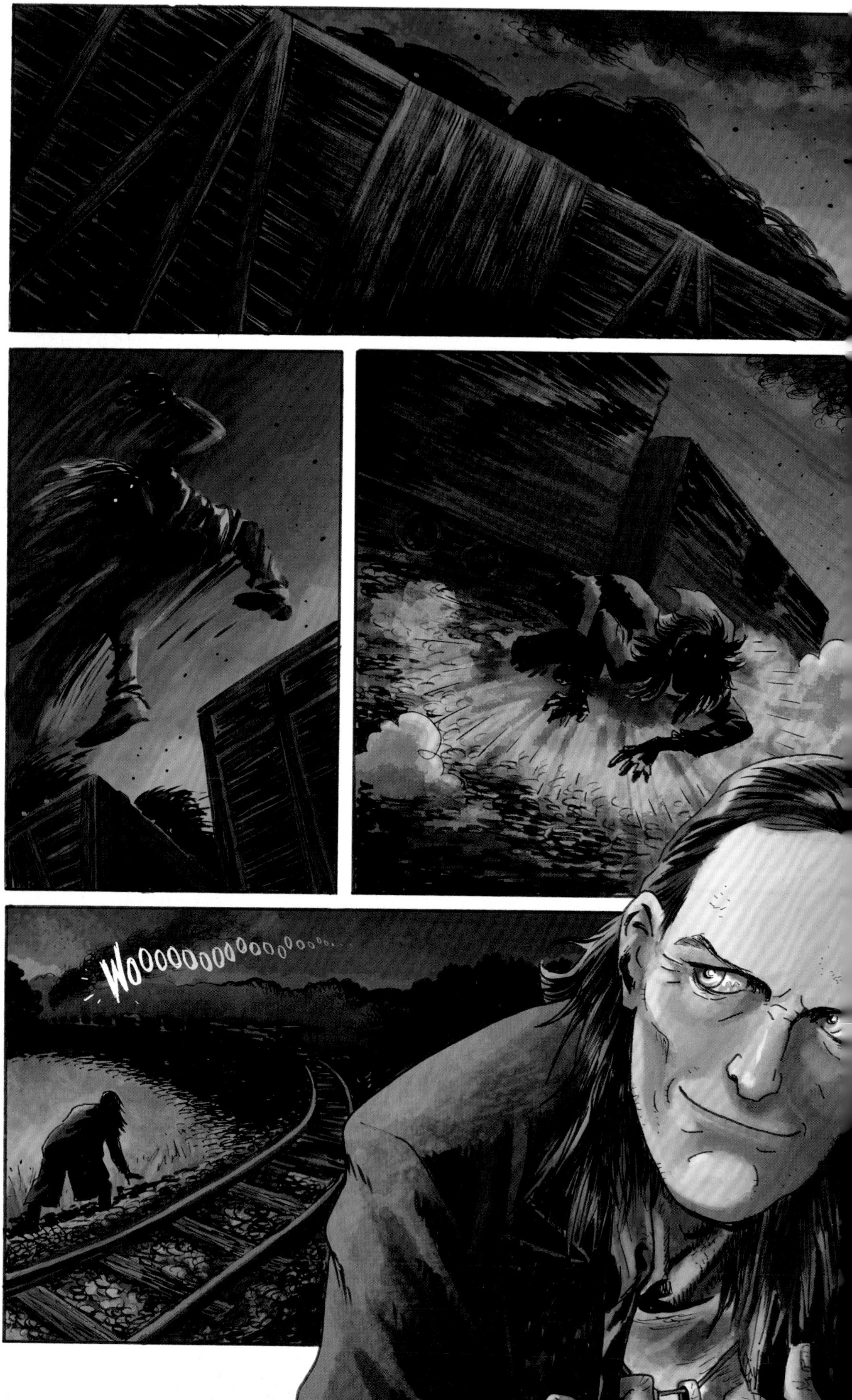
WOOOOOOOOOOOOOOOOO...

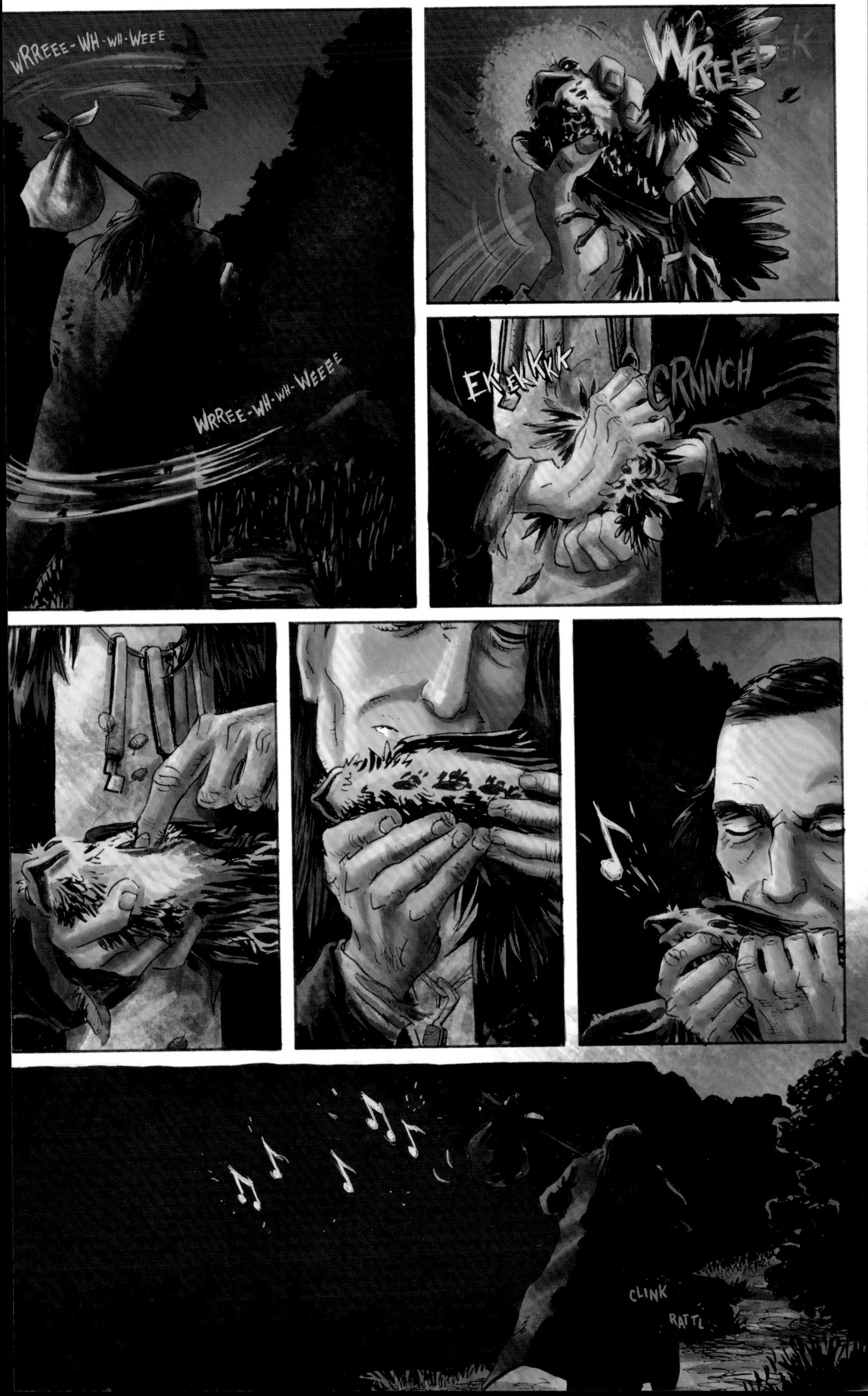

WRREEE-WH-WH-WEEE
WRREE-WH-WH-WEEEE
WREEEEK
EKEKKKK
CRNNCH
CLINK
RATTL

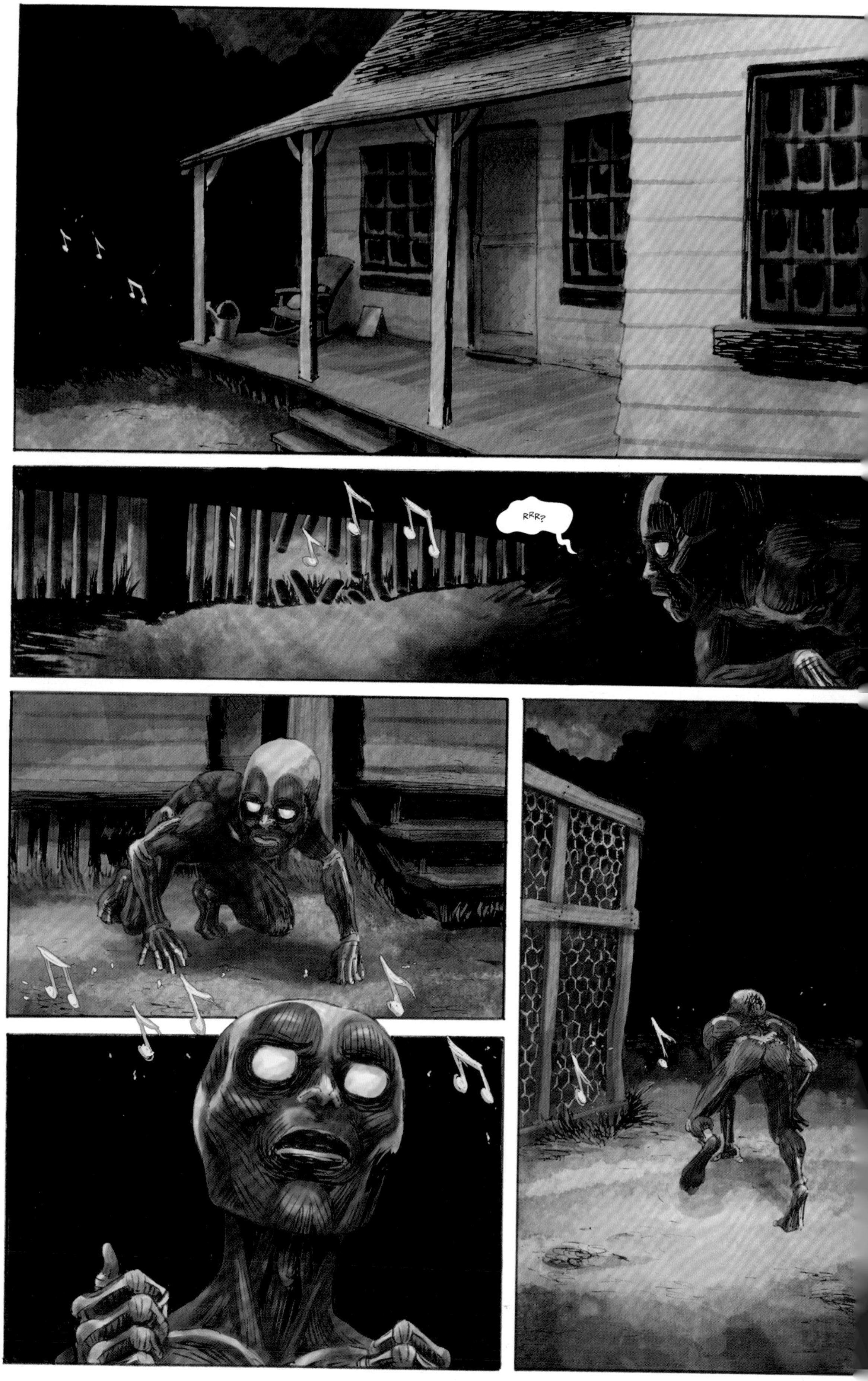
RRR?

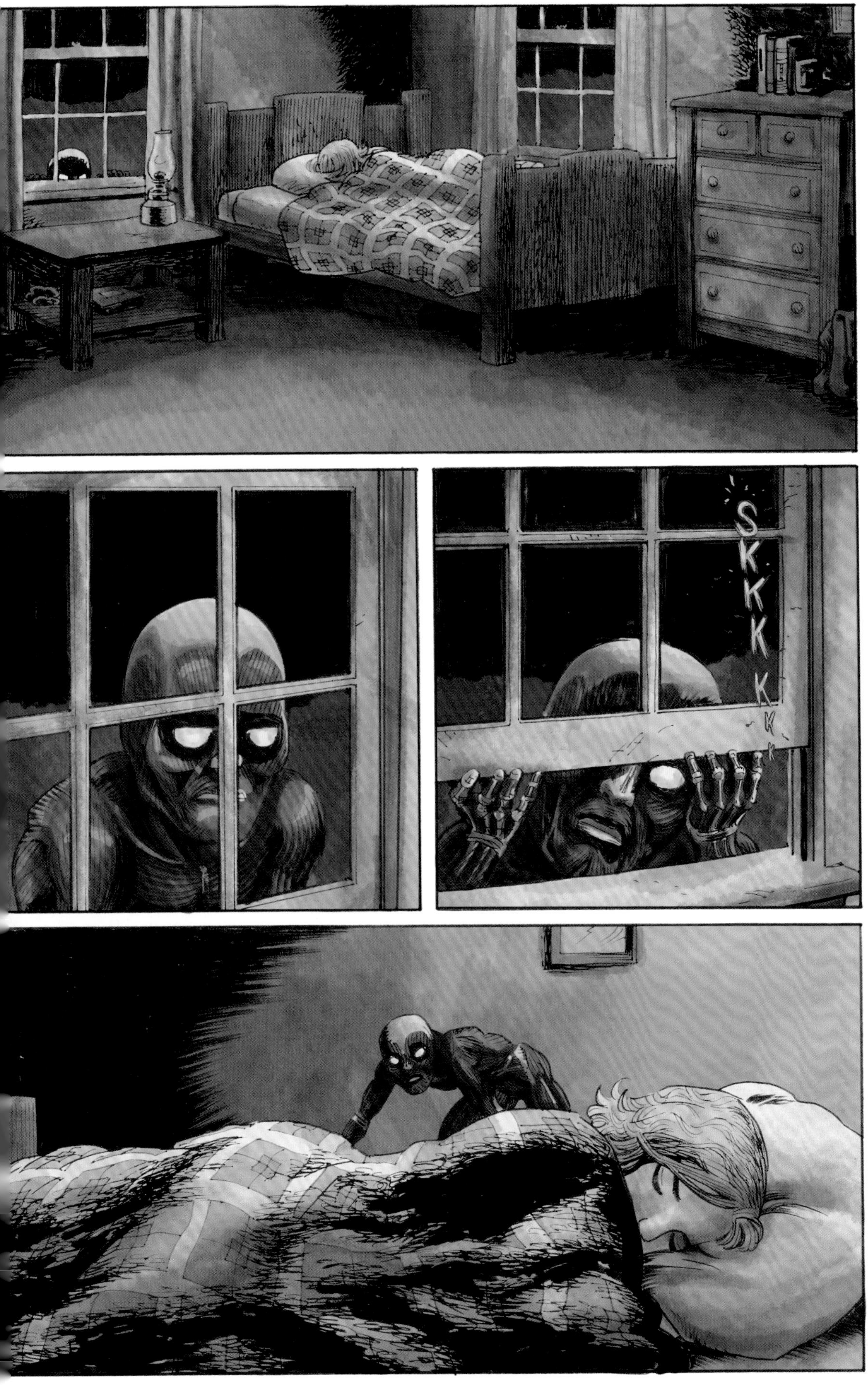
SKKKKK

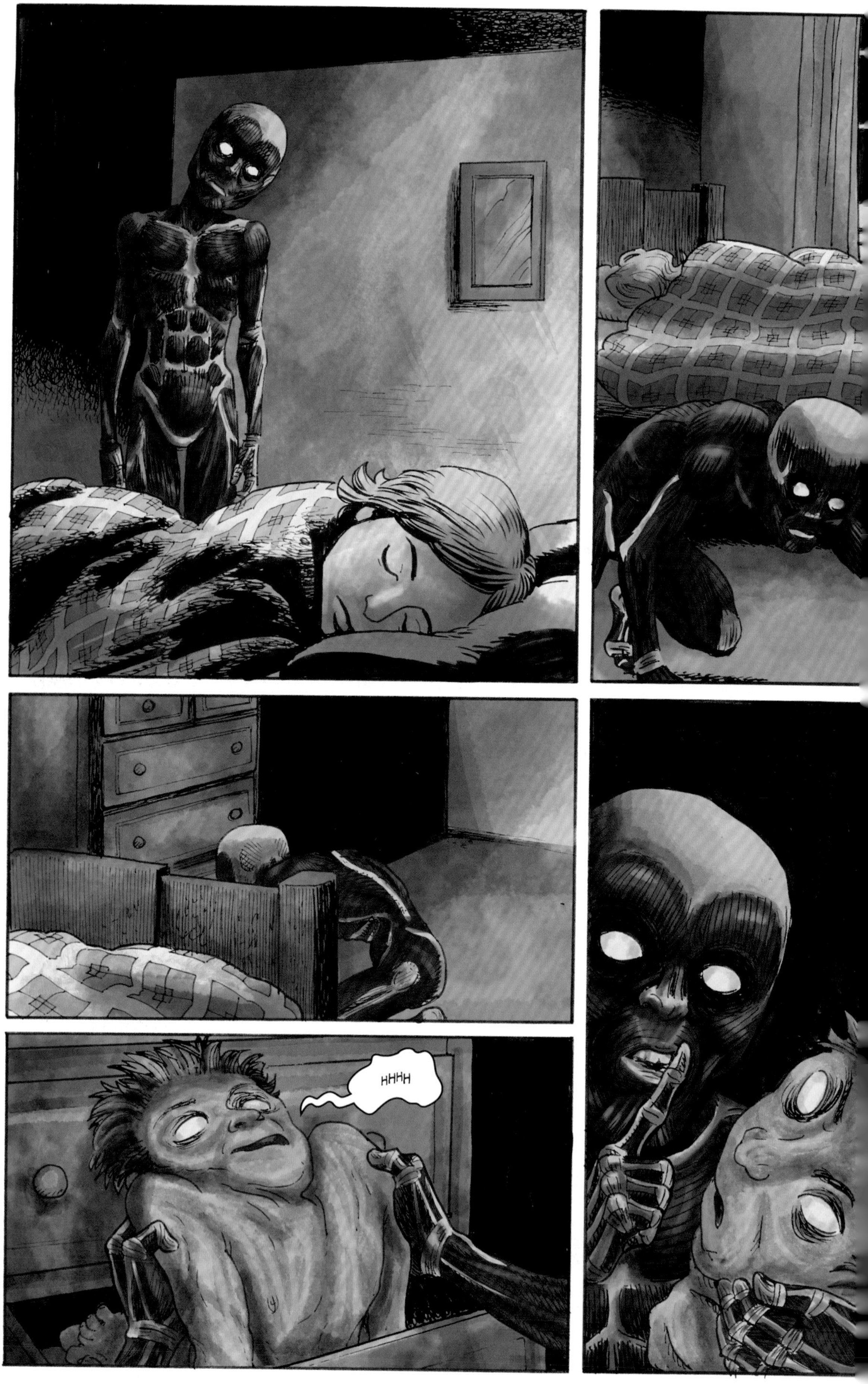
HHHH

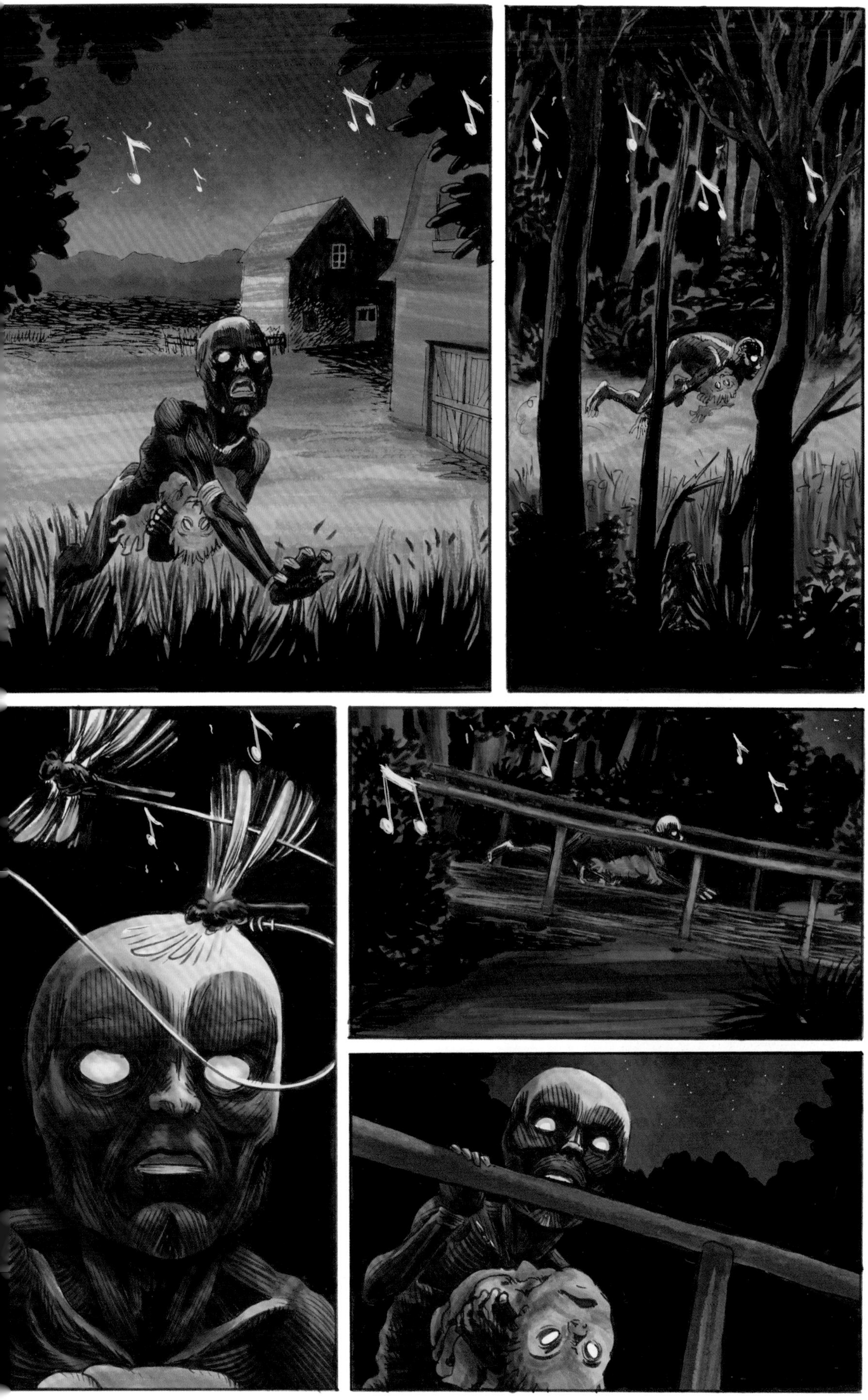

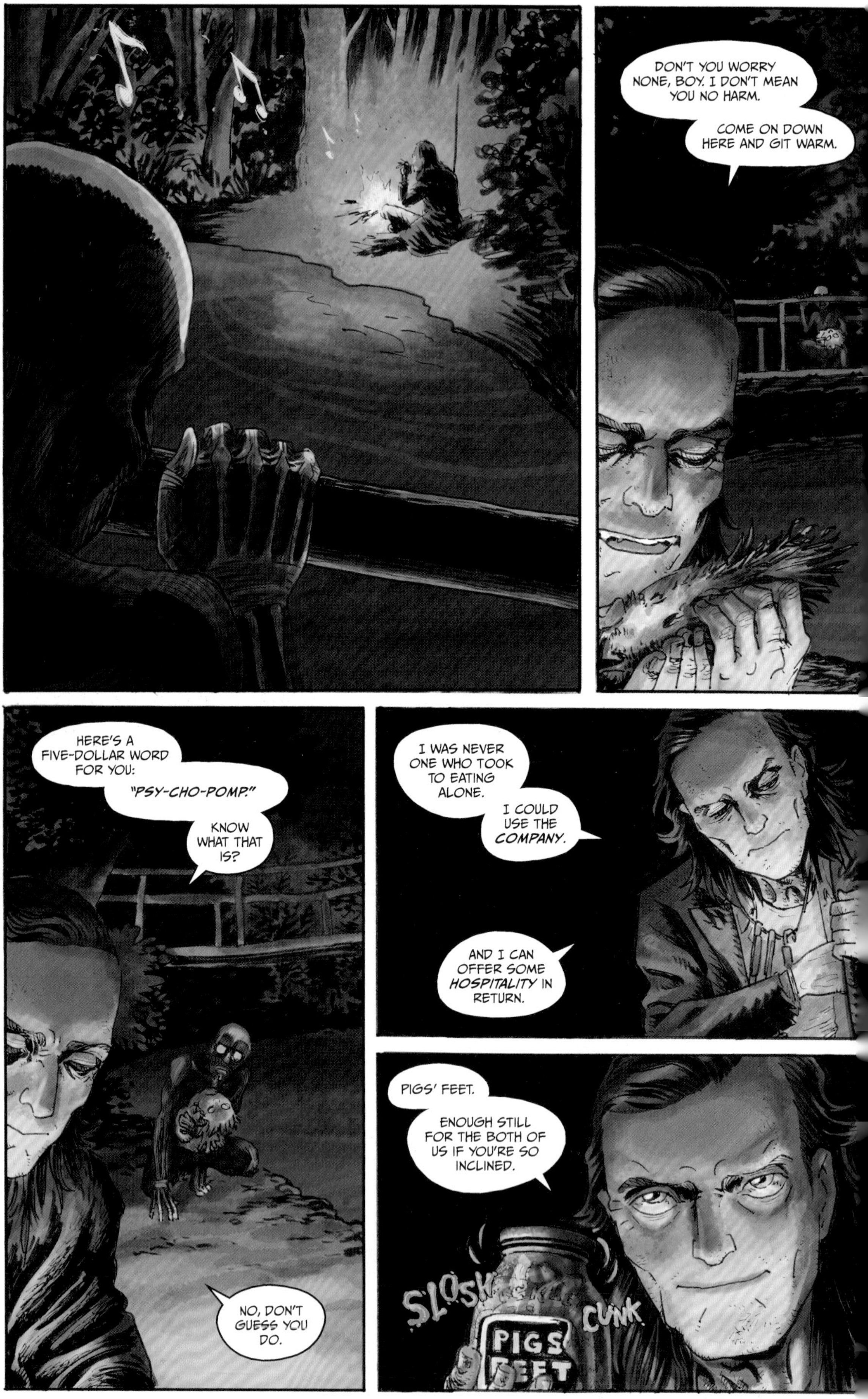
DON'T YOU WORRY NONE, BOY. I DON'T MEAN YOU NO HARM.
COME ON DOWN HERE AND GIT WARM.
HERE'S A FIVE-DOLLAR WORD FOR YOU:
"PSY-CHO-POMP."
KNOW WHAT THAT IS?
NO, DON'T GUESS YOU DO.
I WAS NEVER ONE WHO TOOK TO EATING ALONE.
I COULD USE THE *COMPANY*.
AND I CAN OFFER SOME *HOSPITALITY* IN RETURN.
PIGS' FEET.
ENOUGH STILL FOR THE BOTH OF US IF YOU'RE SO INCLINED.
SLOSH
CUNK
PIGS FEET

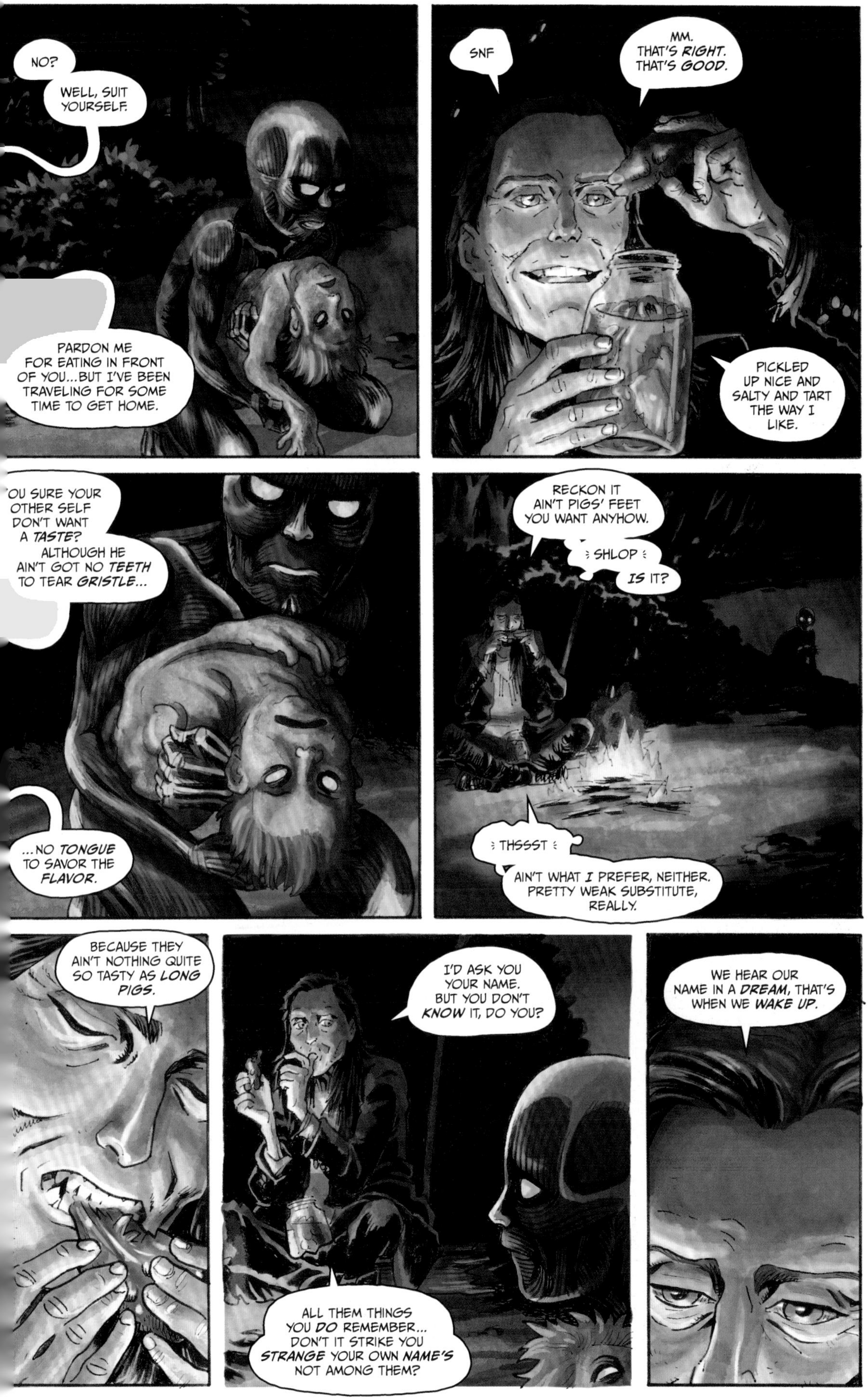
NO?
WELL, SUIT YOURSELF.
PARDON ME FOR EATING IN FRONT OF YOU...BUT I'VE BEEN TRAVELING FOR SOME TIME TO GET HOME.
SNF
MM. THAT'S RIGHT. THAT'S GOOD.
PICKLED UP NICE AND SALTY AND TART THE WAY I LIKE.
OU SURE YOUR OTHER SELF DON'T WANT A TASTE? ALTHOUGH HE AIN'T GOT NO TEETH TO TEAR GRISTLE...
...NO TONGUE TO SAVOR THE FLAVOR.
RECKON IT AIN'T PIGS' FEET YOU WANT ANYHOW.
SHLOP
IS IT?
THSSST
AIN'T WHAT I PREFER, NEITHER. PRETTY WEAK SUBSTITUTE, REALLY.
BECAUSE THEY AIN'T NOTHING QUITE SO TASTY AS LONG PIGS.
I'D ASK YOU YOUR NAME. BUT YOU DON'T KNOW IT, DO YOU?
ALL THEM THINGS YOU DO REMEMBER... DON'T IT STRIKE YOU STRANGE YOUR OWN NAME'S NOT AMONG THEM?
WE HEAR OUR NAME IN A DREAM, THAT'S WHEN WE WAKE UP.

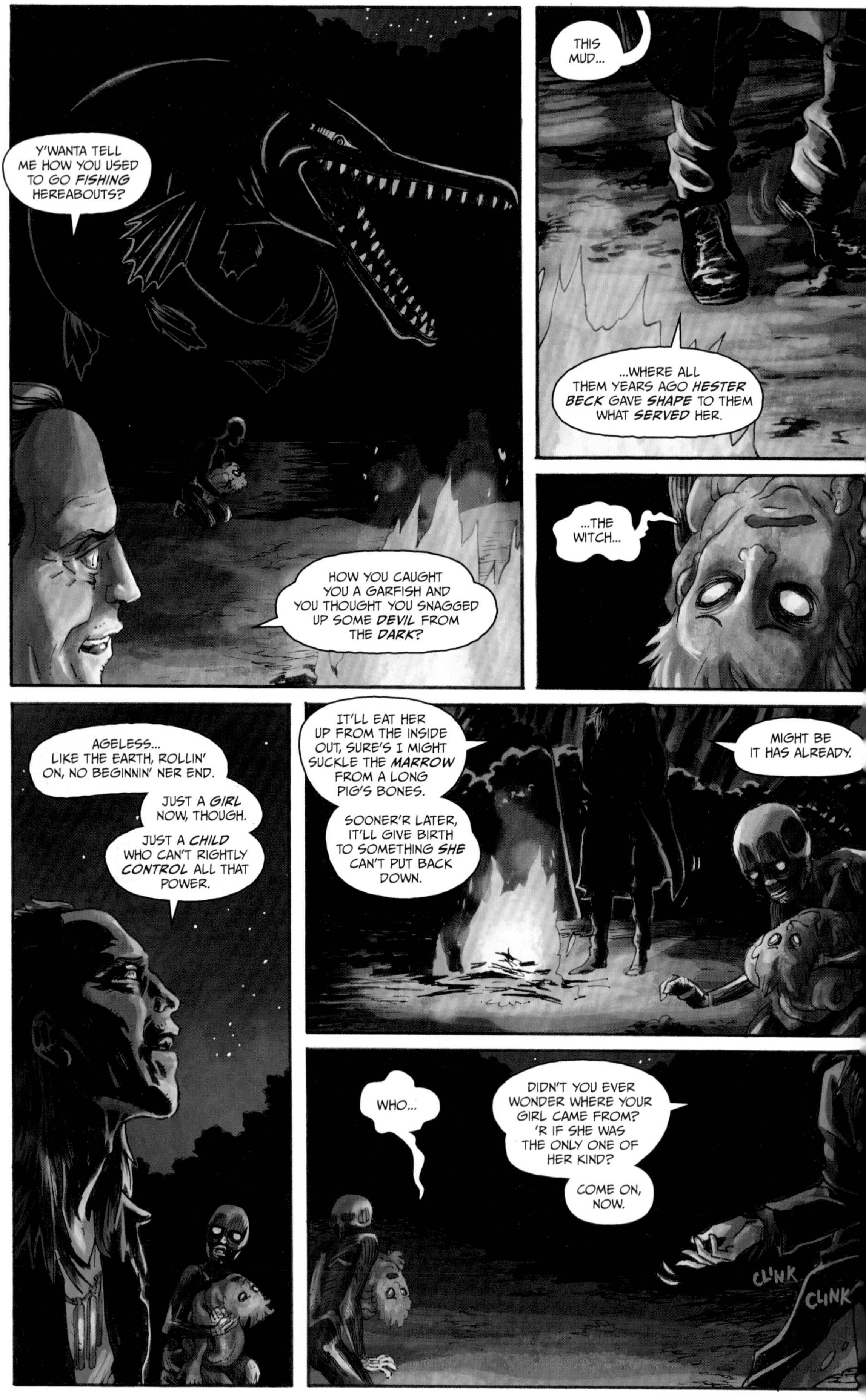
Y'WANTA TELL ME HOW YOU USED TO GO *FISHING* HEREABOUTS?
HOW YOU CAUGHT YOU A GARFISH AND YOU THOUGHT YOU SNAGGED UP SOME *DEVIL* FROM THE *DARK?*
THIS MUD...
...WHERE ALL THEM YEARS AGO *HESTER BECK* GAVE *SHAPE* TO THEM WHAT *SERVED* HER.
...THE WITCH...
AGELESS... LIKE THE EARTH, ROLLIN' ON, NO BEGINNIN' NER END.
JUST A *GIRL* NOW, THOUGH.
JUST A *CHILD* WHO CAN'T RIGHTLY *CONTROL* ALL THAT POWER.
IT'LL EAT HER UP FROM THE INSIDE OUT, SURE'S I MIGHT SUCKLE THE *MARROW* FROM A LONG PIG'S BONES.
SOONER'R LATER, IT'LL GIVE BIRTH TO SOMETHING *SHE* CAN'T PUT BACK DOWN.
MIGHT BE IT HAS ALREADY.
WHO...
DIDN'T YOU EVER WONDER WHERE YOUR GIRL CAME FROM? 'R IF SHE WAS THE ONLY ONE OF HER KIND?
COME ON, NOW.
CLINK
CLINK

THERE'S MUCH TO SEE BEFORE THE NIGHT'S DONE.

SQUEEER!

HHHHHHHH...

YOU THINK YOU REMEMBER THIS, TOO?

YOU REMEMBER CHASING RABBITS?

BUT YOU WEREN'T QUICK ENOUGH TO *CATCH* THEM *BEFORE*, WERE YOU?

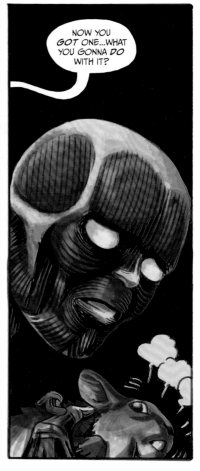

NOW YOU *GOT* ONE...WHAT YOU GONNA *DO* WITH IT?

I RECKON YOU RECOLLECT *THIS* PLACE, *TOO*, DON'T YOU? THE *BRIAR TANGLES*.

THIS IS WHERE YOUR *WITCH* FOUND THAT *SKIN* OF YOURS...

...TATTERED AND TORN AND HANGING IN THE THORNY VINES...

...LIKE THE *WASH* HUNG UP TO *DRY*...

...AMIDST ALL THE *BLOOD*.

BUT YOU REMEMBER SOMETHING *ELSE*, DON'T YOU?

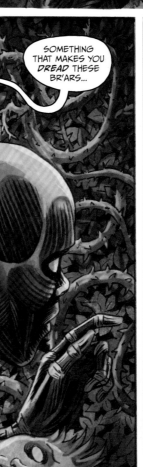

SOMETHING THAT MAKES YOU *DREAD* THESE BR'ARS...

...AND WHAT THEY CAN *DO*.

HSSSSK!

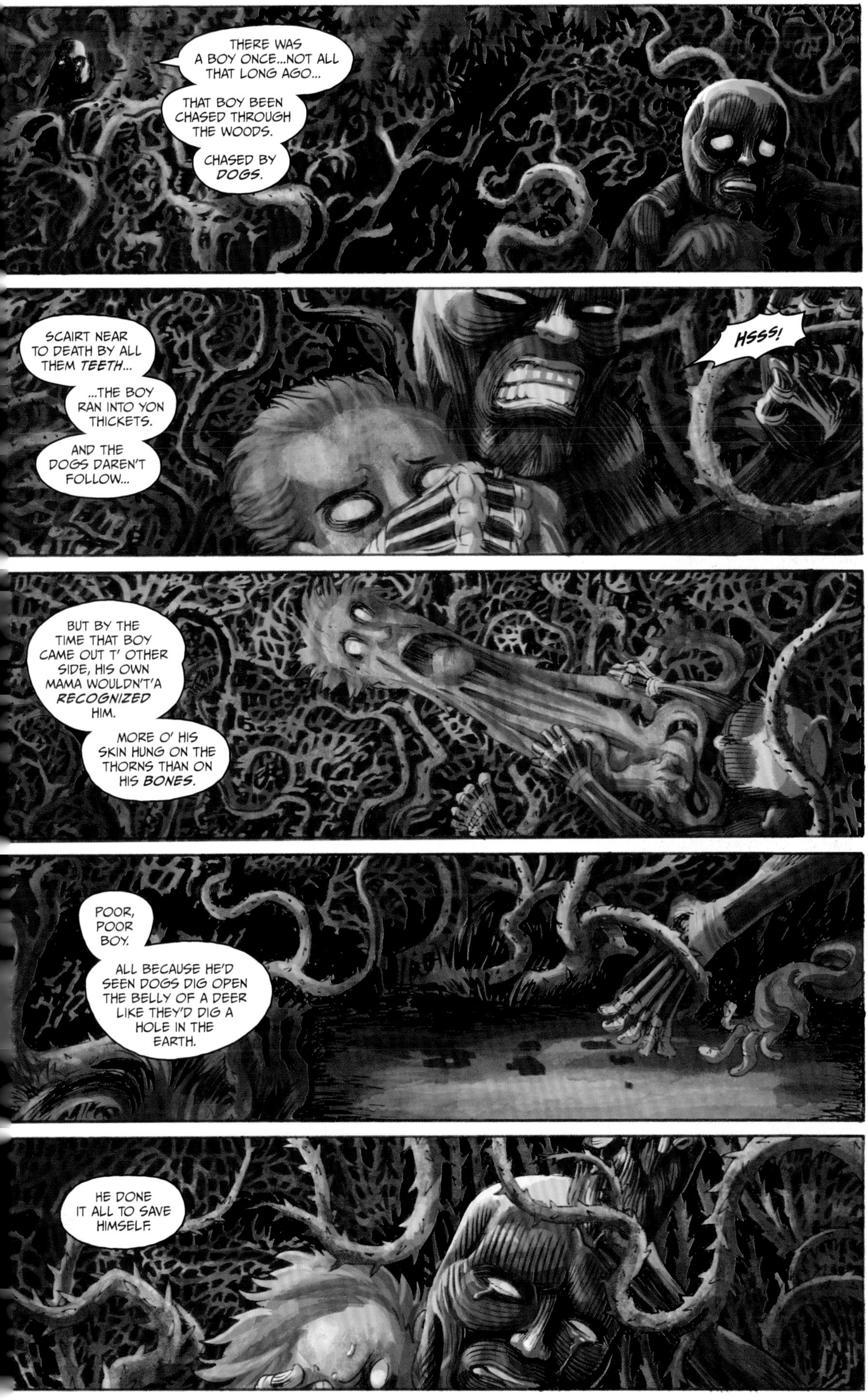
THERE WAS A BOY ONCE...NOT ALL THAT LONG AGO...
THAT BOY BEEN CHASED THROUGH THE WOODS.
CHASED BY *DOGS*.
SCAIRT NEAR TO DEATH BY ALL THEM *TEETH*...
...THE BOY RAN INTO YON THICKETS.
AND THE DOGS DAREN'T FOLLOW...
HSSS!
BUT BY THE TIME THAT BOY CAME OUT T' OTHER SIDE, HIS OWN MAMA WOULDN'T'A *RECOGNIZED* HIM.
MORE O' HIS SKIN HUNG ON THE THORNS THAN ON HIS *BONES*.
POOR, POOR BOY.
ALL BECAUSE HE'D SEEN DOGS DIG OPEN THE BELLY OF A DEER LIKE THEY'D DIG A HOLE IN THE EARTH.
HE DONE IT ALL TO SAVE HIMSELF.

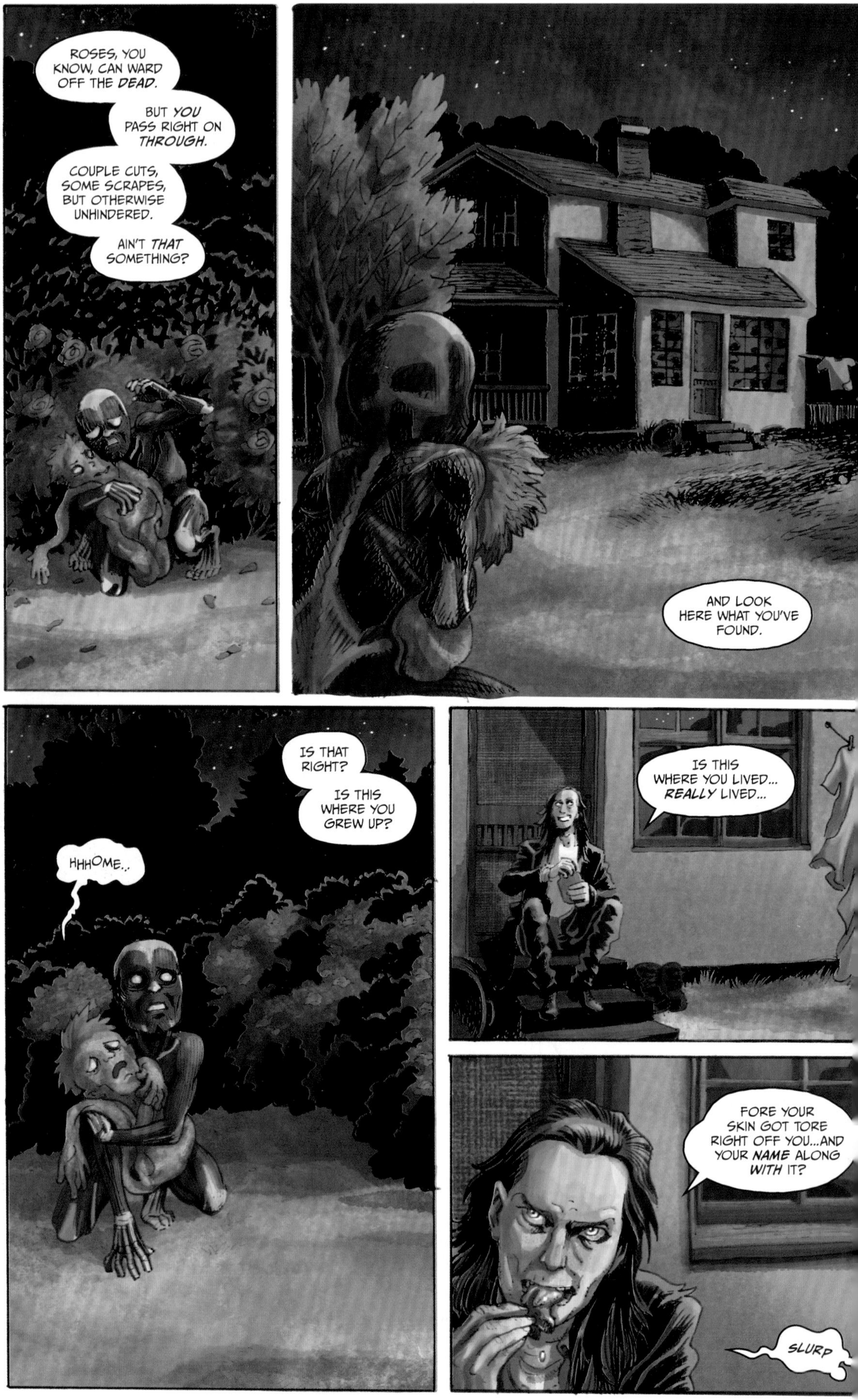
ROSES, YOU KNOW, CAN WARD OFF THE *DEAD*.
BUT *YOU* PASS RIGHT ON *THROUGH*.
COUPLE CUTS, SOME SCRAPES, BUT OTHERWISE UNHINDERED.
AIN'T *THAT* SOMETHING?
AND LOOK HERE WHAT YOU'VE FOUND.
IS THAT RIGHT?
IS THIS WHERE YOU GREW UP?
HHHOME..
IS THIS WHERE YOU LIVED... *REALLY* LIVED...
FORE YOUR SKIN GOT TORE RIGHT OFF YOU...AND YOUR *NAME* ALONG *WITH* IT?
SLURP

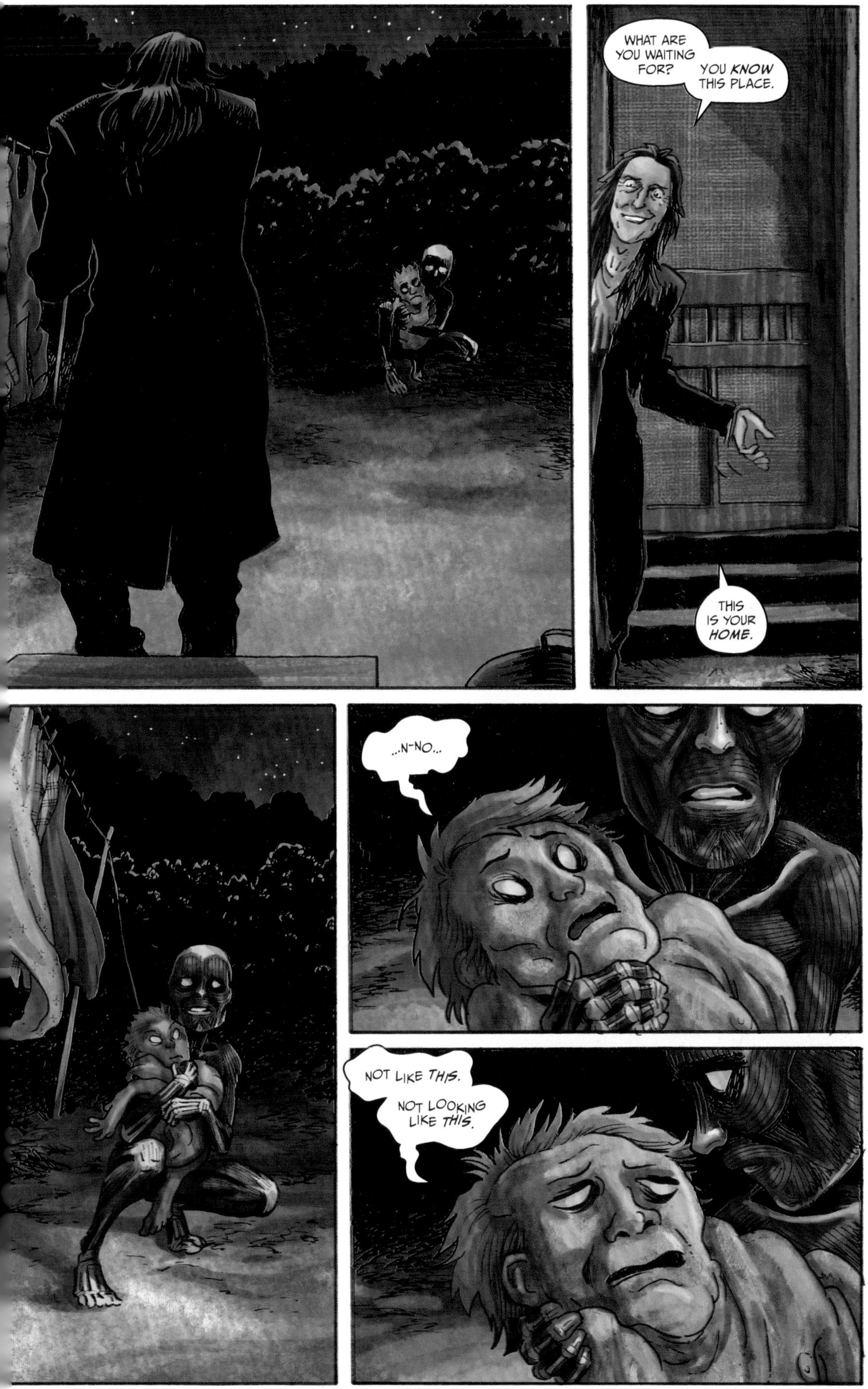
WHAT ARE YOU WAITING FOR?
YOU KNOW THIS PLACE.
THIS IS YOUR HOME.
...N-NO...
NOT LIKE THIS.
NOT LOOKING LIKE THIS.

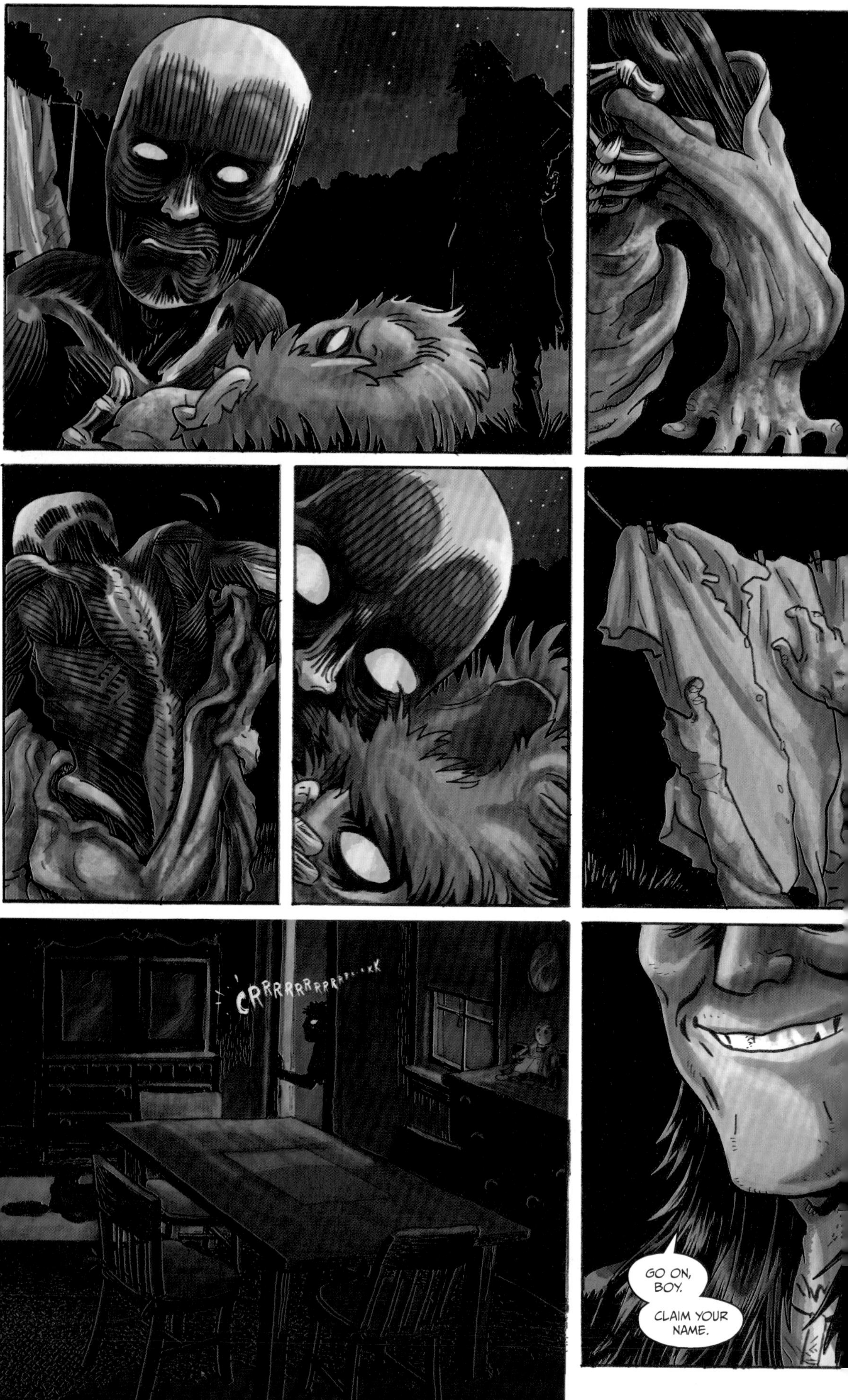
CRRRRRRRRRRR...KK
GO ON, BOY.
CLAIM YOUR NAME.

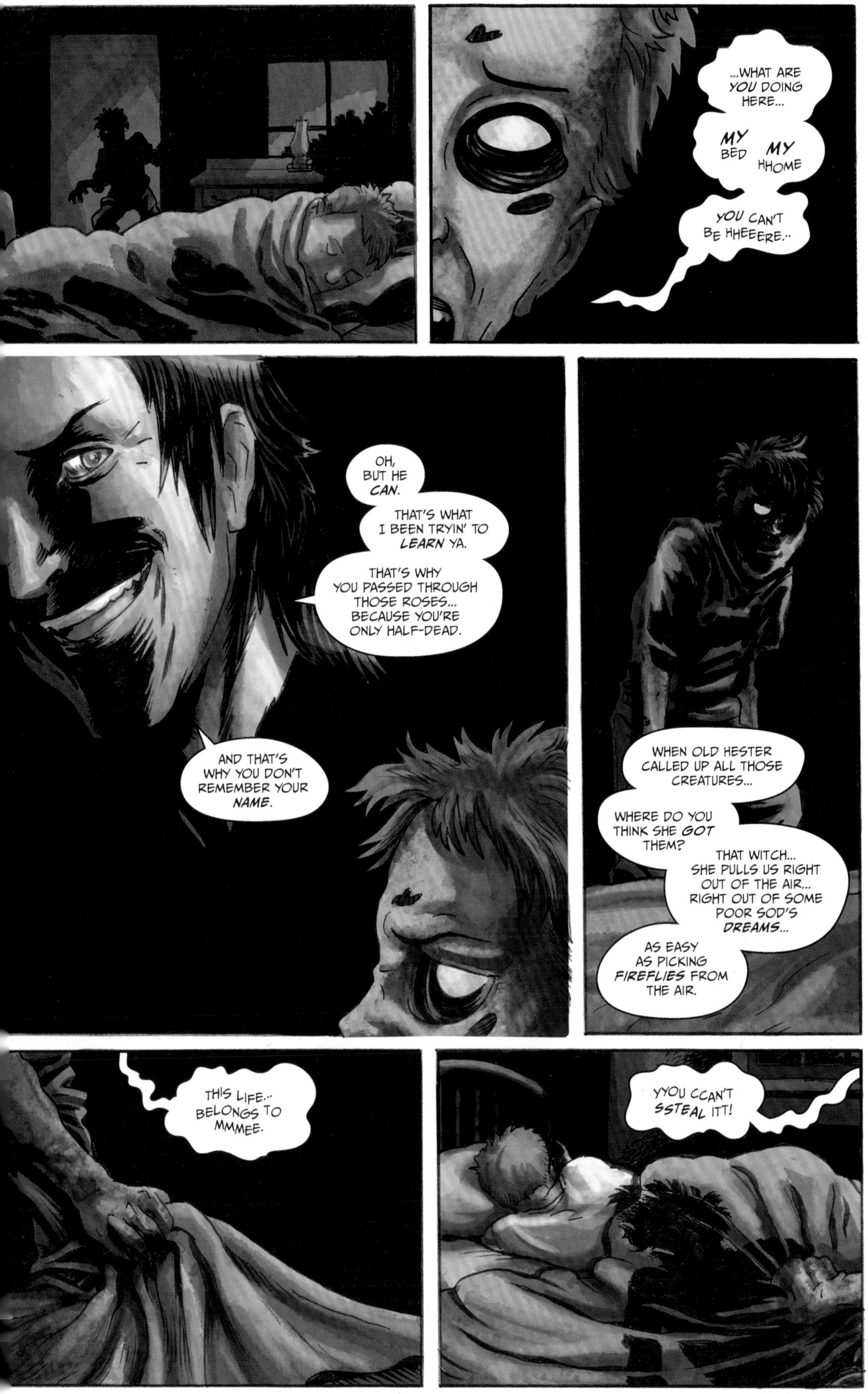
...WHAT ARE YOU DOING HERE...
MY BED MY HHOME
YOU CAN'T BE HHEEERE...
OH, BUT HE CAN.
THAT'S WHAT I BEEN TRYIN' TO LEARN YA.
THAT'S WHY YOU PASSED THROUGH THOSE ROSES... BECAUSE YOU'RE ONLY HALF-DEAD.
AND THAT'S WHY YOU DON'T REMEMBER YOUR NAME.
WHEN OLD HESTER CALLED UP ALL THOSE CREATURES...
WHERE DO YOU THINK SHE GOT THEM?
THAT WITCH... SHE PULLS US RIGHT OUT OF THE AIR... RIGHT OUT OF SOME POOR SOD'S DREAMS...
AS EASY AS PICKING FIREFLIES FROM THE AIR.
THIS LIFE... BELONGS TO MMMEE.
YYOU CCAN'T SSTEAL ITT!

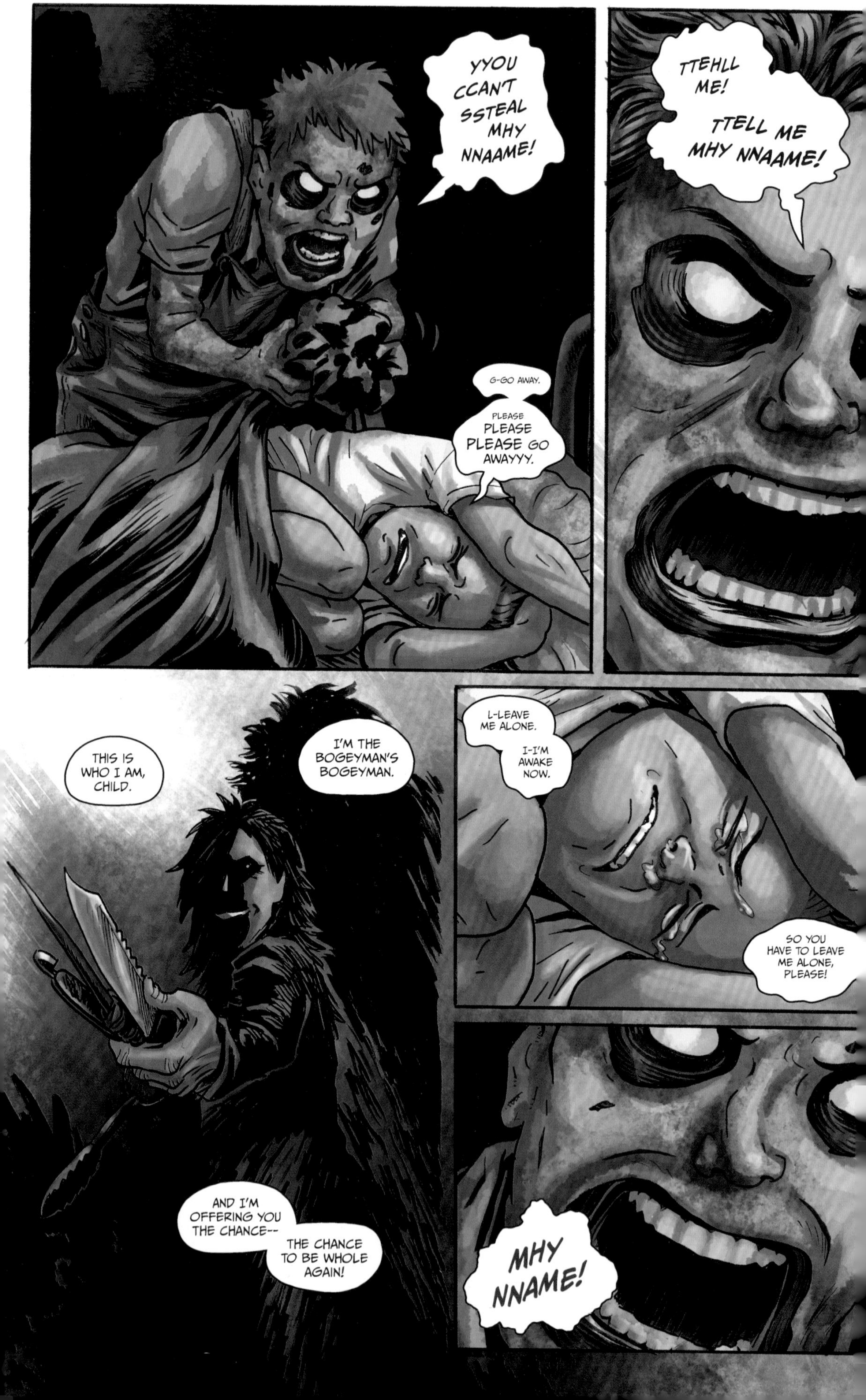
YYOU CCAN'T SSTEAL MHY NNAAME!
G-GO AWAY.
PLEASE PLEASE PLEASE GO AWAYYY.
TTEHLL ME!
TTELL ME MHY NNAAME!
THIS IS WHO I AM, CHILD.
I'M THE BOGEYMAN'S BOGEYMAN.
AND I'M OFFERING YOU THE CHANCE--
THE CHANCE TO BE WHOLE AGAIN!
L-LEAVE ME ALONE.
I-I'M AWAKE NOW.
SO YOU HAVE TO LEAVE ME ALONE, PLEASE!
MHY NNAME!

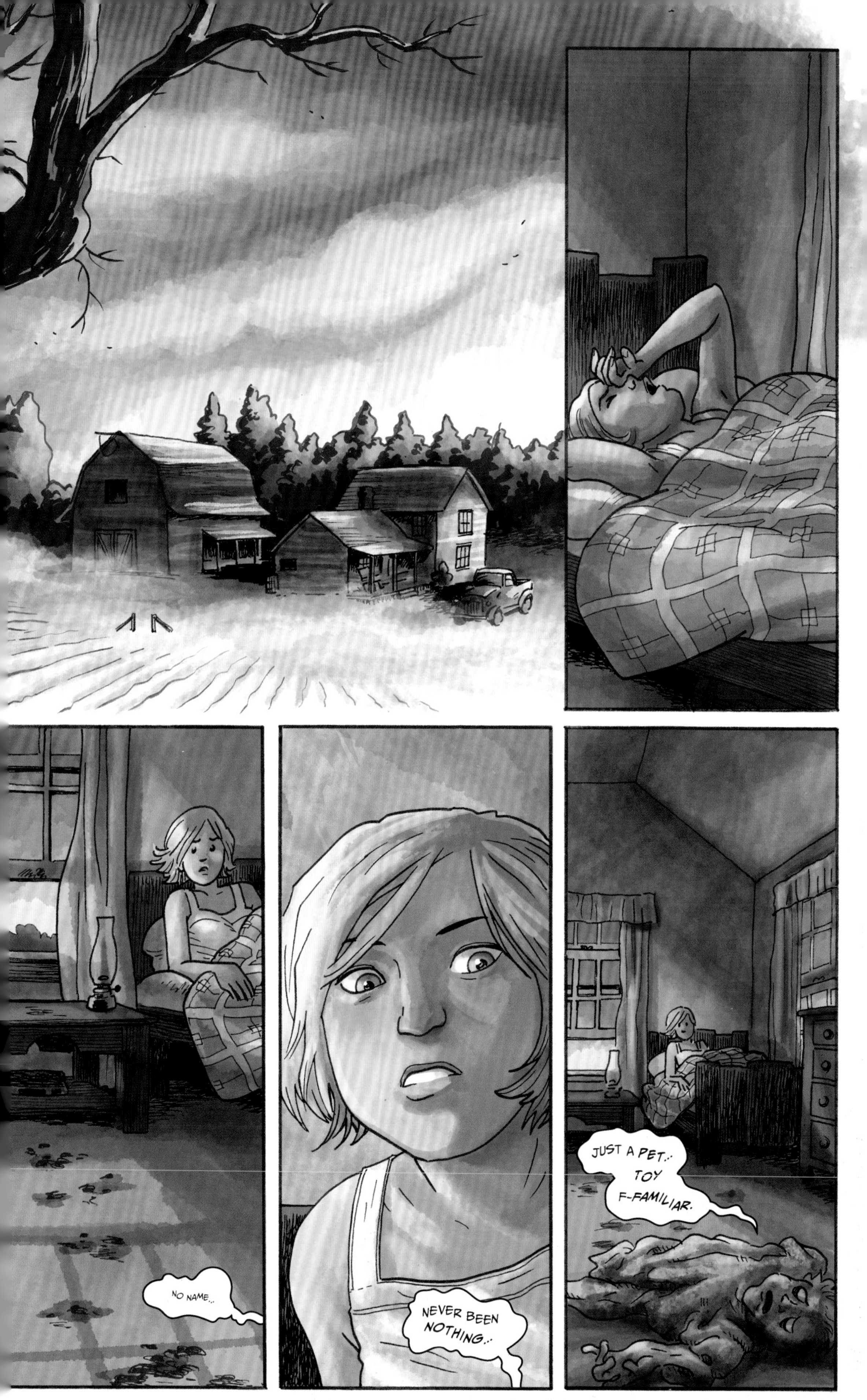
NO NAME...
NEVER BEEN NOTHING...
JUST A PET... TOY F-FAMILIAR.

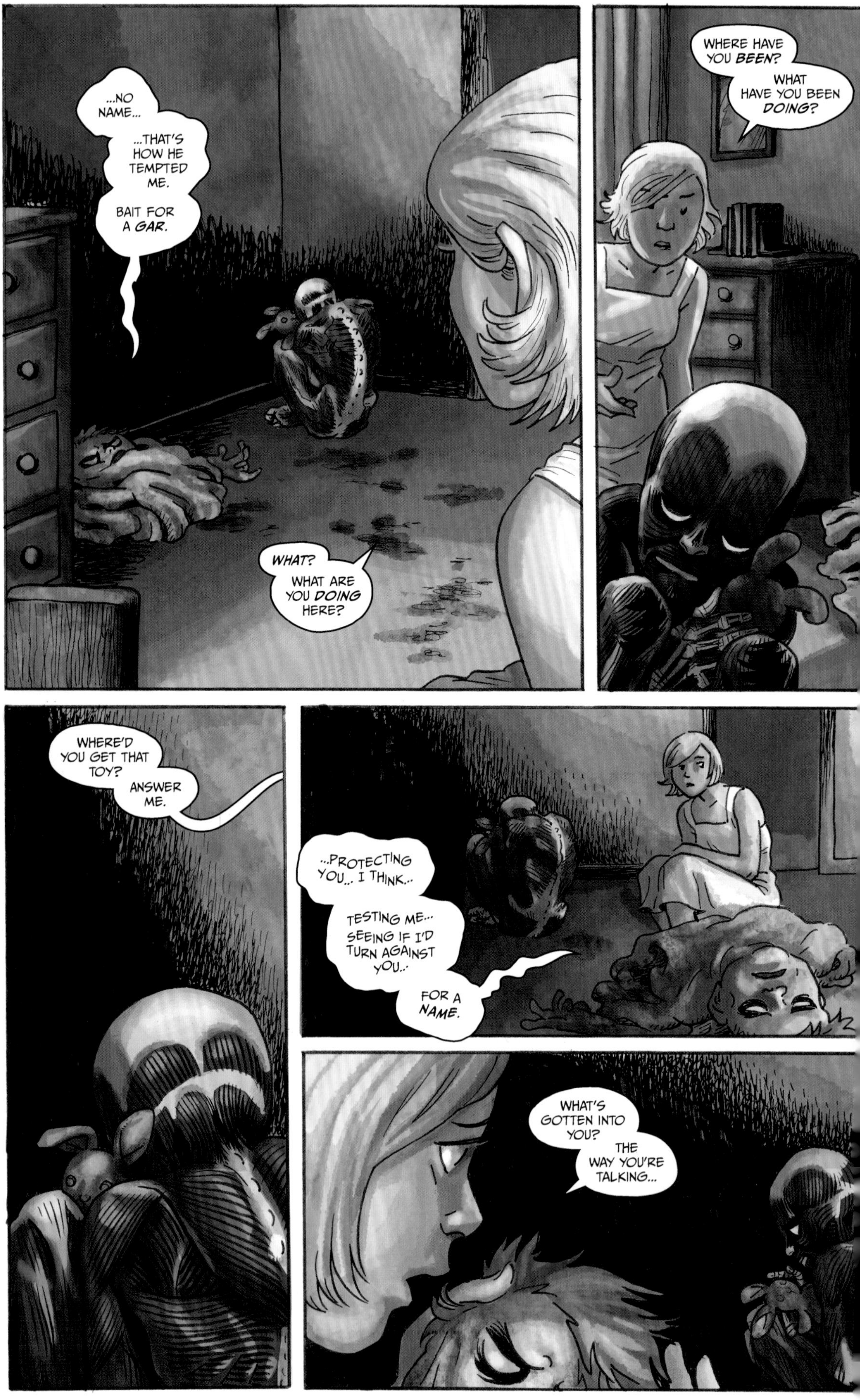
...NO NAME...
...THAT'S HOW HE TEMPTED ME.
BAIT FOR A GAR.
WHAT?
WHAT ARE YOU DOING HERE?
WHERE HAVE YOU BEEN?
WHAT HAVE YOU BEEN DOING?
WHERE'D YOU GET THAT TOY?
ANSWER ME.
...PROTECTING YOU... I THINK...
TESTING ME... SEEING IF I'D TURN AGAINST YOU...
FOR A NAME.
WHAT'S GOTTEN INTO YOU?
THE WAY YOU'RE TALKING...

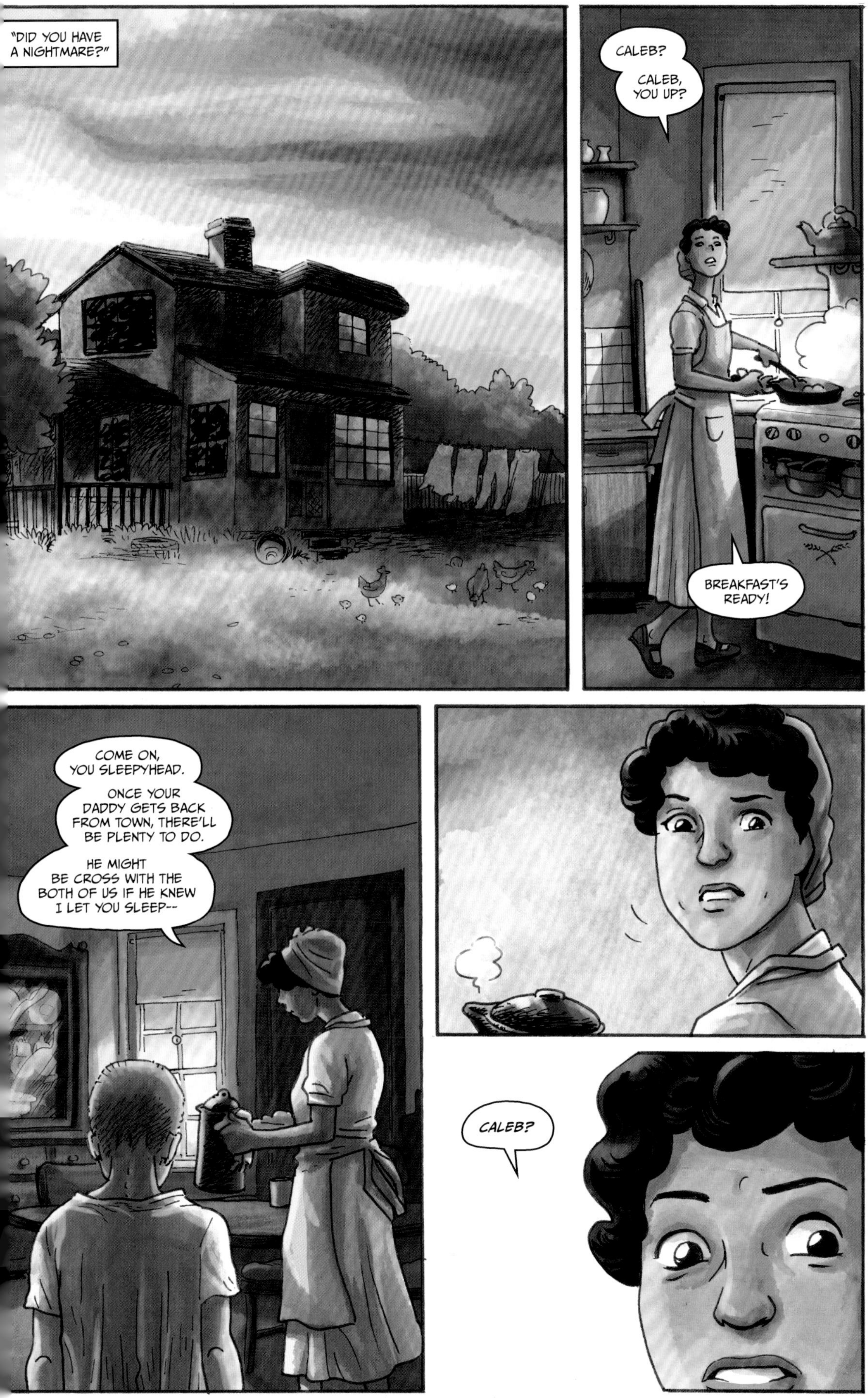
"DID YOU HAVE A NIGHTMARE?"
CALEB?
CALEB, YOU UP?
BREAKFAST'S READY!
COME ON, YOU SLEEPYHEAD.
ONCE YOUR DADDY GETS BACK FROM TOWN, THERE'LL BE PLENTY TO DO.
HE MIGHT BE CROSS WITH THE BOTH OF US IF HE KNEW I LET YOU SLEEP--
CALEB?

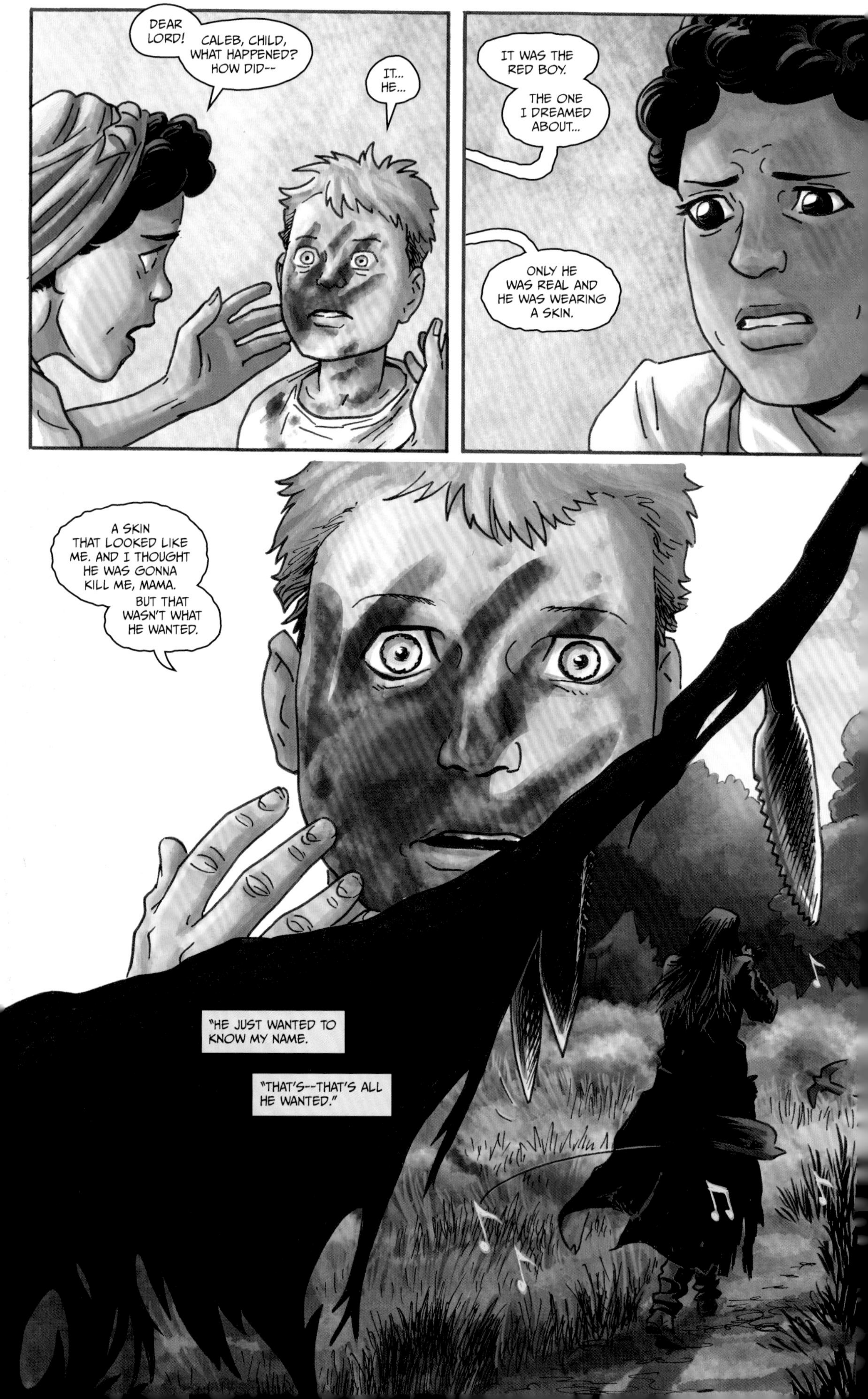
DEAR LORD!
CALEB, CHILD, WHAT HAPPENED? HOW DID--
IT... HE...
IT WAS THE RED BOY.
THE ONE I DREAMED ABOUT...
ONLY HE WAS REAL AND HE WAS WEARING A SKIN.
A SKIN THAT LOOKED LIKE ME. AND I THOUGHT HE WAS GONNA KILL ME, MAMA.
BUT THAT WASN'T WHAT HE WANTED.
"HE JUST WANTED TO KNOW MY NAME.
"THAT'S--THAT'S ALL HE WANTED."

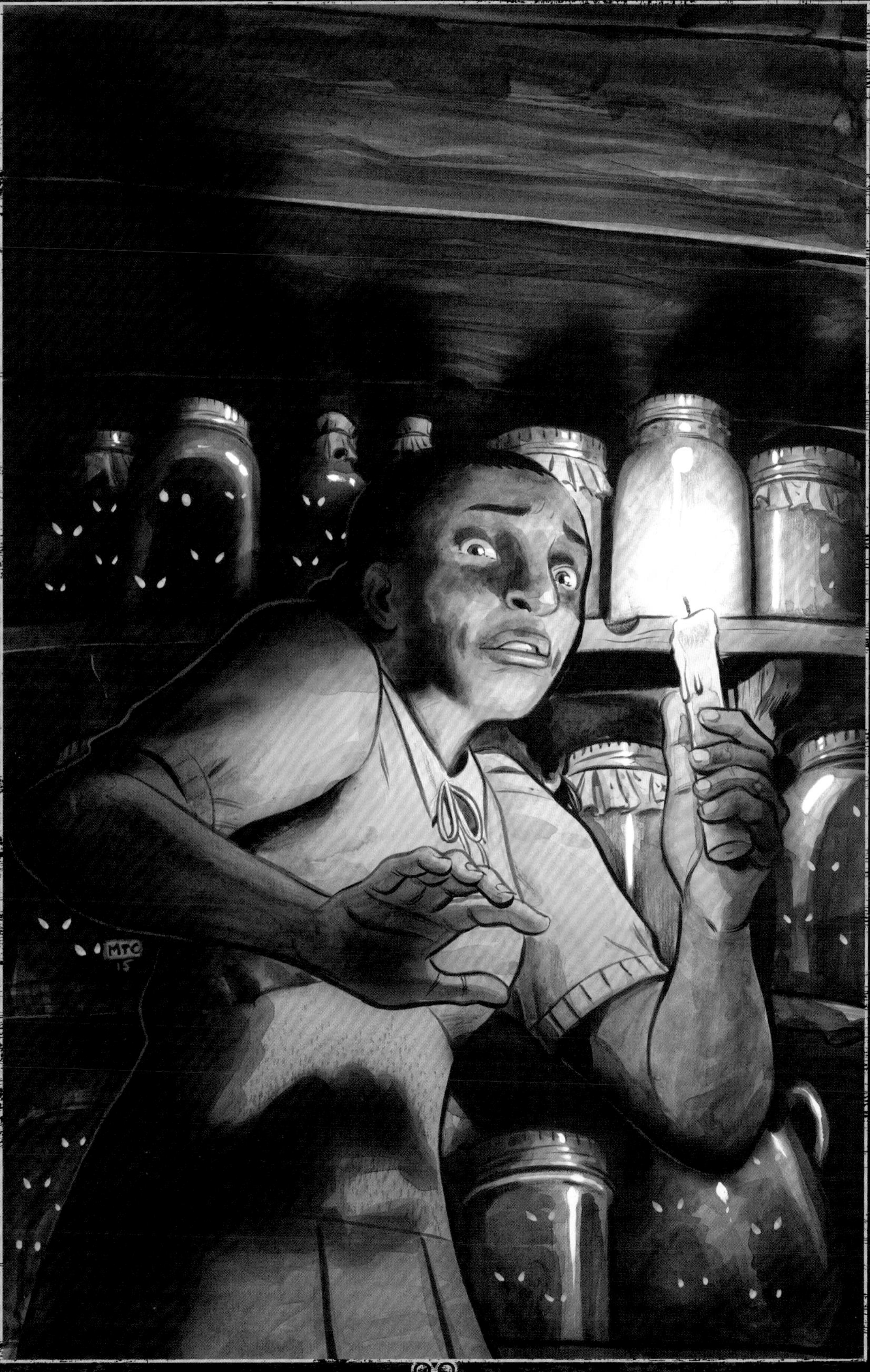
MTC
15

TWO

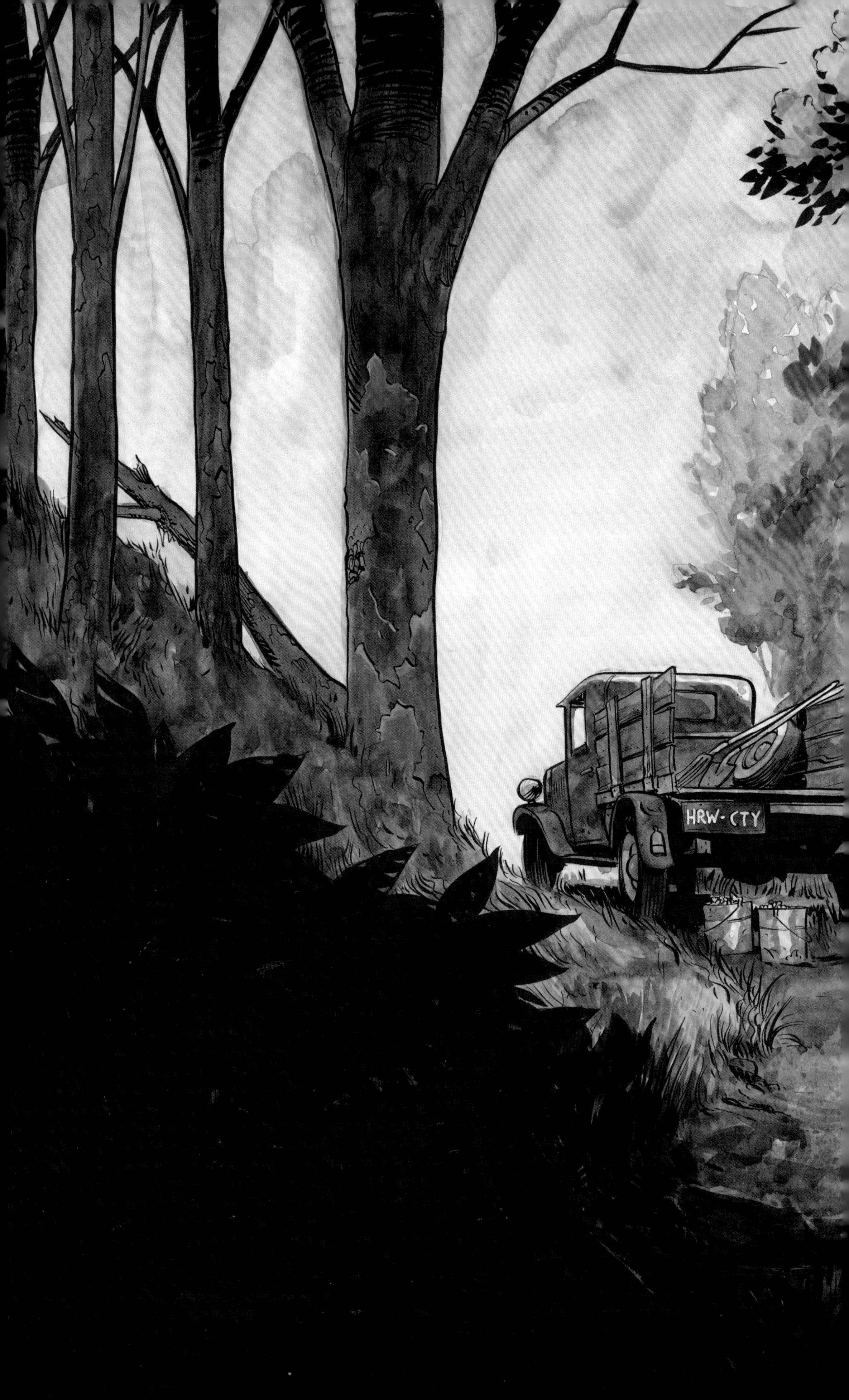
HRW-CTY

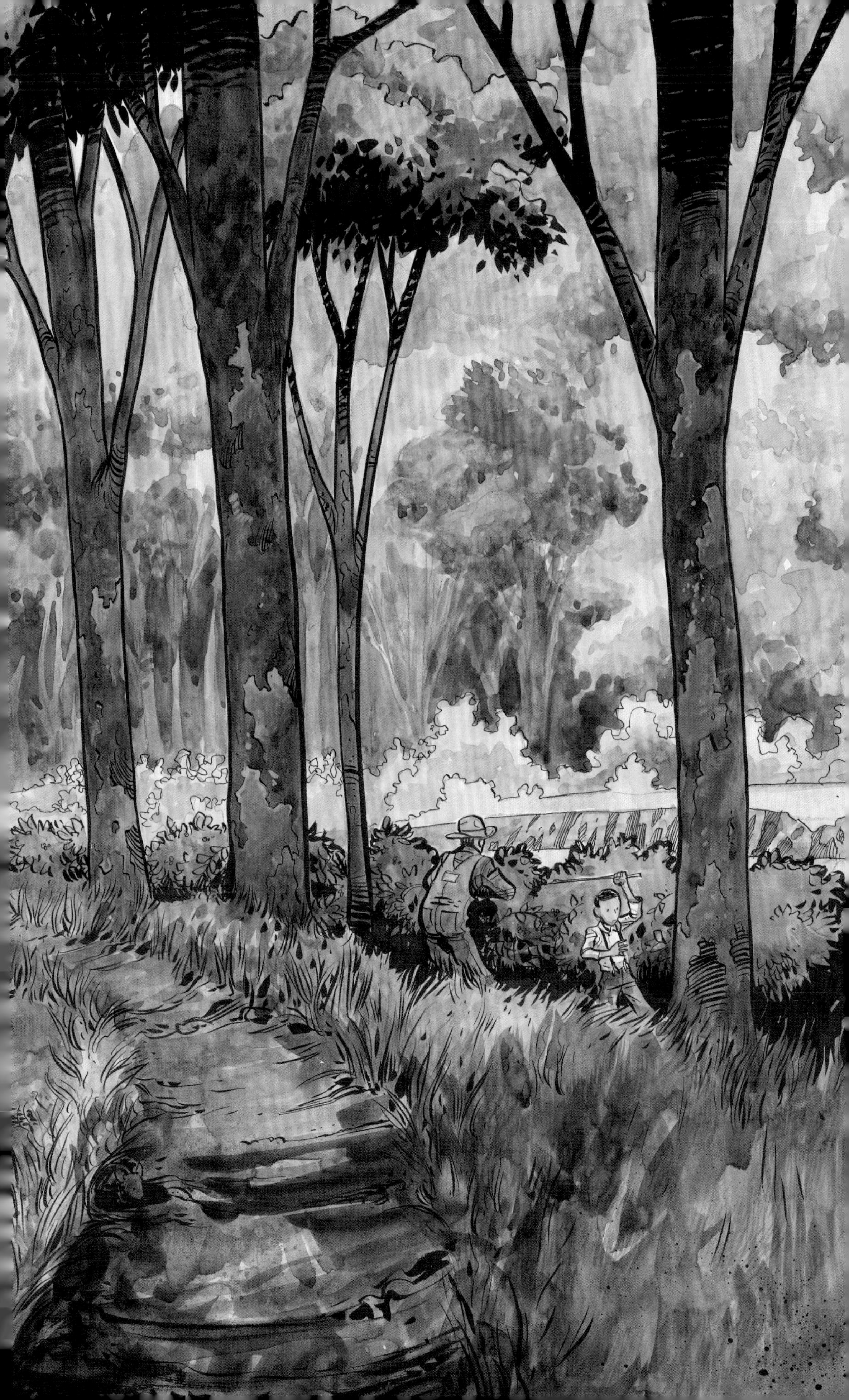

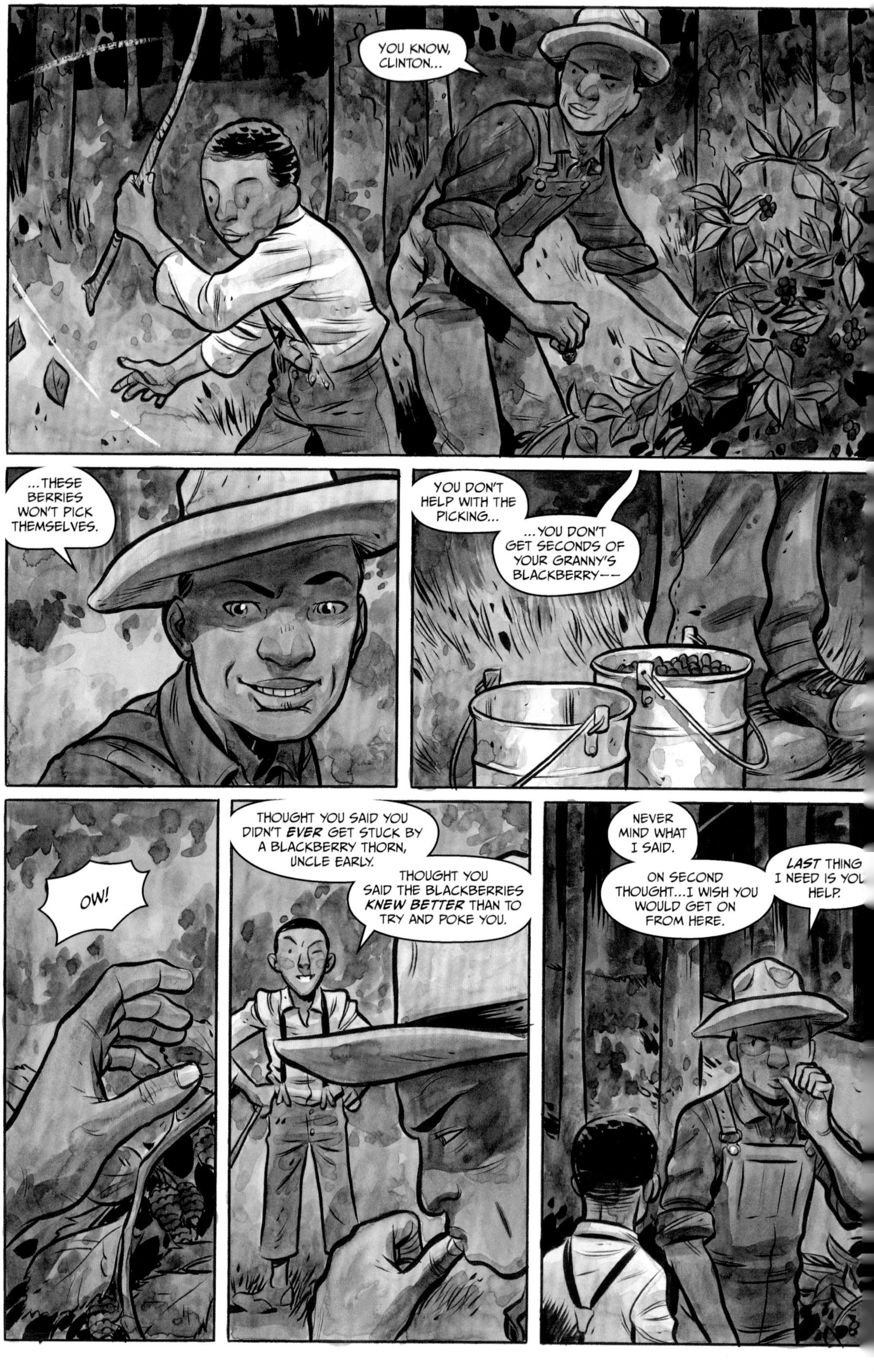
YOU KNOW, CLINTON...
...THESE BERRIES WON'T PICK THEMSELVES.
YOU DON'T HELP WITH THE PICKING...
...YOU DON'T GET SECONDS OF YOUR GRANNY'S BLACKBERRY--
OW!
THOUGHT YOU SAID YOU DIDN'T EVER GET STUCK BY A BLACKBERRY THORN, UNCLE EARLY.
THOUGHT YOU SAID THE BLACKBERRIES KNEW BETTER THAN TO TRY AND POKE YOU.
NEVER MIND WHAT I SAID.
ON SECOND THOUGHT...I WISH YOU WOULD GET ON FROM HERE.
LAST THING I NEED IS YOU HELP.

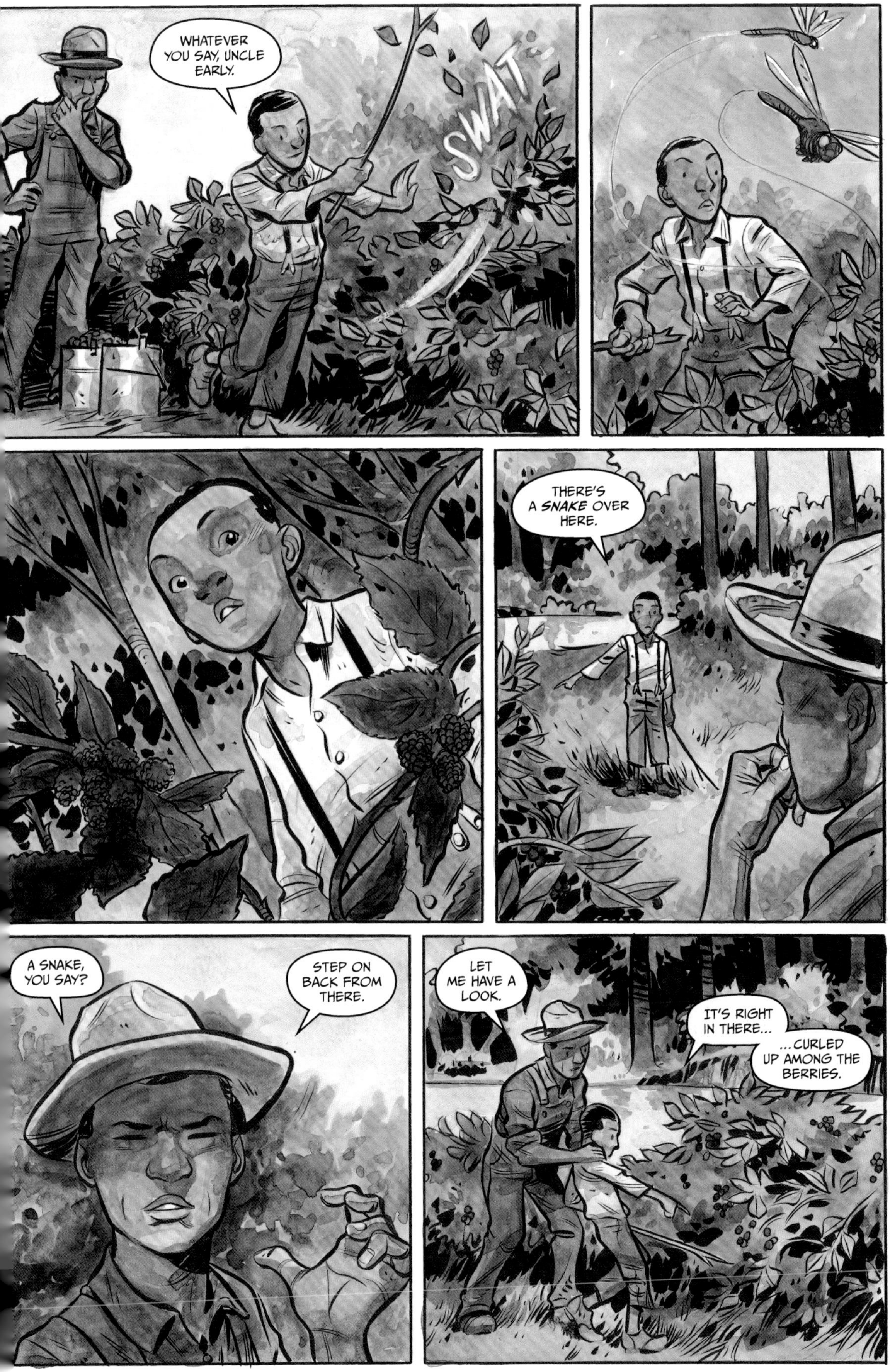
WHATEVER YOU SAY, UNCLE EARLY.
SWAT
THERE'S A SNAKE OVER HERE.
A SNAKE, YOU SAY?
STEP ON BACK FROM THERE.
LET ME HAVE A LOOK.
IT'S RIGHT IN THERE...
...CURLED UP AMONG THE BERRIES.

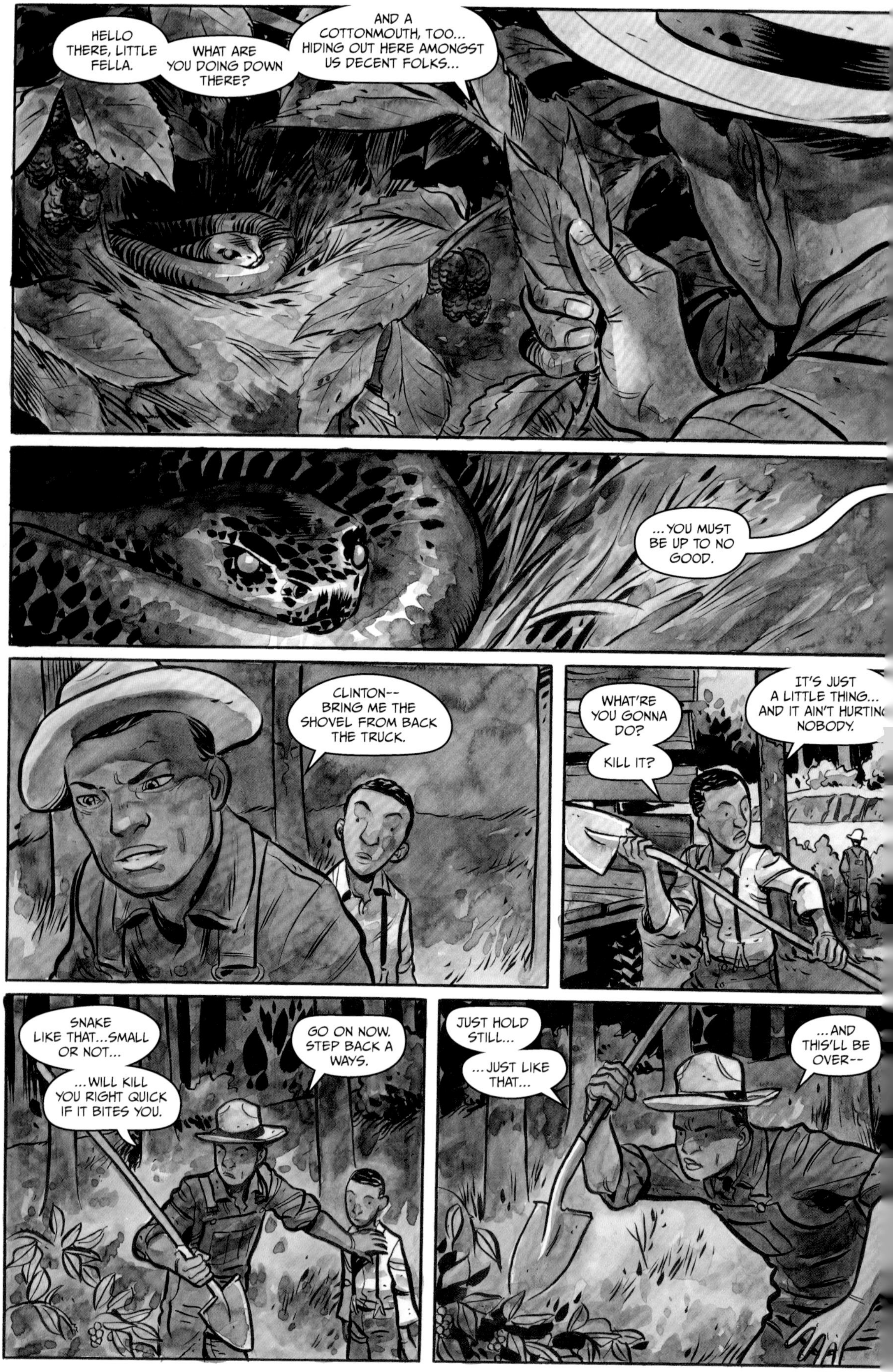
HELLO THERE, LITTLE FELLA.
WHAT ARE YOU DOING DOWN THERE?
AND A COTTONMOUTH, TOO... HIDING OUT HERE AMONGST US DECENT FOLKS...
...YOU MUST BE UP TO NO GOOD.
CLINTON-- BRING ME THE SHOVEL FROM BACK THE TRUCK.
WHAT'RE YOU GONNA DO?
KILL IT?
IT'S JUST A LITTLE THING... AND IT AIN'T HURTING NOBODY.
SNAKE LIKE THAT...SMALL OR NOT...
...WILL KILL YOU RIGHT QUICK IF IT BITES YOU.
GO ON NOW. STEP BACK A WAYS.
JUST HOLD STILL...
...JUST LIKE THAT...
...AND THIS'LL BE OVER--

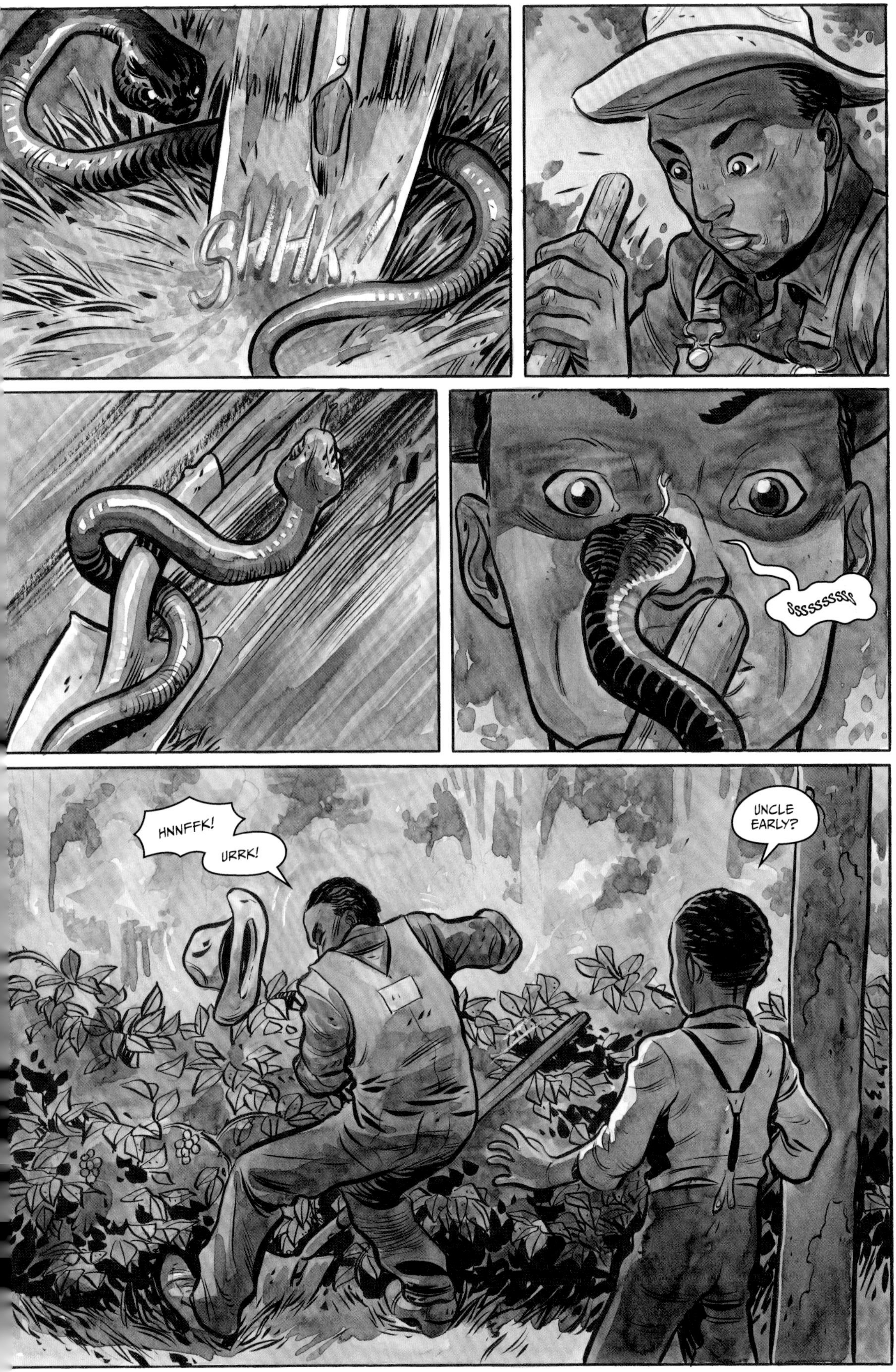
SHHK
SSSSSSSSS
HNNFFK!
URRK!
UNCLE EARLY?

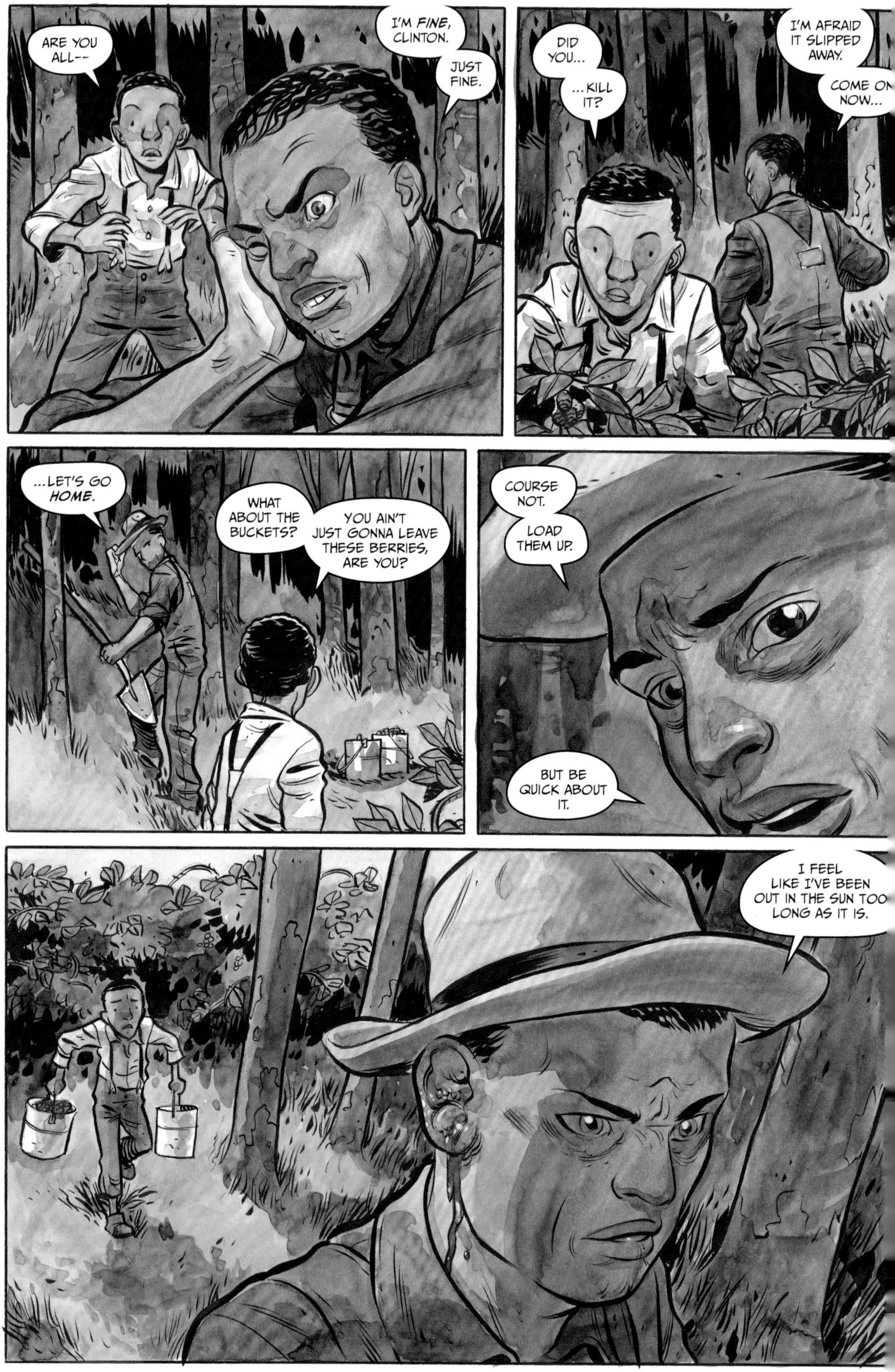
ARE YOU ALL--
I'M *FINE*, CLINTON.
JUST FINE.
DID YOU...
...KILL IT?
I'M AFRAID IT SLIPPED AWAY.
COME ON NOW...
...LET'S GO *HOME*.
WHAT ABOUT THE BUCKETS?
YOU AIN'T JUST GONNA LEAVE THESE BERRIES, ARE YOU?
COURSE NOT.
LOAD THEM UP.
BUT BE QUICK ABOUT IT.
I FEEL LIKE I'VE BEEN OUT IN THE SUN TOO LONG AS IT IS.

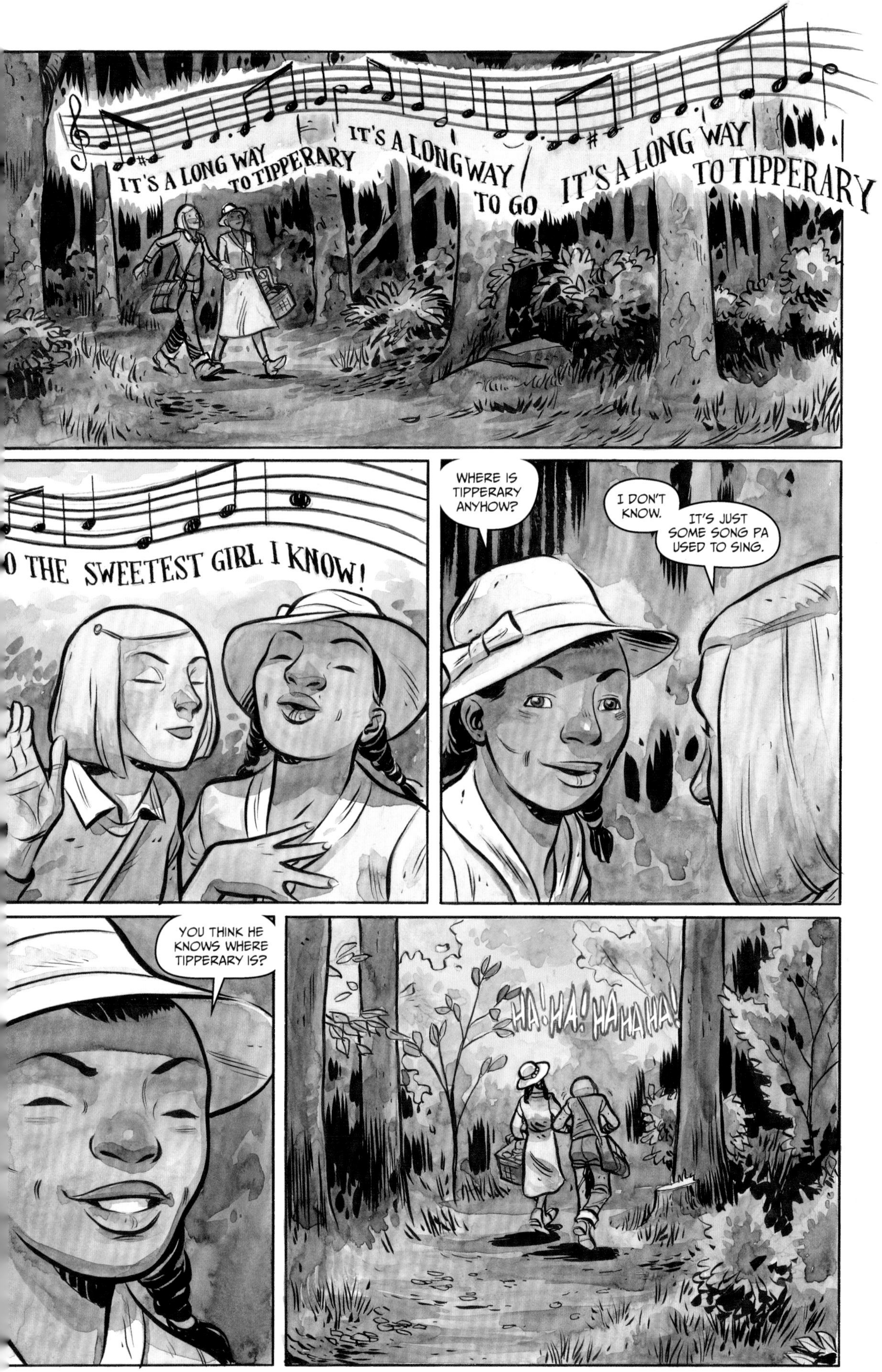
IT'S A LONG WAY
TO TIPPERARY
IT'S A LONG WAY
TO GO
IT'S A LONG WAY
TO TIPPERARY
O THE SWEETEST GIRL I KNOW!
WHERE IS TIPPERARY ANYHOW?
I DON'T KNOW.
IT'S JUST SOME SONG PA USED TO SING.
YOU THINK HE KNOWS WHERE TIPPERARY IS?
HA! HA! HAHAHA!

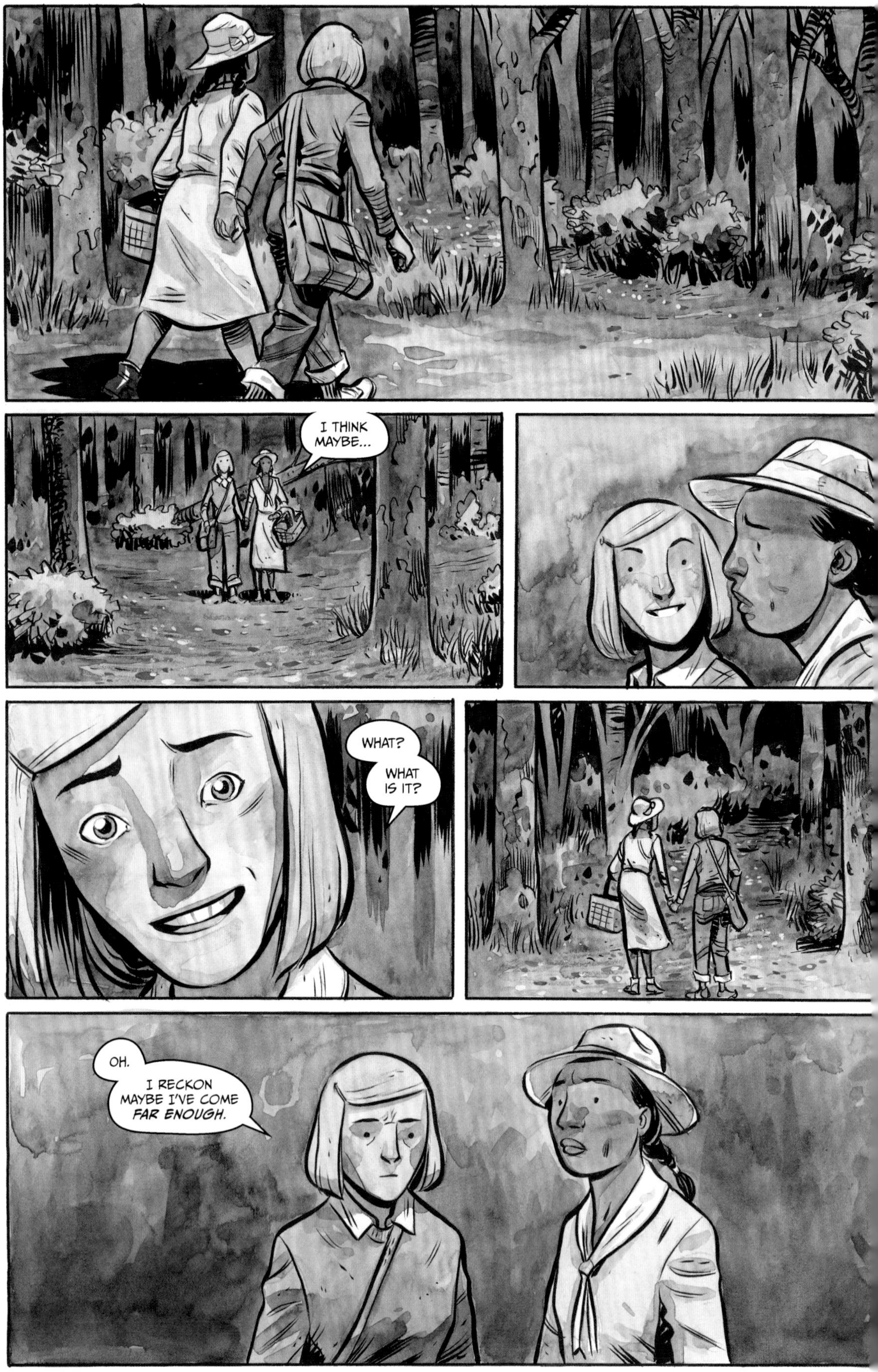
I THINK MAYBE...
WHAT?
WHAT IS IT?
OH.
I RECKON MAYBE I'VE COME *FAR ENOUGH*.

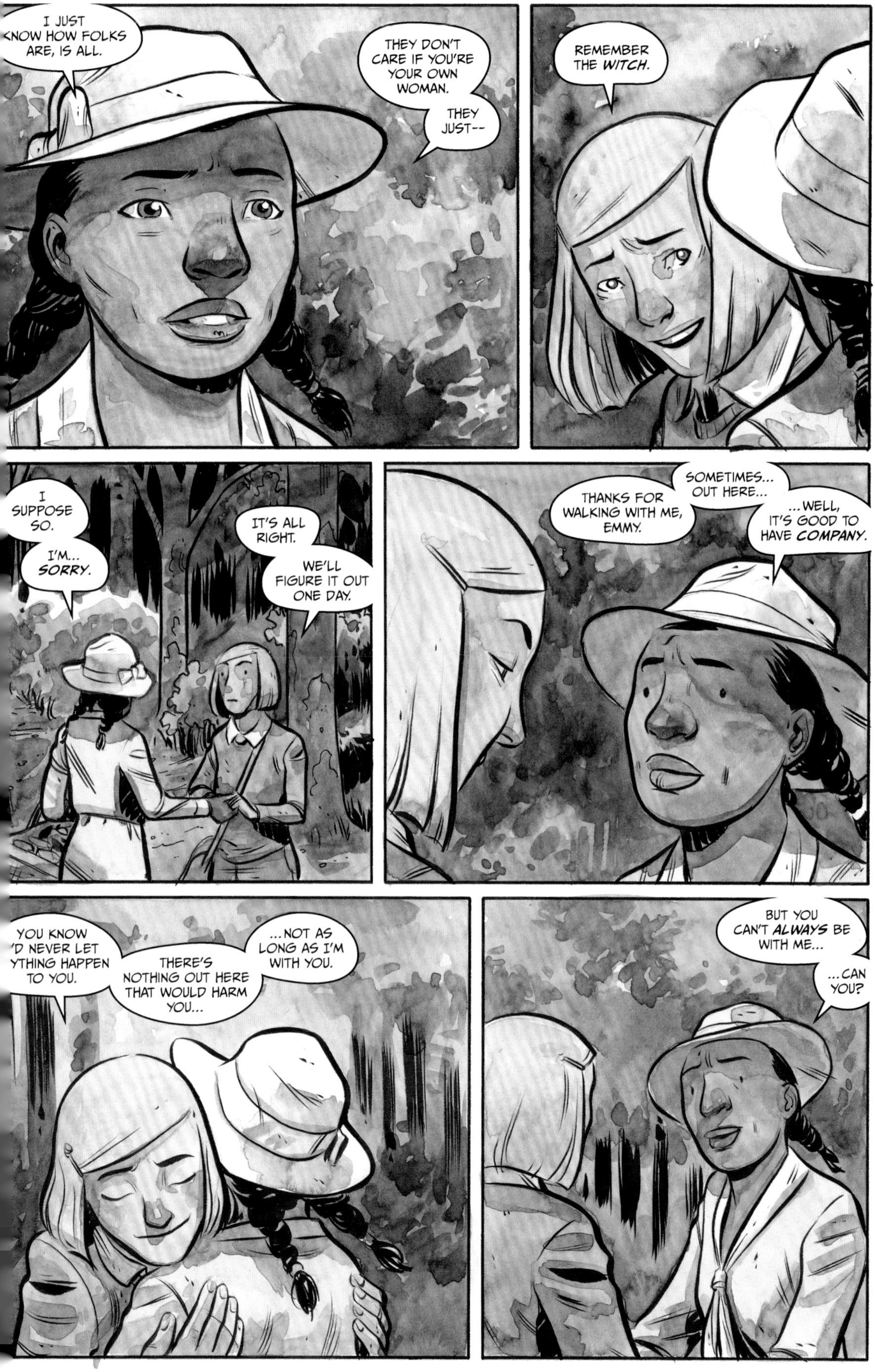
I JUST
KNOW HOW FOLKS ARE, IS ALL.
THEY DON'T CARE IF YOU'RE YOUR OWN WOMAN.
THEY JUST--
REMEMBER THE *WITCH.*
I SUPPOSE SO.
I'M... *SORRY.*
IT'S ALL RIGHT.
WE'LL FIGURE IT OUT ONE DAY.
THANKS FOR WALKING WITH ME, EMMY.
SOMETIMES... OUT HERE...
...WELL, IT'S GOOD TO HAVE *COMPANY.*
YOU KNOW
'D NEVER LET
YTHING HAPPEN TO YOU.
THERE'S NOTHING OUT HERE THAT WOULD HARM YOU...
...NOT AS LONG AS I'M WITH YOU.
BUT YOU CAN'T *ALWAYS* BE WITH ME...
...CAN YOU?

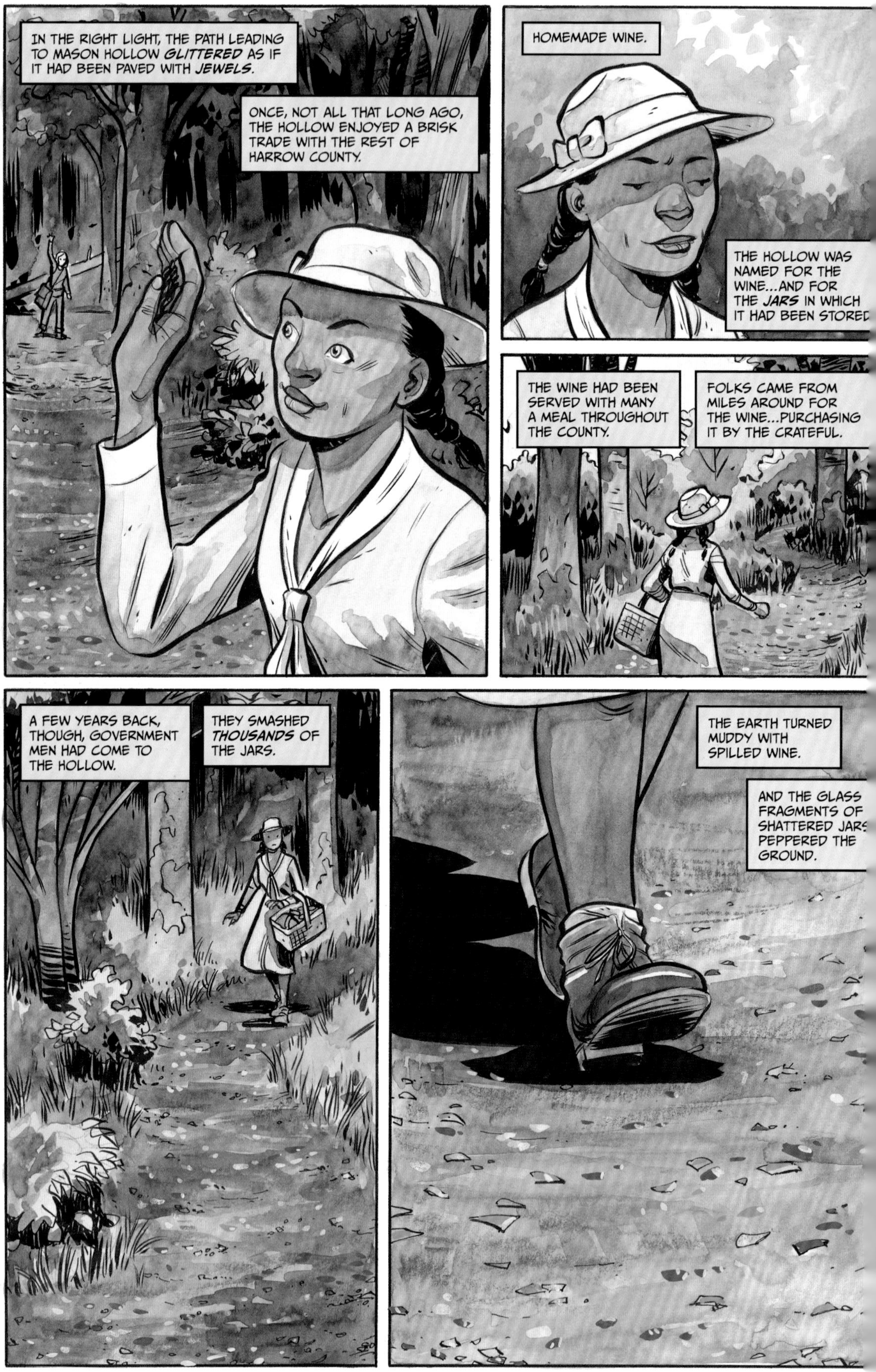
IN THE RIGHT LIGHT, THE PATH LEADING TO MASON HOLLOW GLITTERED AS IF IT HAD BEEN PAVED WITH JEWELS.
ONCE, NOT ALL THAT LONG AGO, THE HOLLOW ENJOYED A BRISK TRADE WITH THE REST OF HARROW COUNTY.
HOMEMADE WINE.
THE HOLLOW WAS NAMED FOR THE WINE...AND FOR THE JARS IN WHICH IT HAD BEEN STORED
THE WINE HAD BEEN SERVED WITH MANY A MEAL THROUGHOUT THE COUNTY.
FOLKS CAME FROM MILES AROUND FOR THE WINE...PURCHASING IT BY THE CRATEFUL.
A FEW YEARS BACK, THOUGH, GOVERNMENT MEN HAD COME TO THE HOLLOW.
THEY SMASHED THOUSANDS OF THE JARS.
THE EARTH TURNED MUDDY WITH SPILLED WINE.
AND THE GLASS FRAGMENTS OF SHATTERED JARS PEPPERED THE GROUND.

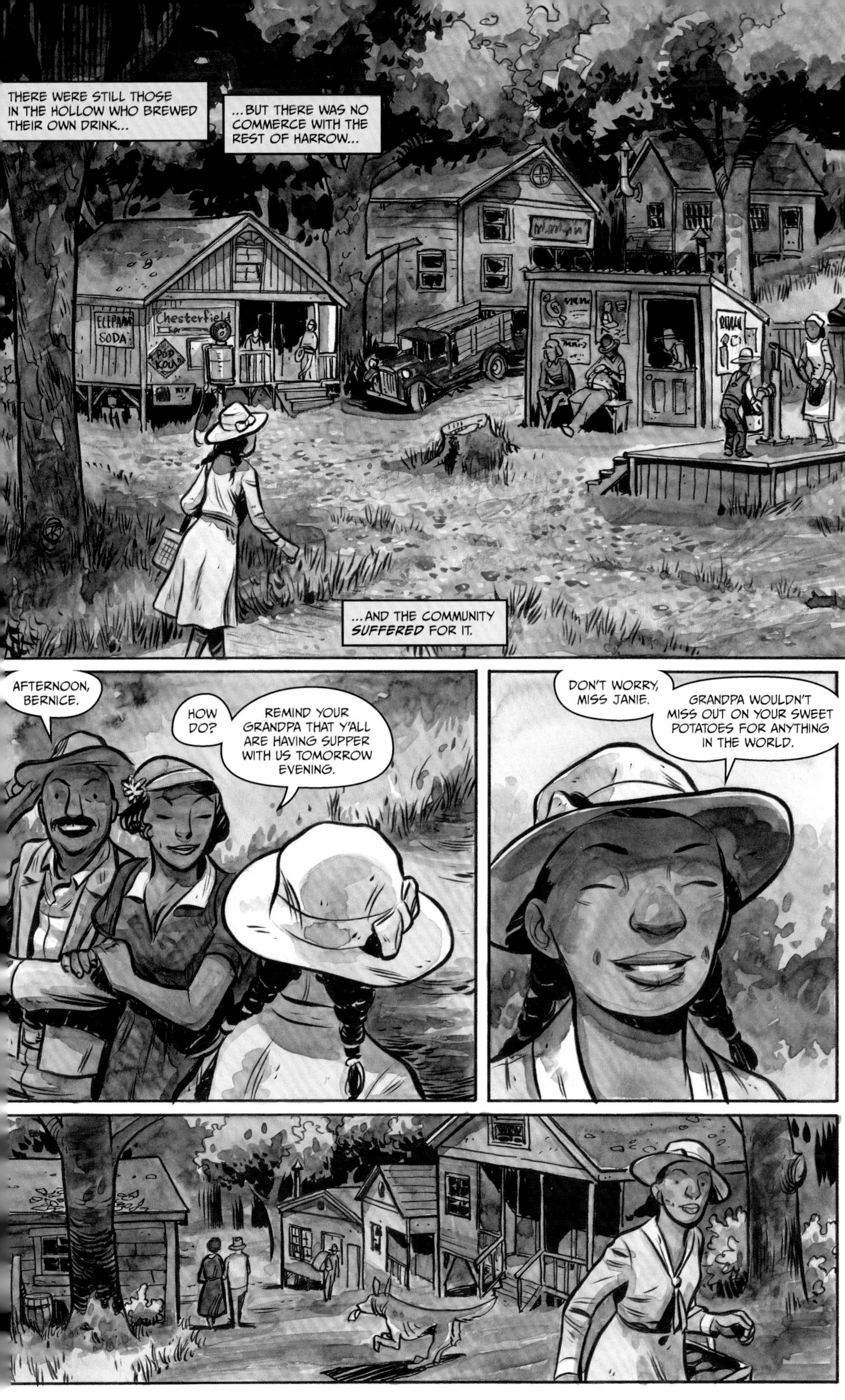
THERE WERE STILL THOSE IN THE HOLLOW WHO BREWED THEIR OWN DRINK...
...BUT THERE WAS NO COMMERCE WITH THE REST OF HARROW...
Chesterfield
SODA
...AND THE COMMUNITY *SUFFERED* FOR IT.
AFTERNOON, BERNICE.
HOW DO?
REMIND YOUR GRANDPA THAT Y'ALL ARE HAVING SUPPER WITH US TOMORROW EVENING.
DON'T WORRY, MISS JANIE.
GRANDPA WOULDN'T MISS OUT ON YOUR SWEET POTATOES FOR ANYTHING IN THE WORLD.

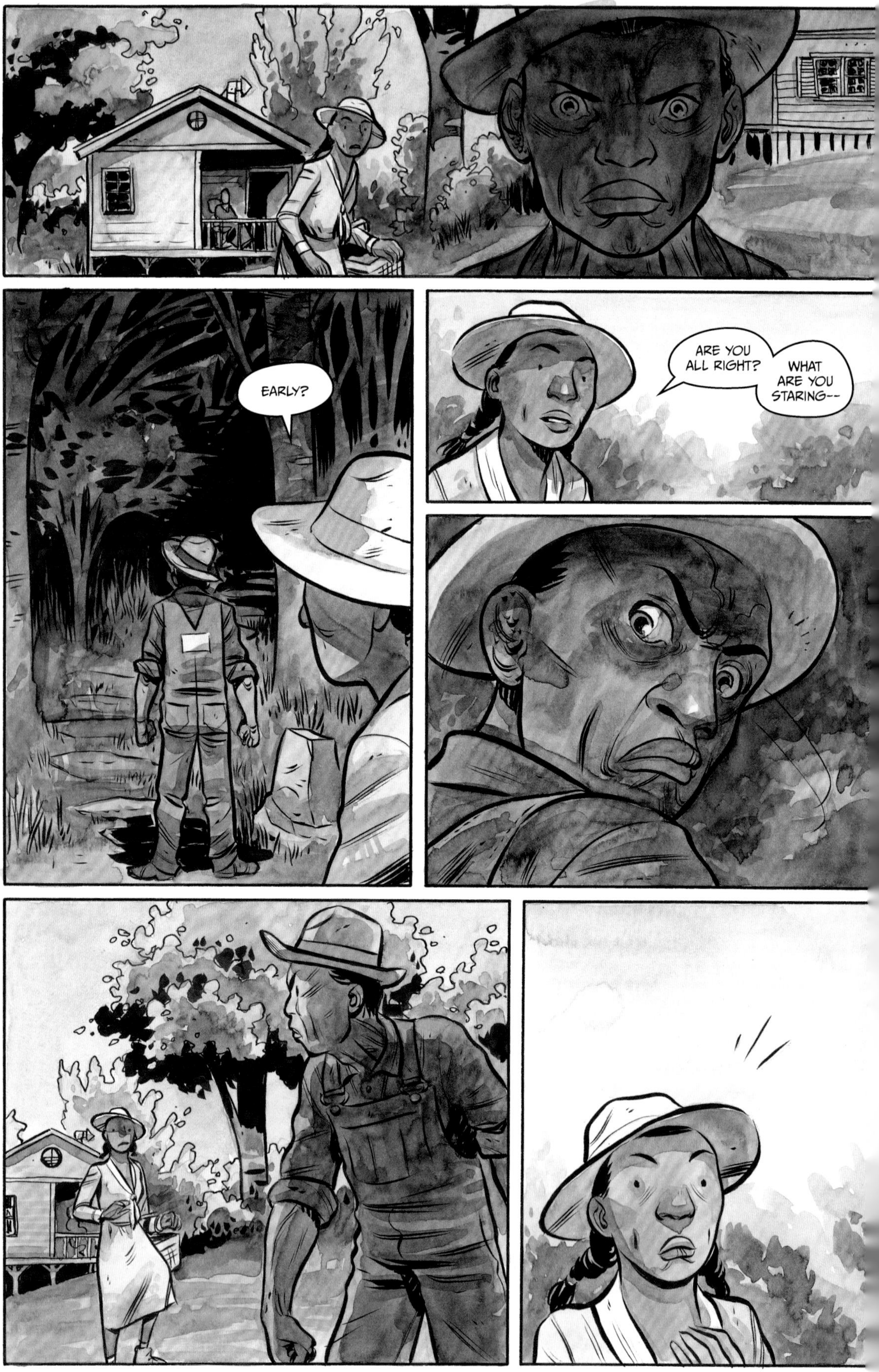
EARLY?
ARE YOU ALL RIGHT?
WHAT ARE YOU STARING--

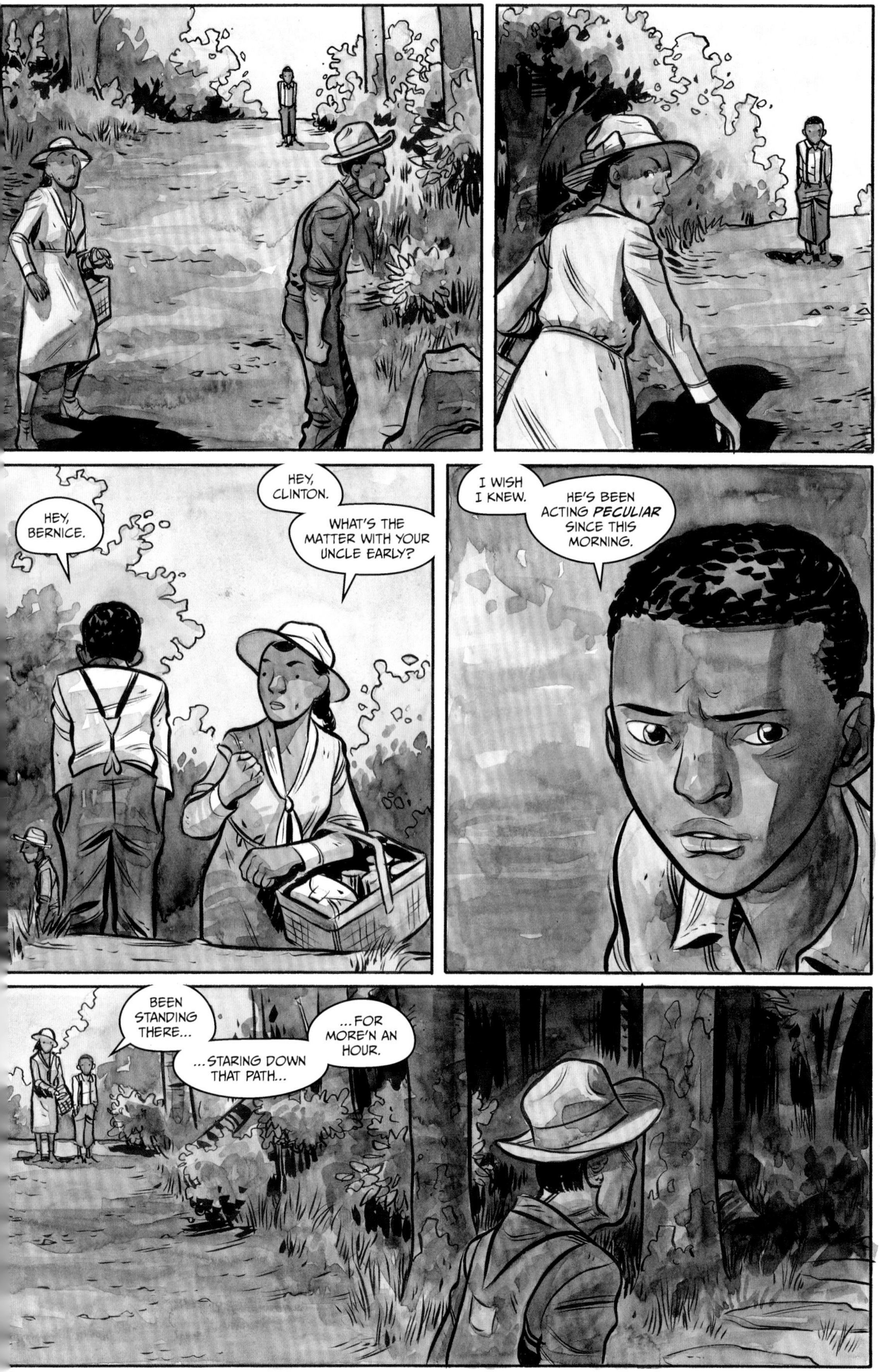
HEY, BERNICE.
HEY, CLINTON.
WHAT'S THE MATTER WITH YOUR UNCLE EARLY?
I WISH I KNEW.
HE'S BEEN ACTING PECULIAR SINCE THIS MORNING.
BEEN STANDING THERE...
...STARING DOWN THAT PATH...
...FOR MORE'N AN HOUR.

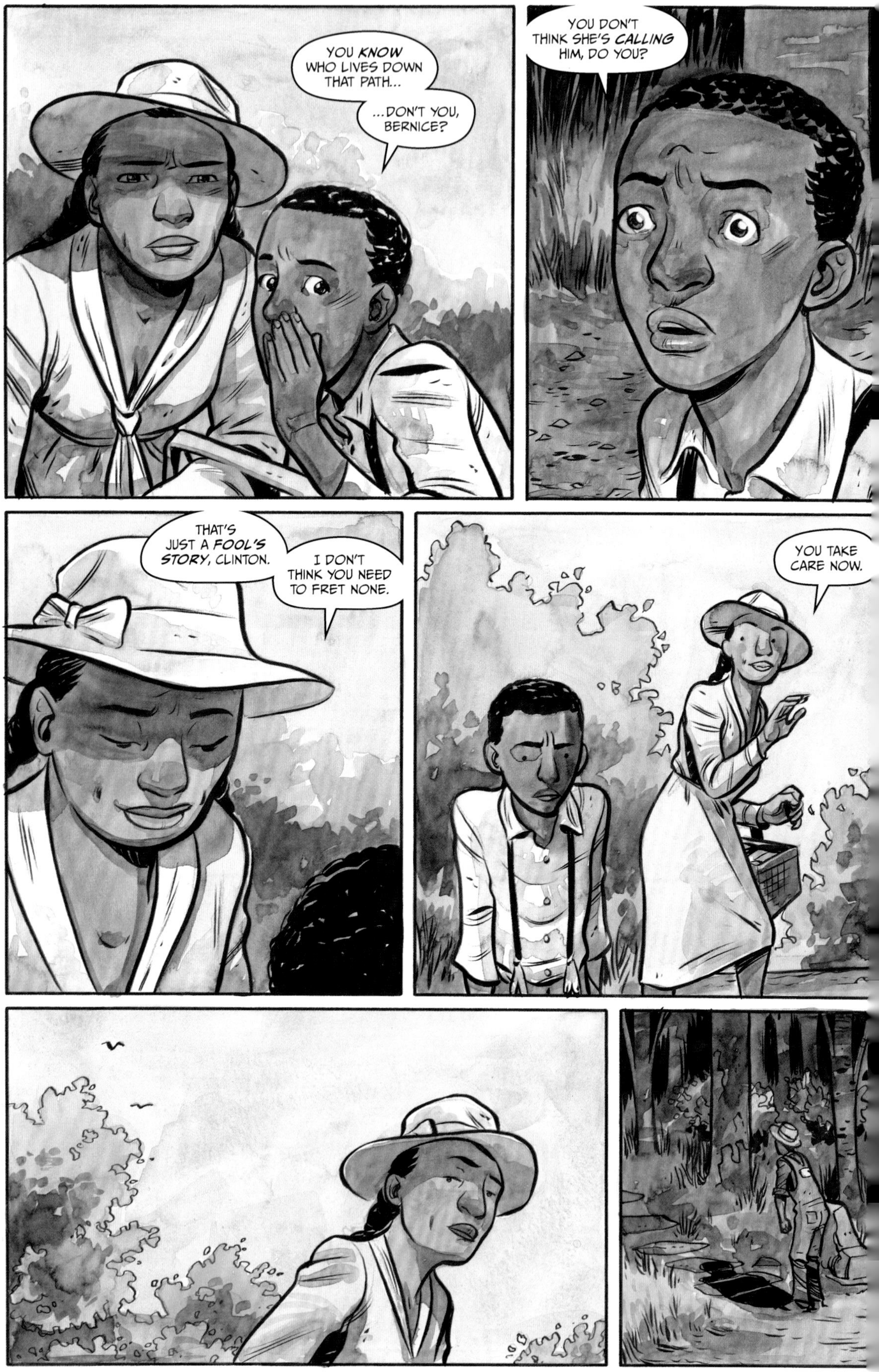
YOU KNOW WHO LIVES DOWN THAT PATH...
...DON'T YOU, BERNICE?
YOU DON'T THINK SHE'S CALLING HIM, DO YOU?
THAT'S JUST A FOOL'S STORY, CLINTON.
I DON'T THINK YOU NEED TO FRET NONE.
YOU TAKE CARE NOW.

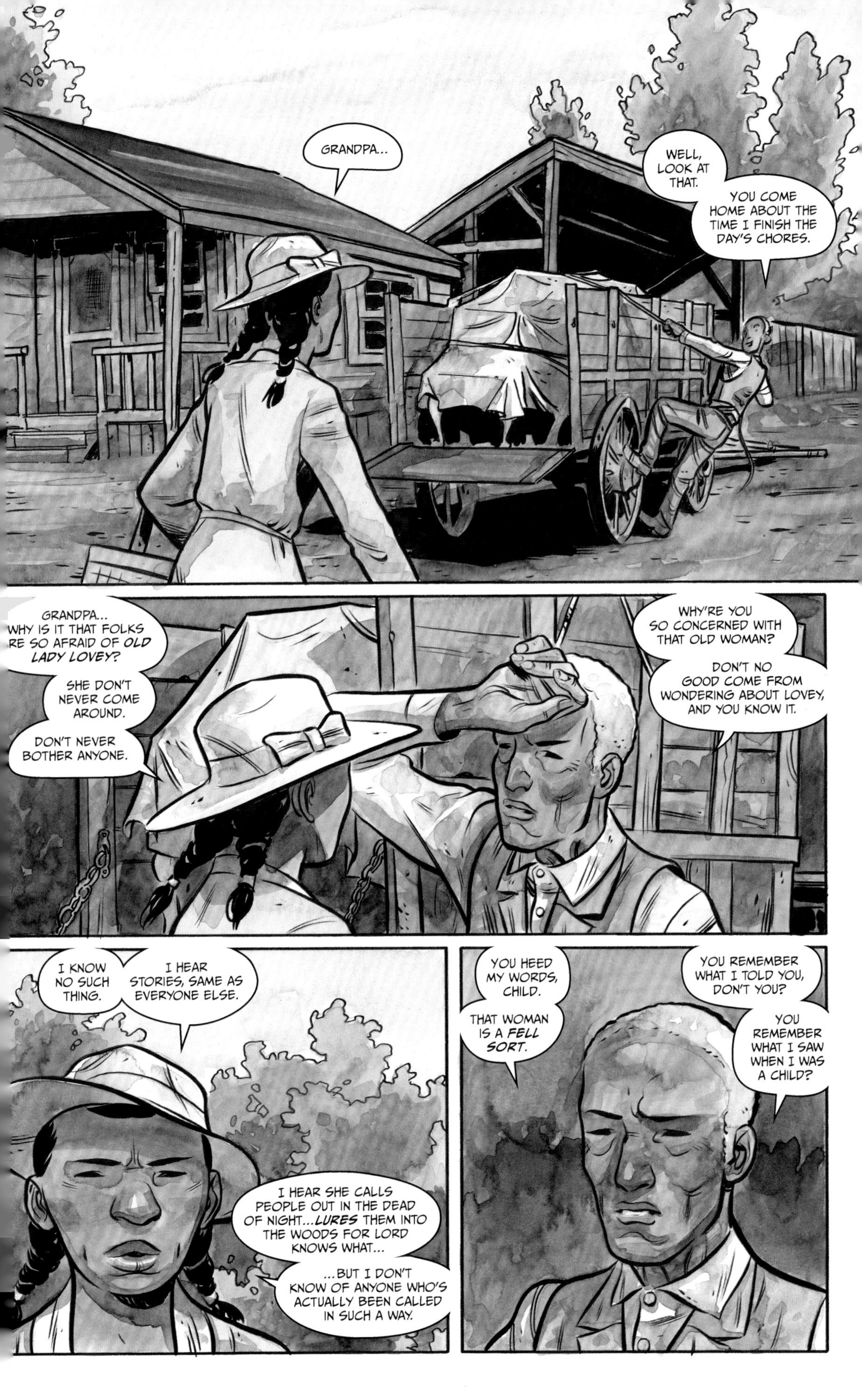
GRANDPA...
WELL, LOOK AT THAT.
YOU COME HOME ABOUT THE TIME I FINISH THE DAY'S CHORES.
GRANDPA... WHY IS IT THAT FOLKS RE SO AFRAID OF *OLD LADY LOVEY*?
SHE DON'T NEVER COME AROUND.
DON'T NEVER BOTHER ANYONE.
WHY'RE YOU SO CONCERNED WITH THAT OLD WOMAN?
DON'T NO GOOD COME FROM WONDERING ABOUT LOVEY, AND YOU KNOW IT.
I KNOW NO SUCH THING.
I HEAR STORIES, SAME AS EVERYONE ELSE.
I HEAR SHE CALLS PEOPLE OUT IN THE DEAD OF NIGHT...*LURES* THEM INTO THE WOODS FOR LORD KNOWS WHAT...
...BUT I DON'T KNOW OF ANYONE WHO'S ACTUALLY BEEN CALLED IN SUCH A WAY.
YOU HEED MY WORDS, CHILD.
THAT WOMAN IS A *FELL SORT*.
YOU REMEMBER WHAT I TOLD YOU, DON'T YOU?
YOU REMEMBER WHAT I SAW WHEN I WAS A CHILD?

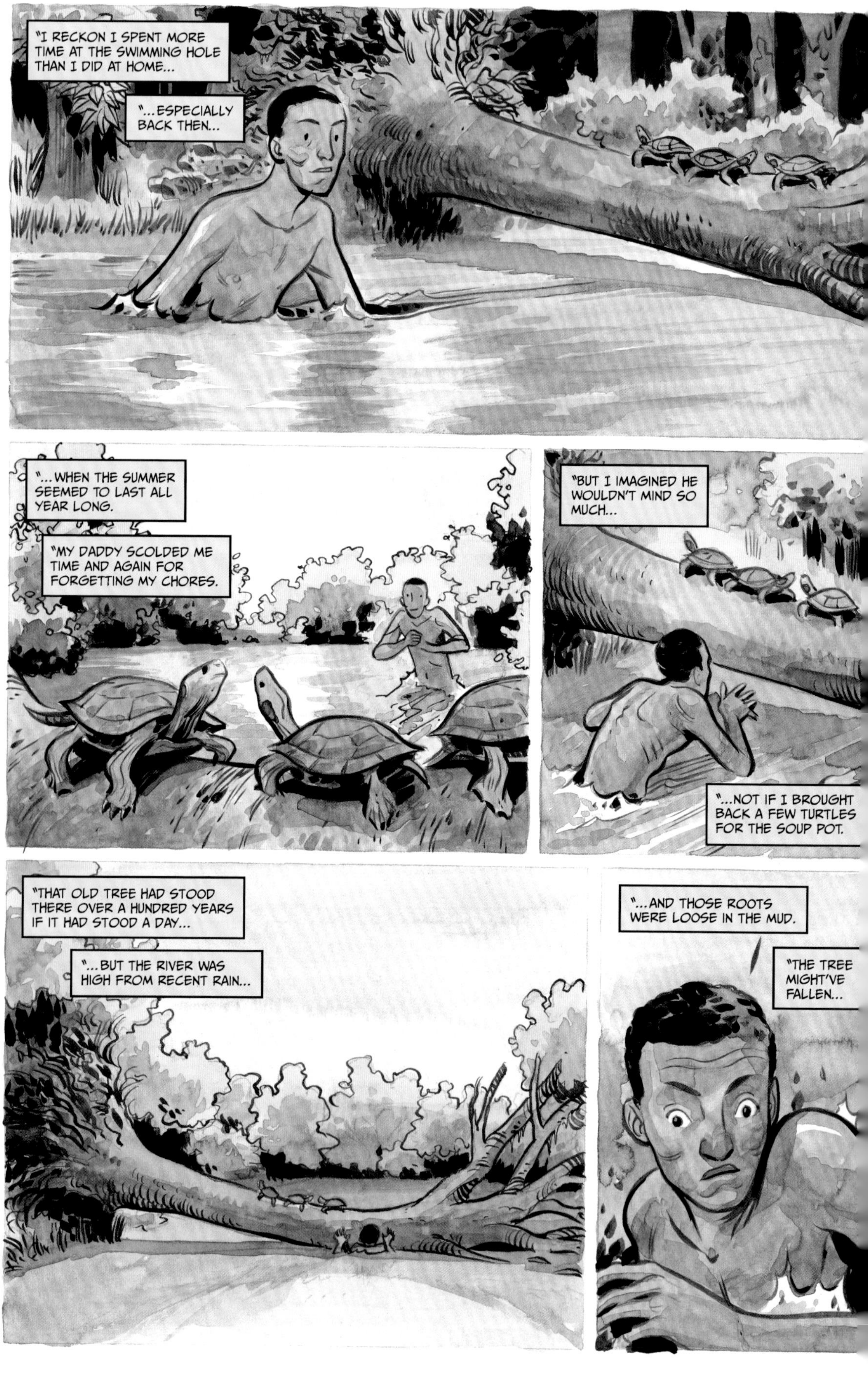
"I RECKON I SPENT MORE TIME AT THE SWIMMING HOLE THAN I DID AT HOME...
"...ESPECIALLY BACK THEN...
"...WHEN THE SUMMER SEEMED TO LAST ALL YEAR LONG.
"MY DADDY SCOLDED ME TIME AND AGAIN FOR FORGETTING MY CHORES.
"BUT I IMAGINED HE WOULDN'T MIND SO MUCH...
"...NOT IF I BROUGHT BACK A FEW TURTLES FOR THE SOUP POT.
"THAT OLD TREE HAD STOOD THERE OVER A HUNDRED YEARS IF IT HAD STOOD A DAY...
"...BUT THE RIVER WAS HIGH FROM RECENT RAIN...
"...AND THOSE ROOTS WERE LOOSE IN THE MUD.
"THE TREE MIGHT'VE FALLEN...

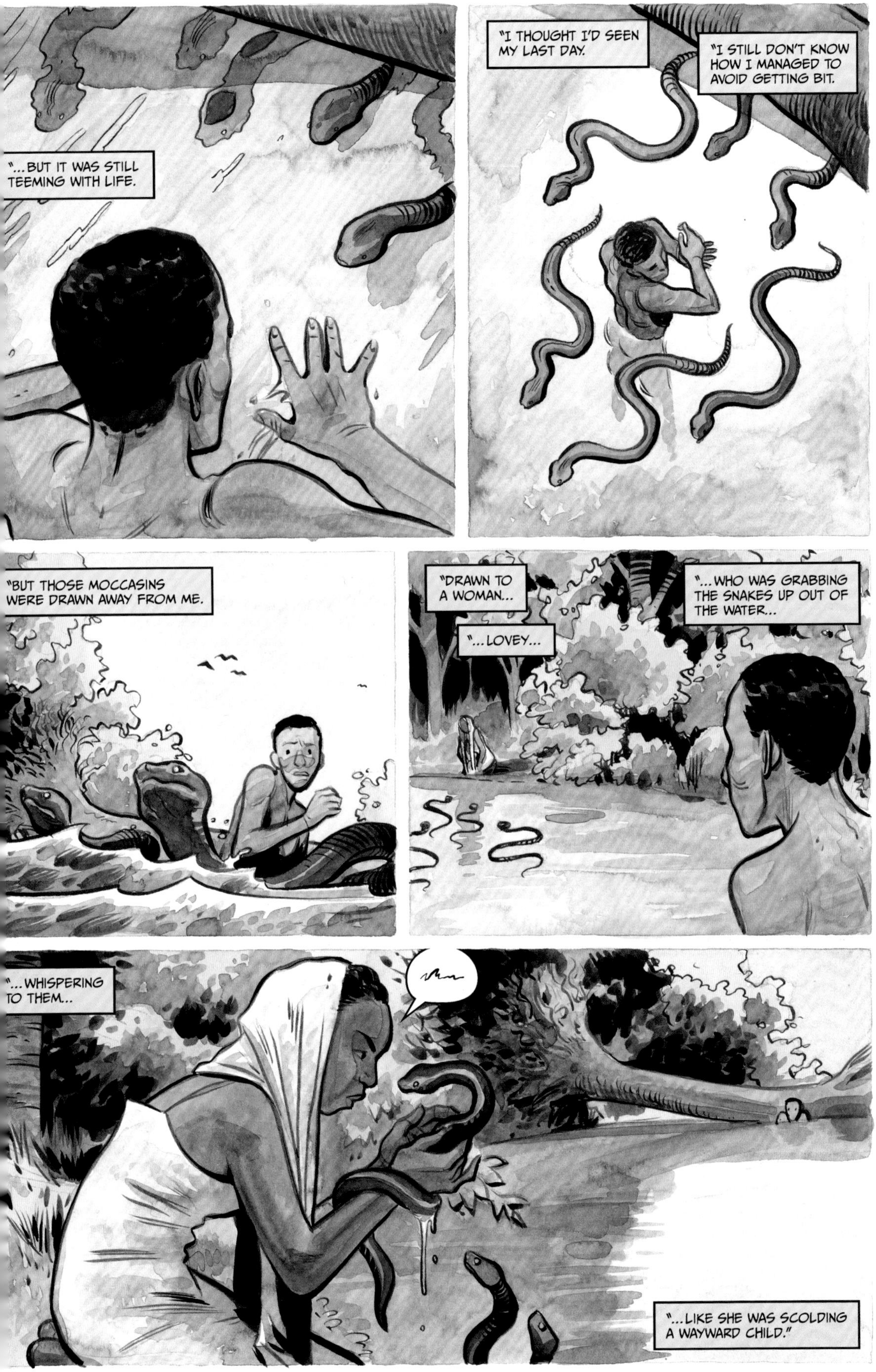
"...BUT IT WAS STILL TEEMING WITH LIFE.
"I THOUGHT I'D SEEN MY LAST DAY.
"I STILL DON'T KNOW HOW I MANAGED TO AVOID GETTING BIT.
"BUT THOSE MOCCASINS WERE DRAWN AWAY FROM ME.
"DRAWN TO A WOMAN...
"...LOVEY...
"...WHO WAS GRABBING THE SNAKES UP OUT OF THE WATER...
"...WHISPERING TO THEM...
"...LIKE SHE WAS SCOLDING A WAYWARD CHILD."

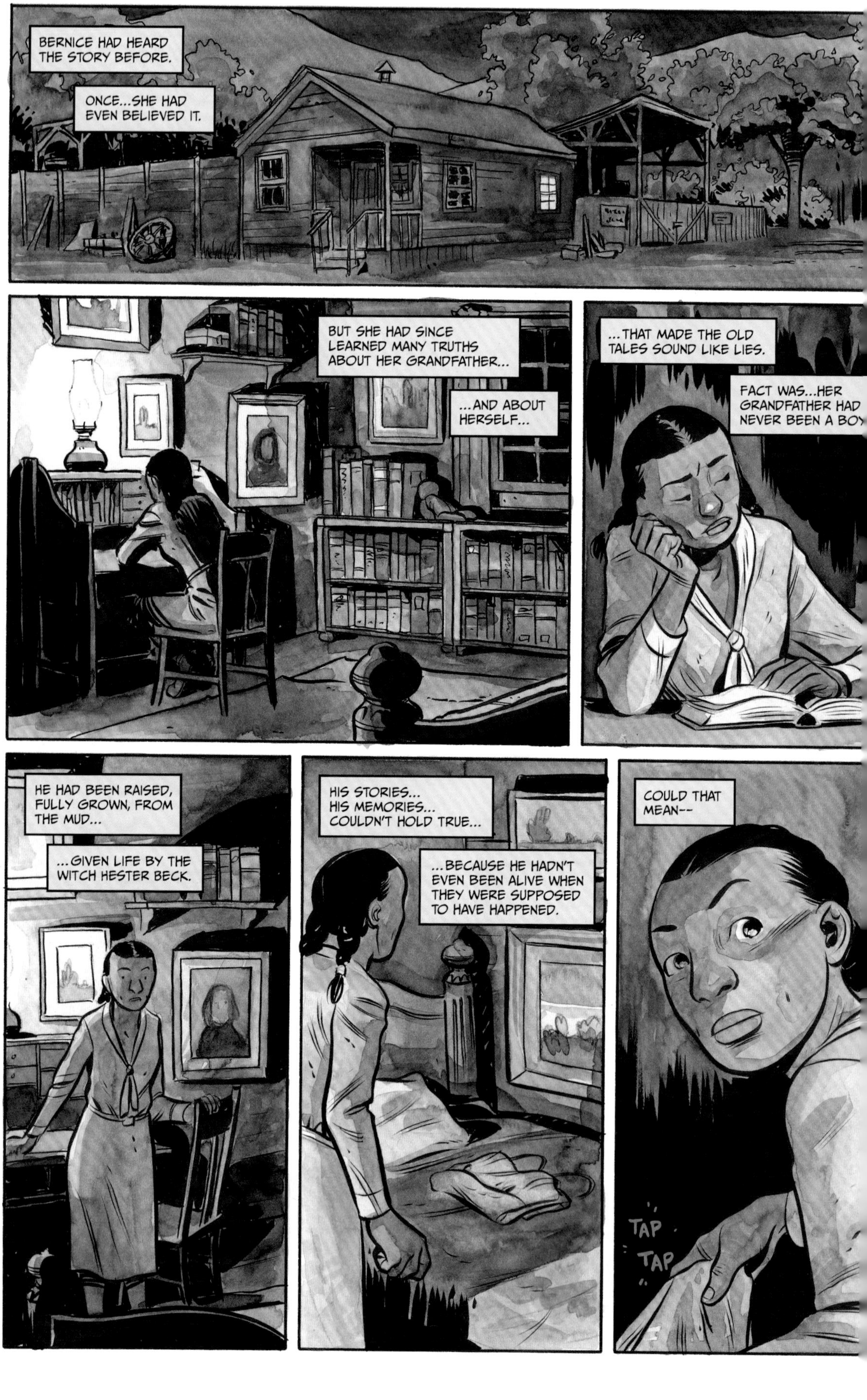
BERNICE HAD HEARD THE STORY BEFORE.
ONCE...SHE HAD EVEN BELIEVED IT.
BUT SHE HAD SINCE LEARNED MANY TRUTHS ABOUT HER GRANDFATHER...
...AND ABOUT HERSELF...
...THAT MADE THE OLD TALES SOUND LIKE LIES.
FACT WAS...HER GRANDFATHER HAD NEVER BEEN A BOY
HE HAD BEEN RAISED, FULLY GROWN, FROM THE MUD...
...GIVEN LIFE BY THE WITCH HESTER BECK.
HIS STORIES... HIS MEMORIES... COULDN'T HOLD TRUE...
...BECAUSE HE HADN'T EVEN BEEN ALIVE WHEN THEY WERE SUPPOSED TO HAVE HAPPENED.
COULD THAT MEAN--
TAP
TAP

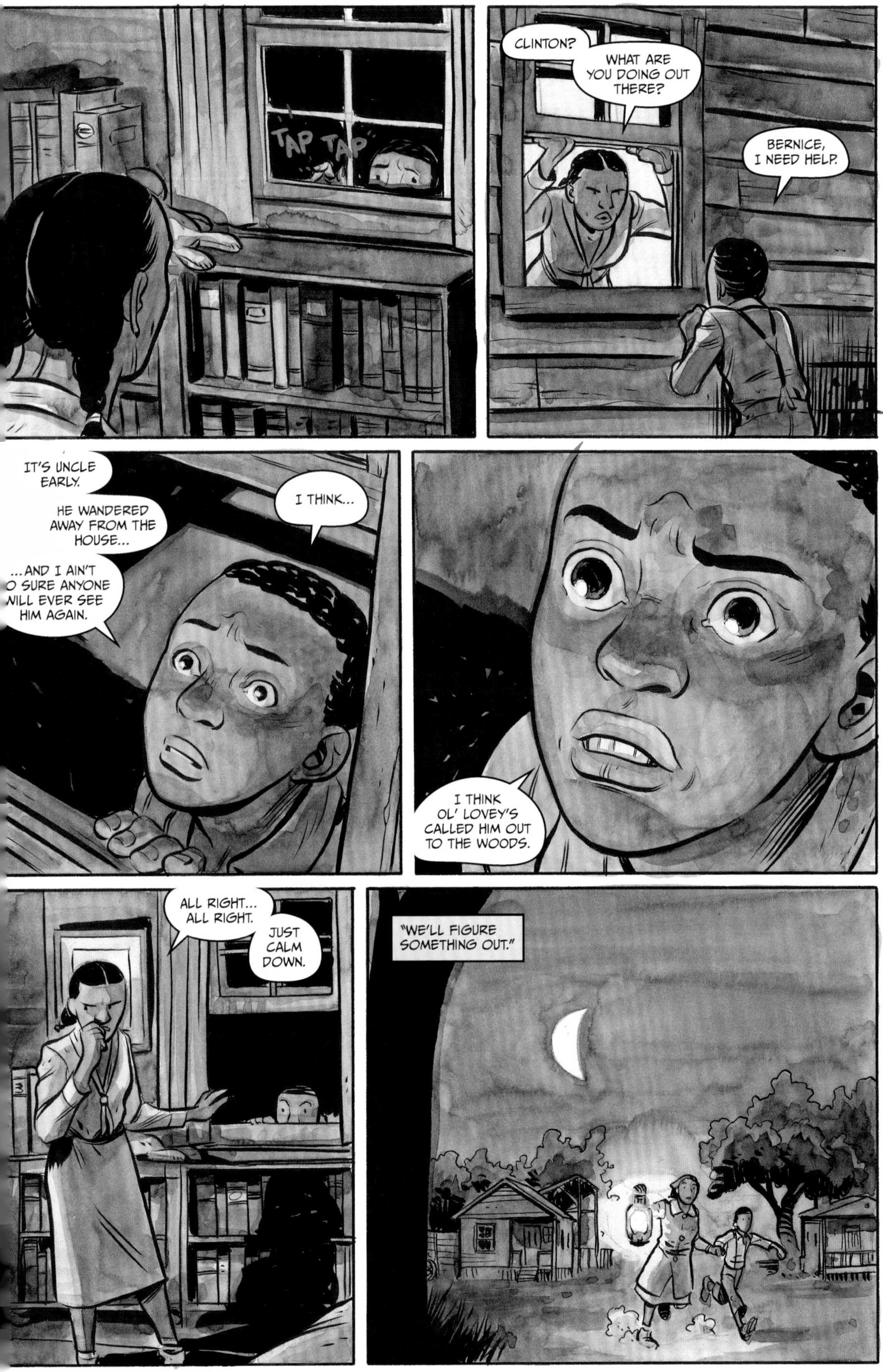
TAP TAP
CLINTON?
WHAT ARE YOU DOING OUT THERE?
BERNICE, I NEED HELP.
IT'S UNCLE EARLY.
HE WANDERED AWAY FROM THE HOUSE...
...AND I AIN'T SO SURE ANYONE WILL EVER SEE HIM AGAIN.
I THINK...
I THINK OL' LOVEY'S CALLED HIM OUT TO THE WOODS.
ALL RIGHT... ALL RIGHT.
JUST CALM DOWN.
"WE'LL FIGURE SOMETHING OUT."

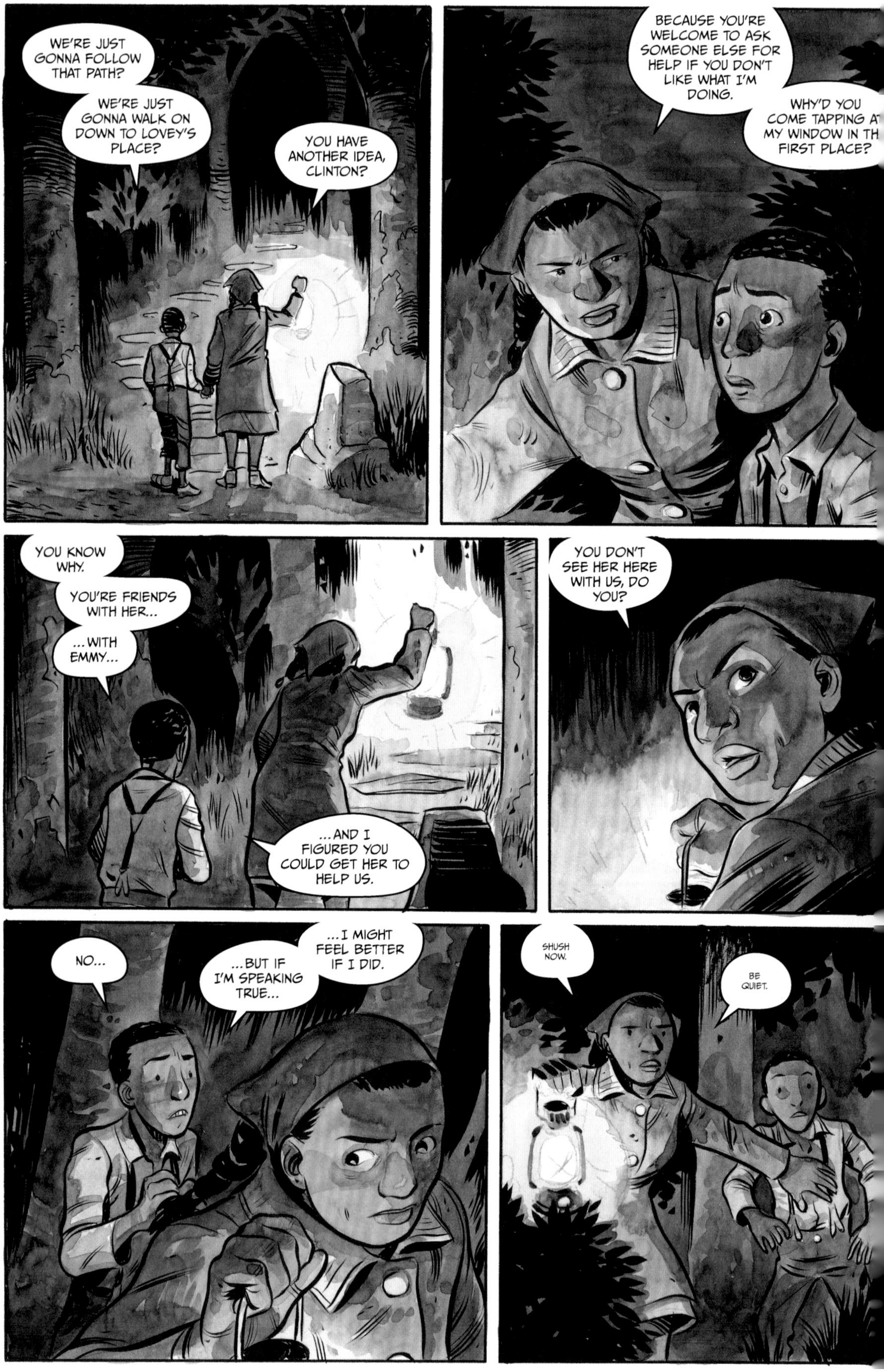
WE'RE JUST GONNA FOLLOW THAT PATH?
WE'RE JUST GONNA WALK ON DOWN TO LOVEY'S PLACE?
YOU HAVE ANOTHER IDEA, CLINTON?
BECAUSE YOU'RE WELCOME TO ASK SOMEONE ELSE FOR HELP IF YOU DON'T LIKE WHAT I'M DOING.
WHY'D YOU COME TAPPING AT MY WINDOW IN THE FIRST PLACE?
YOU KNOW WHY.
YOU'RE FRIENDS WITH HER...
...WITH EMMY...
...AND I FIGURED YOU COULD GET HER TO HELP US.
YOU DON'T SEE HER HERE WITH US, DO YOU?
NO...
...BUT IF I'M SPEAKING TRUE...
...I MIGHT FEEL BETTER IF I DID.
SHUSH NOW.
BE QUIET.

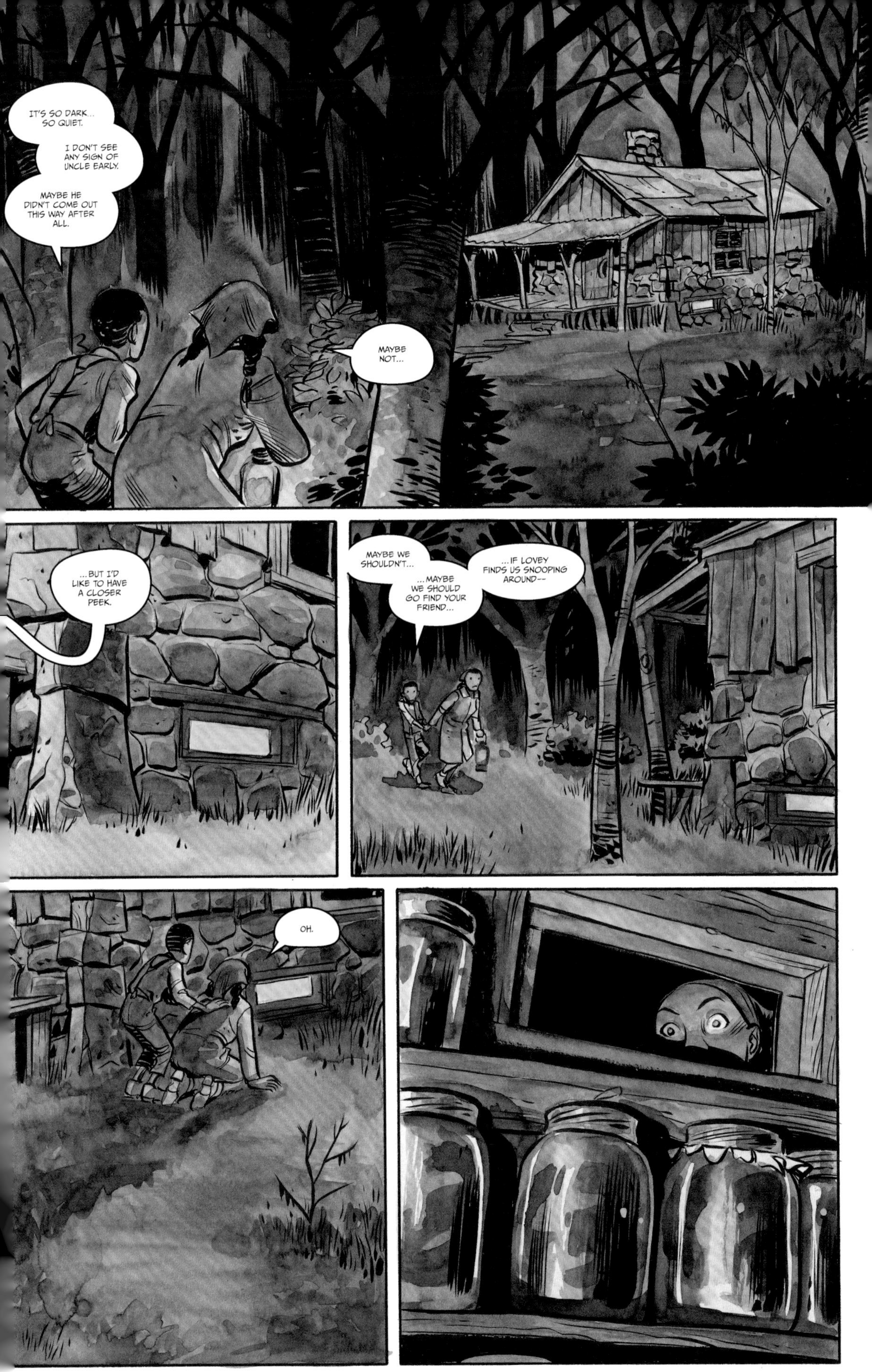
IT'S SO DARK... SO QUIET.
I DON'T SEE ANY SIGN OF UNCLE EARLY.
MAYBE HE DIDN'T COME OUT THIS WAY AFTER ALL.
MAYBE NOT...
...BUT I'D LIKE TO HAVE A CLOSER PEEK.
MAYBE WE SHOULDN'T...
...IF LOVEY FINDS US SNOOPING AROUND--
...MAYBE WE SHOULD GO FIND YOUR FRIEND...
OH.

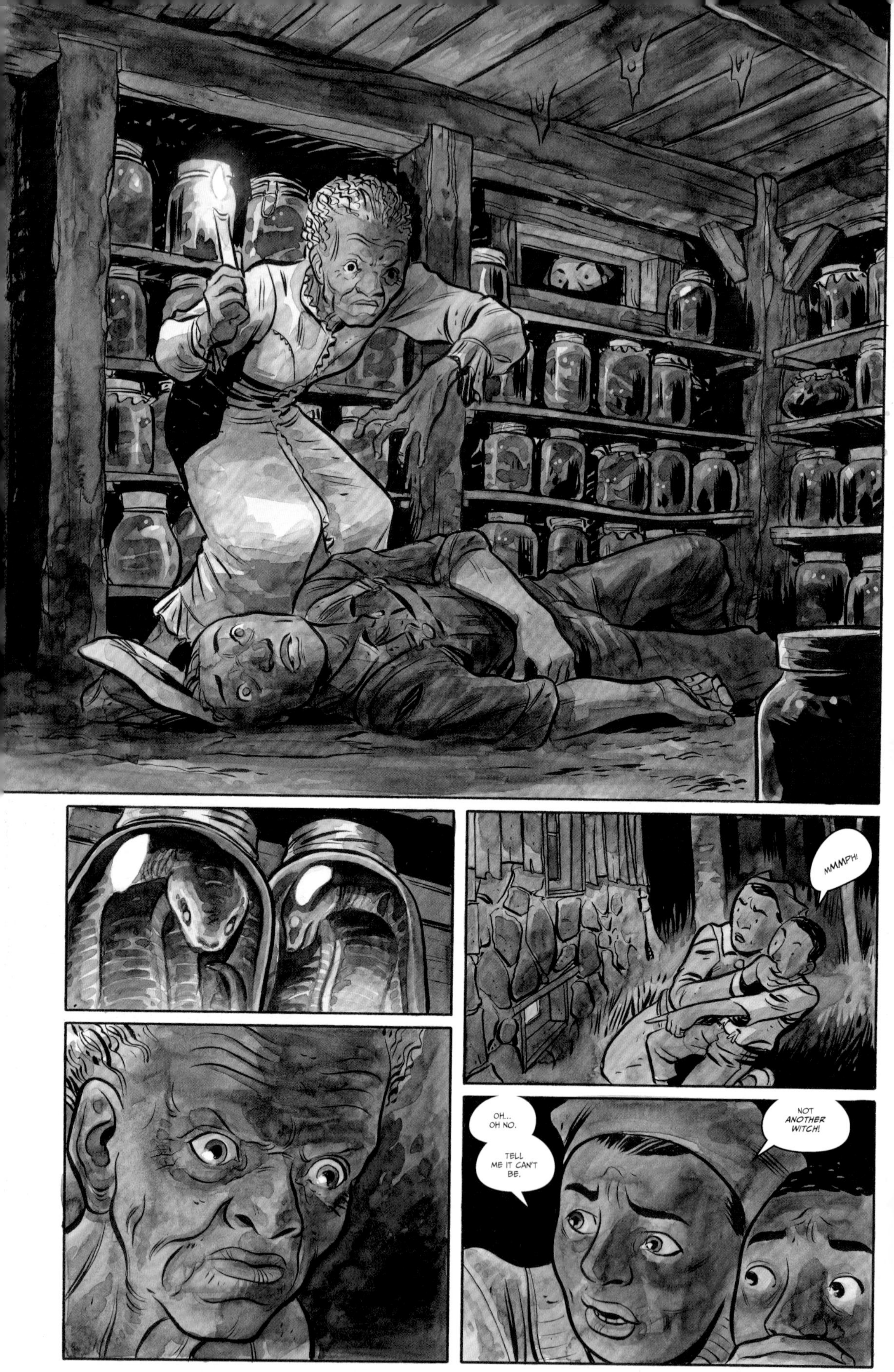
MMMPH!
OH... OH NO.
TELL ME IT CAN'T BE.
NOT ANOTHER WITCH!

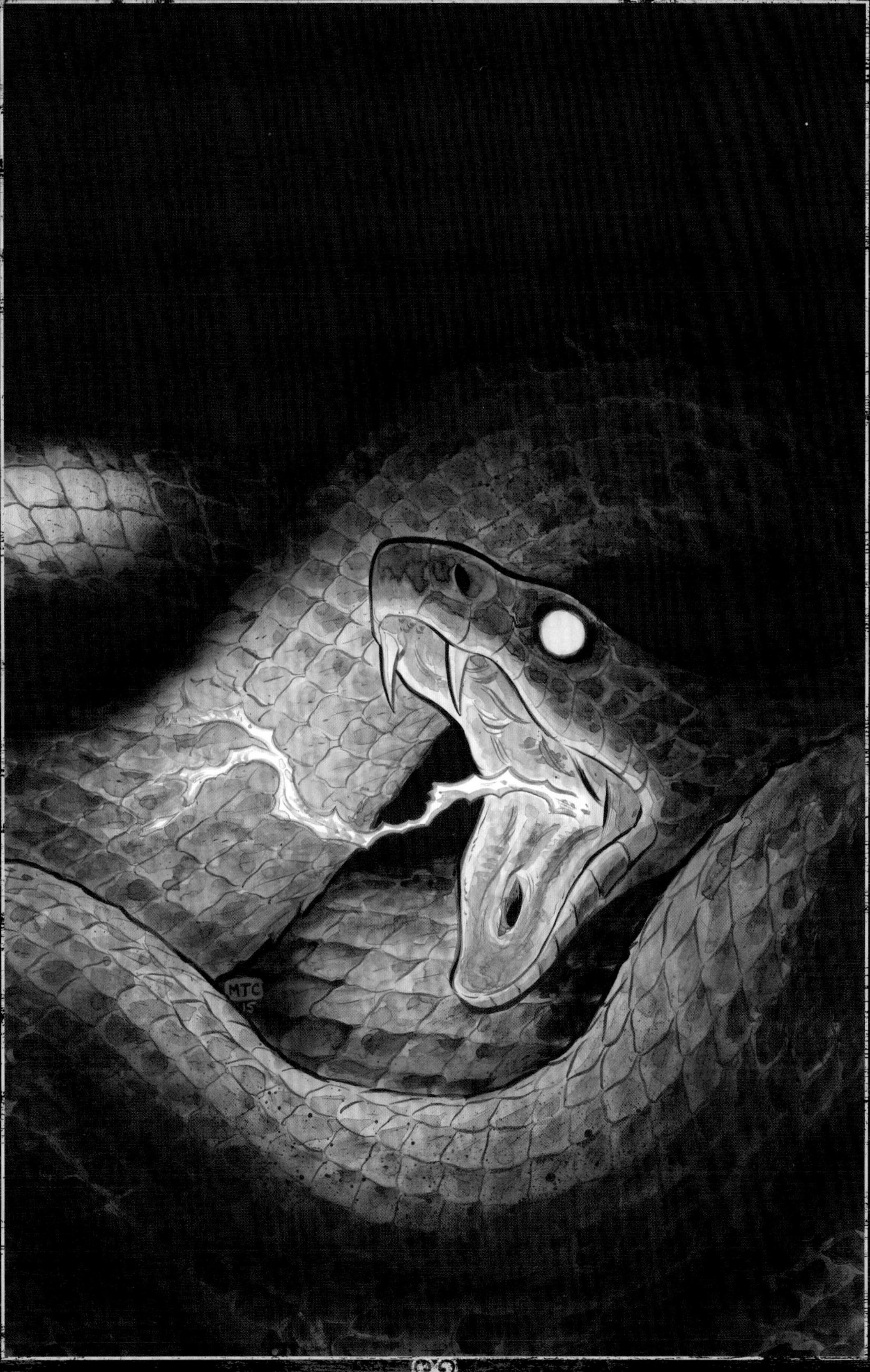
MTC
15

THREE

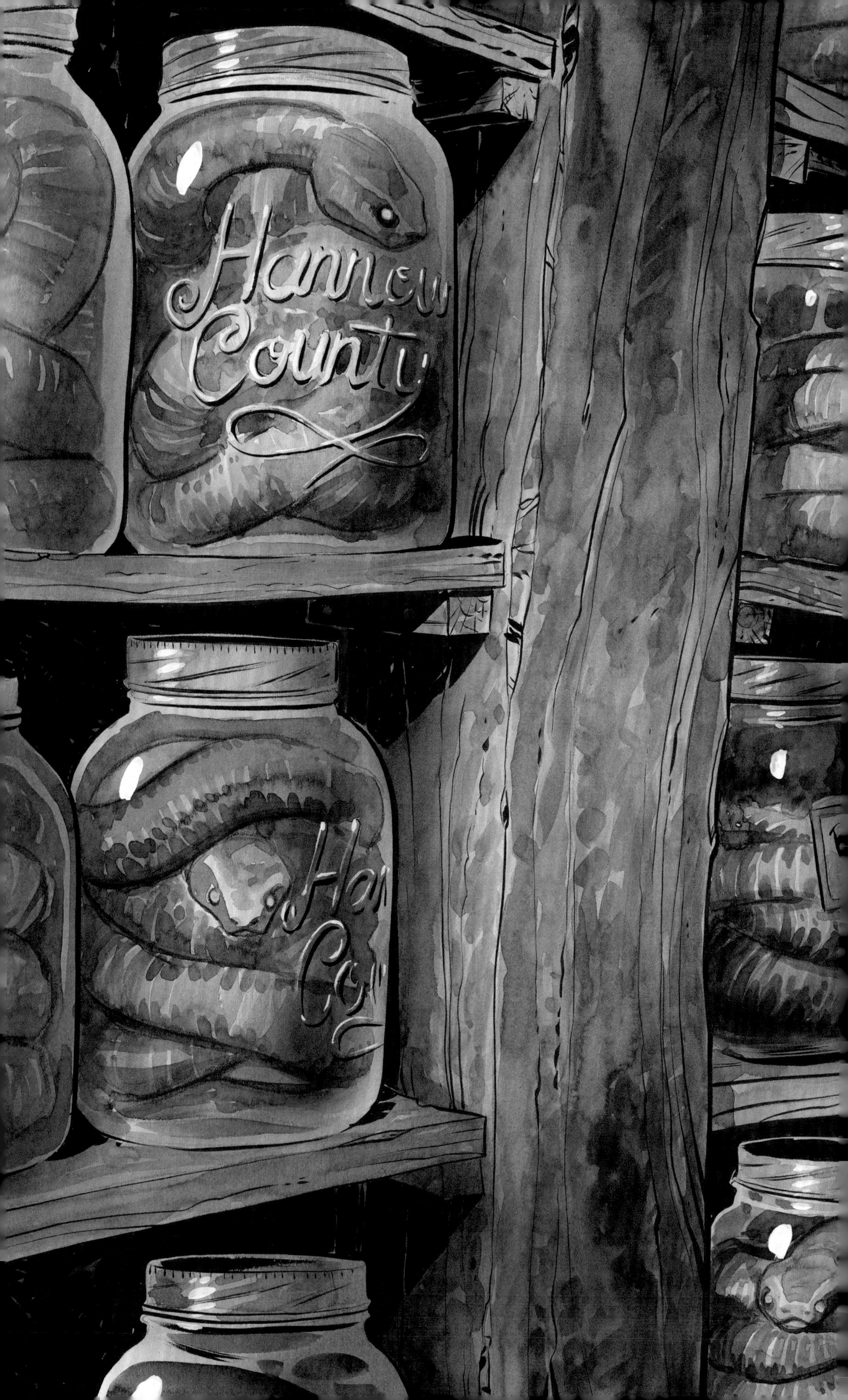
Harrow County

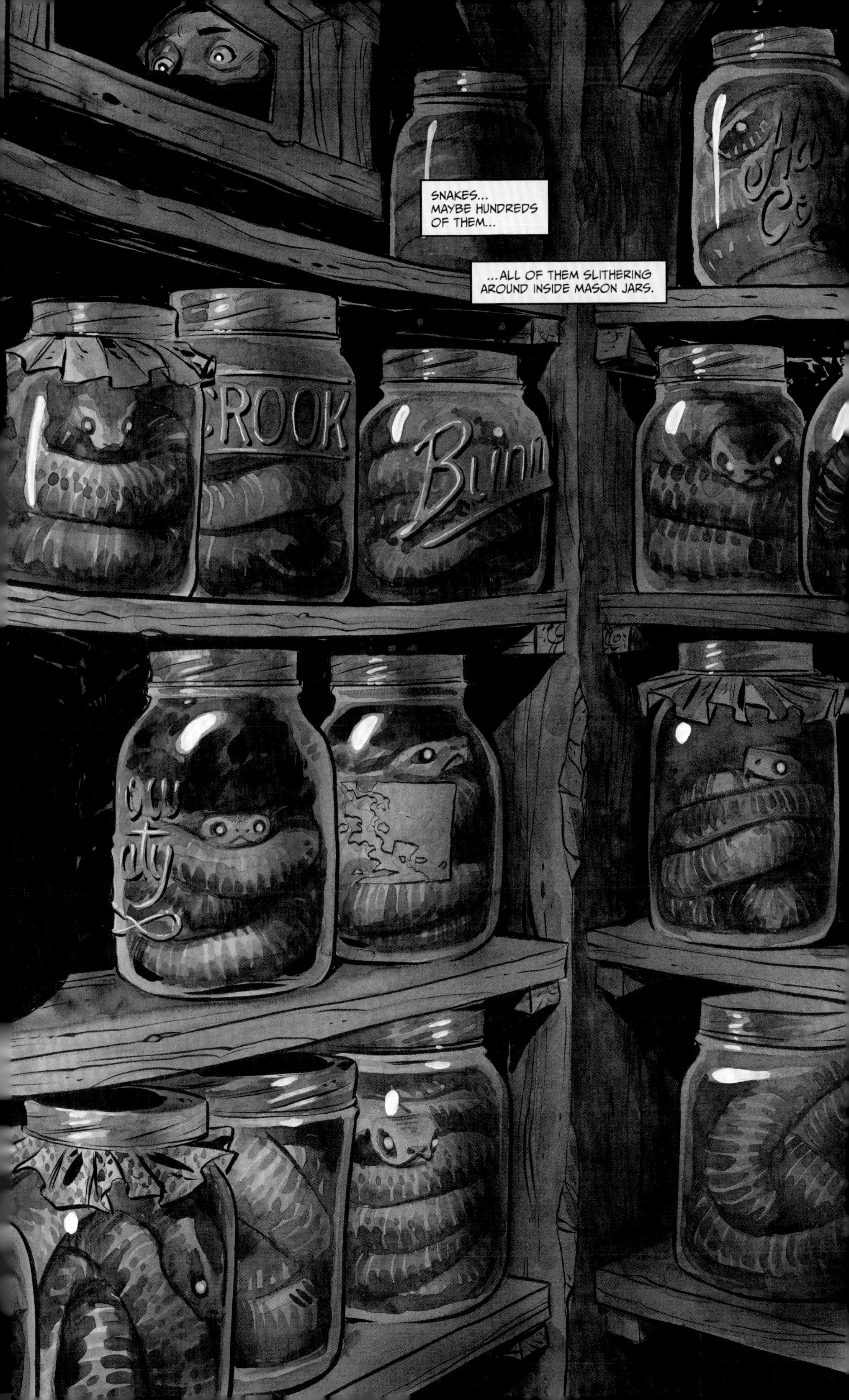
SNAKES... MAYBE HUNDREDS OF THEM...
...ALL OF THEM SLITHERING AROUND INSIDE MASON JARS.

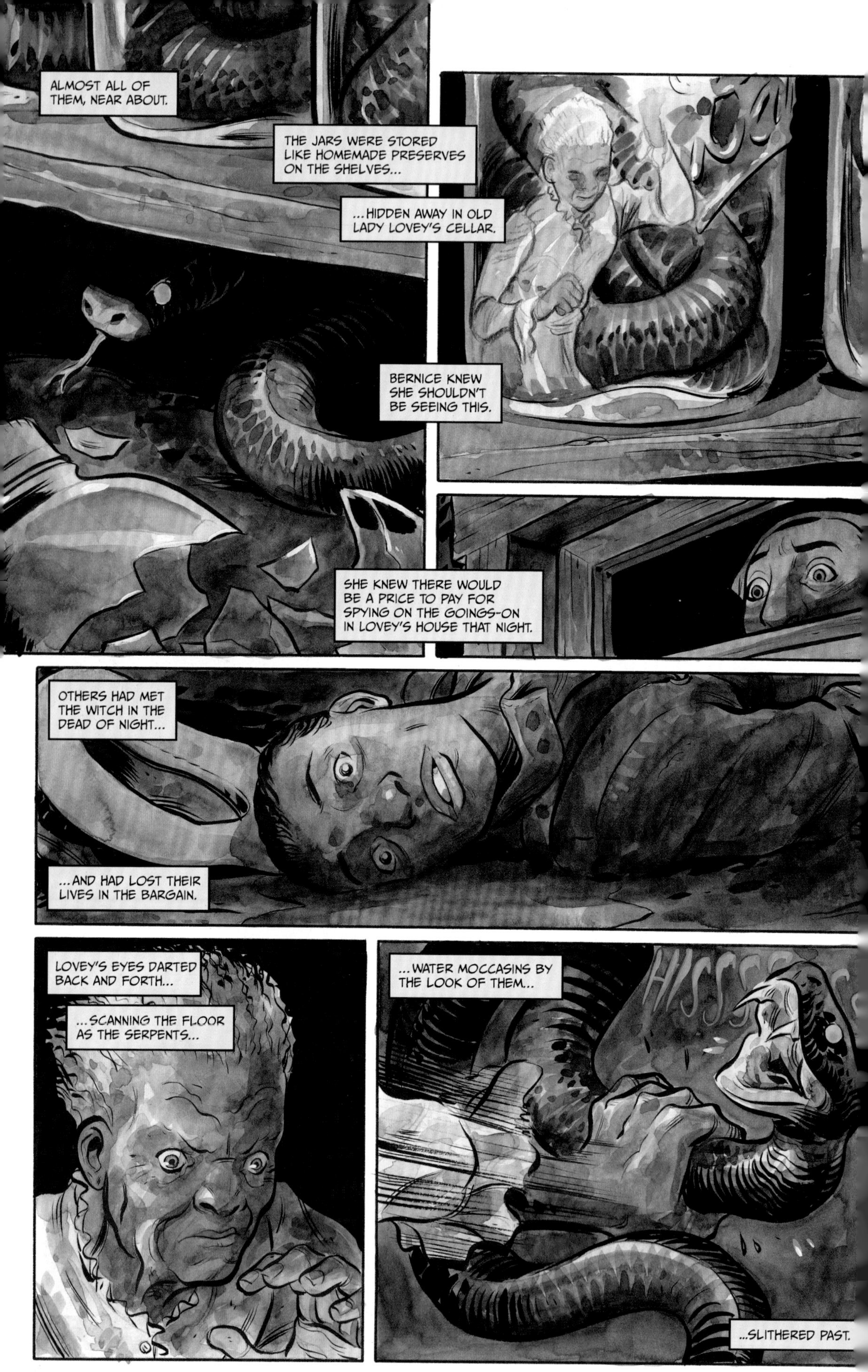
ALMOST ALL OF THEM, NEAR ABOUT.
THE JARS WERE STORED LIKE HOMEMADE PRESERVES ON THE SHELVES...
...HIDDEN AWAY IN OLD LADY LOVEY'S CELLAR.
BERNICE KNEW SHE SHOULDN'T BE SEEING THIS.
SHE KNEW THERE WOULD BE A PRICE TO PAY FOR SPYING ON THE GOINGS-ON IN LOVEY'S HOUSE THAT NIGHT.
OTHERS HAD MET THE WITCH IN THE DEAD OF NIGHT...
...AND HAD LOST THEIR LIVES IN THE BARGAIN.
LOVEY'S EYES DARTED BACK AND FORTH...
...SCANNING THE FLOOR AS THE SERPENTS...
...WATER MOCCASINS BY THE LOOK OF THEM...
...SLITHERED PAST.

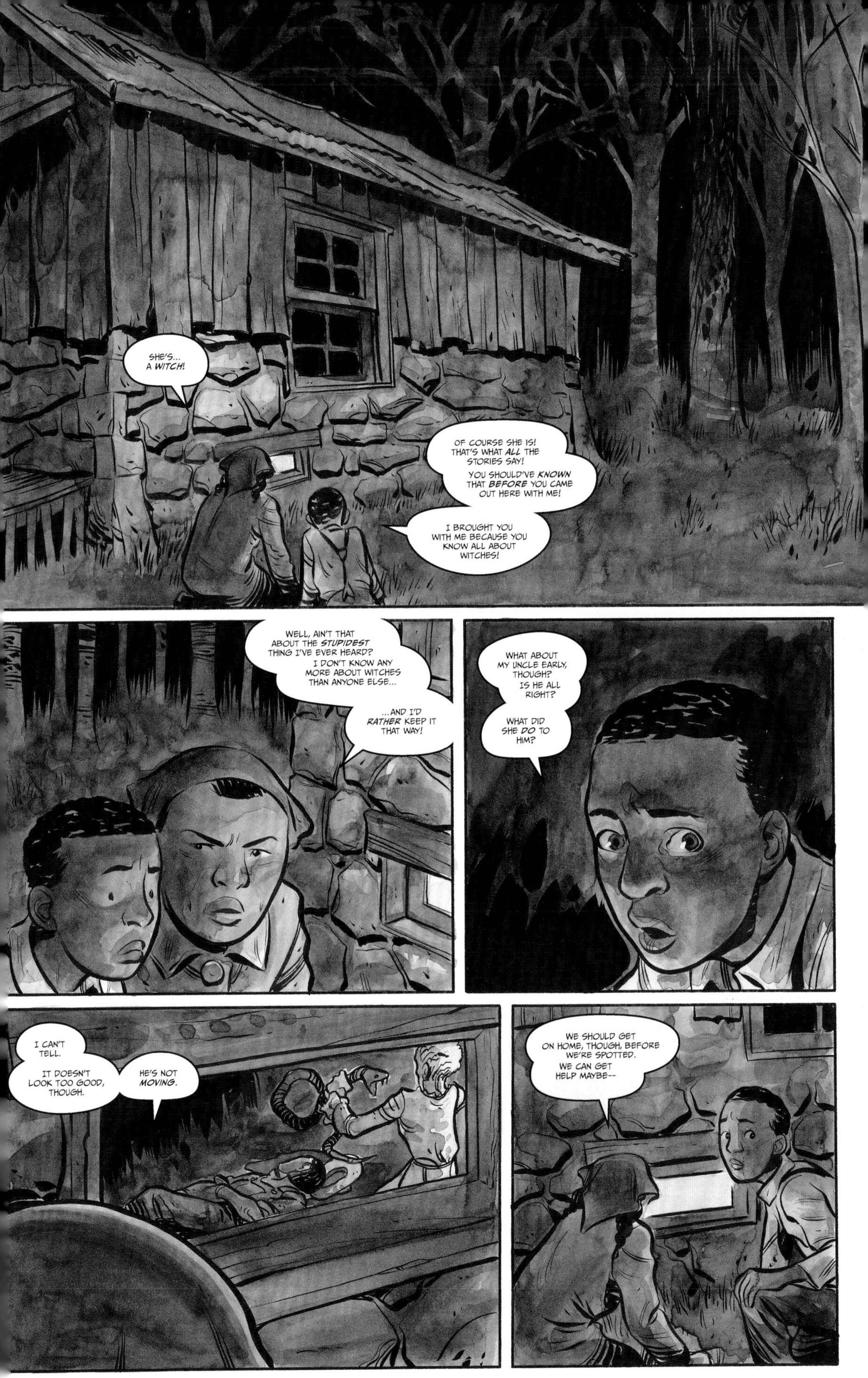
SHE'S... A WITCH!
OF COURSE SHE IS! THAT'S WHAT ALL THE STORIES SAY!
YOU SHOULD'VE KNOWN THAT BEFORE YOU CAME OUT HERE WITH ME!
I BROUGHT YOU WITH ME BECAUSE YOU KNOW ALL ABOUT WITCHES!
WELL, AIN'T THAT ABOUT THE STUPIDEST THING I'VE EVER HEARD?
I DON'T KNOW ANY MORE ABOUT WITCHES THAN ANYONE ELSE...
...AND I'D RATHER KEEP IT THAT WAY!
WHAT ABOUT MY UNCLE EARLY, THOUGH?
IS HE ALL RIGHT?
WHAT DID SHE DO TO HIM?
I CAN'T TELL.
IT DOESN'T LOOK TOO GOOD, THOUGH.
HE'S NOT MOVING.
WE SHOULD GET ON HOME, THOUGH, BEFORE WE'RE SPOTTED.
WE CAN GET HELP MAYBE--

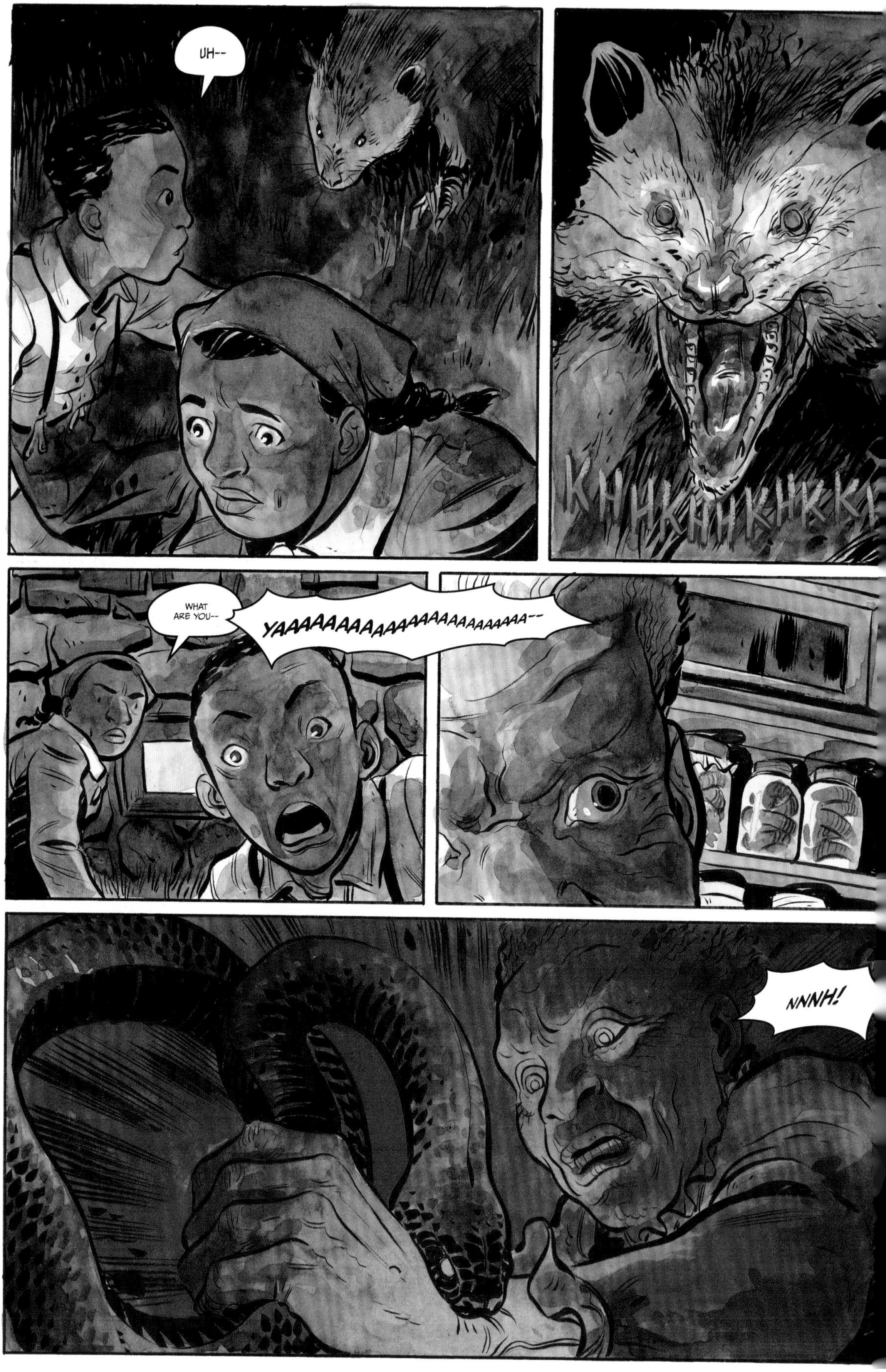
UH--
KHHKHHKHKK!
WHAT ARE YOU--
YAAAAAAAAAAAAAAAAAAAAAAA--
NNNH!

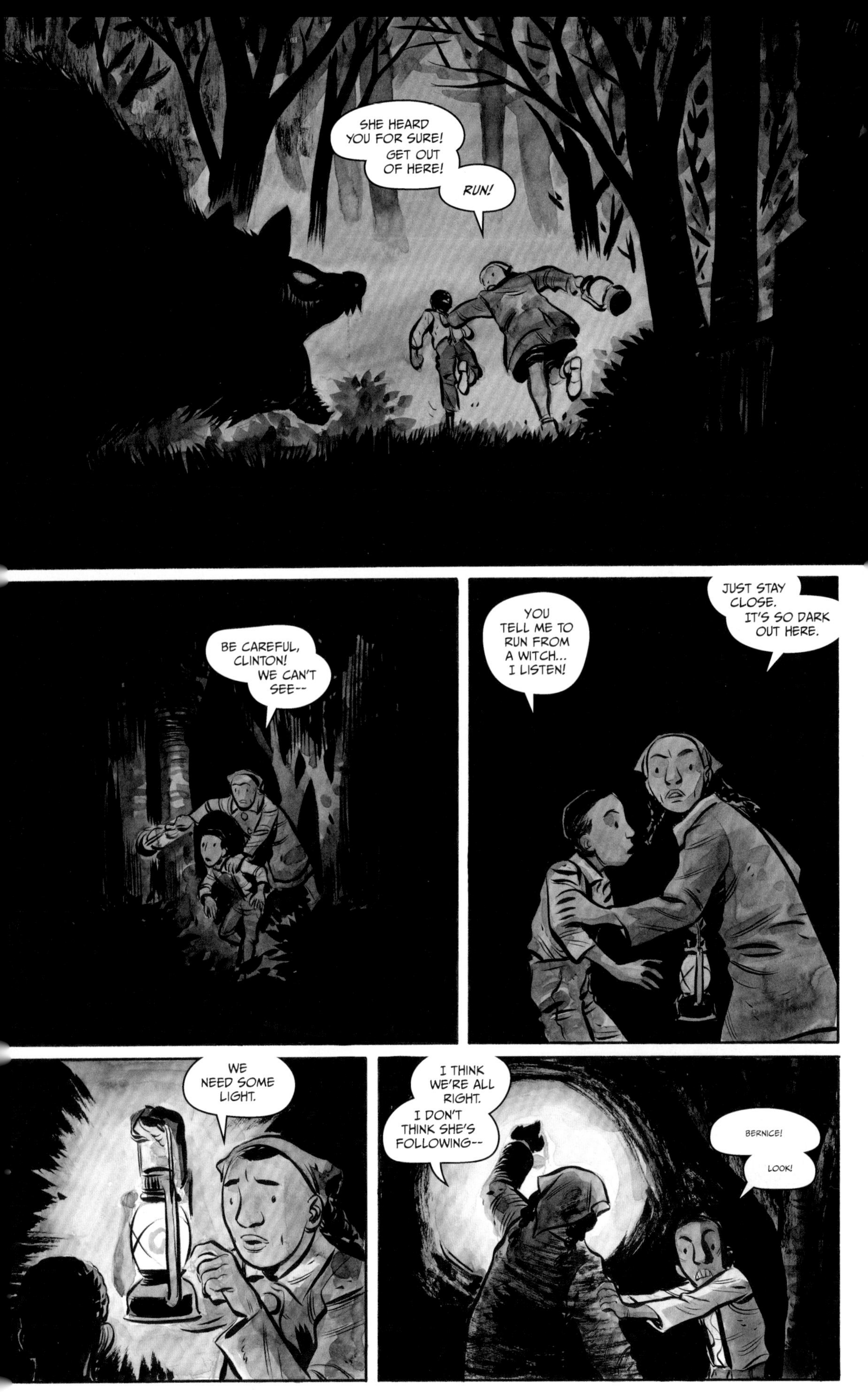
SHE HEARD YOU FOR SURE! GET OUT OF HERE!
RUN!
BE CAREFUL, CLINTON! WE CAN'T SEE--
YOU TELL ME TO RUN FROM A WITCH... I LISTEN!
JUST STAY CLOSE. IT'S SO DARK OUT HERE.
WE NEED SOME LIGHT.
I THINK WE'RE ALL RIGHT. I DON'T THINK SHE'S FOLLOWING--
BERNICE!
LOOK!

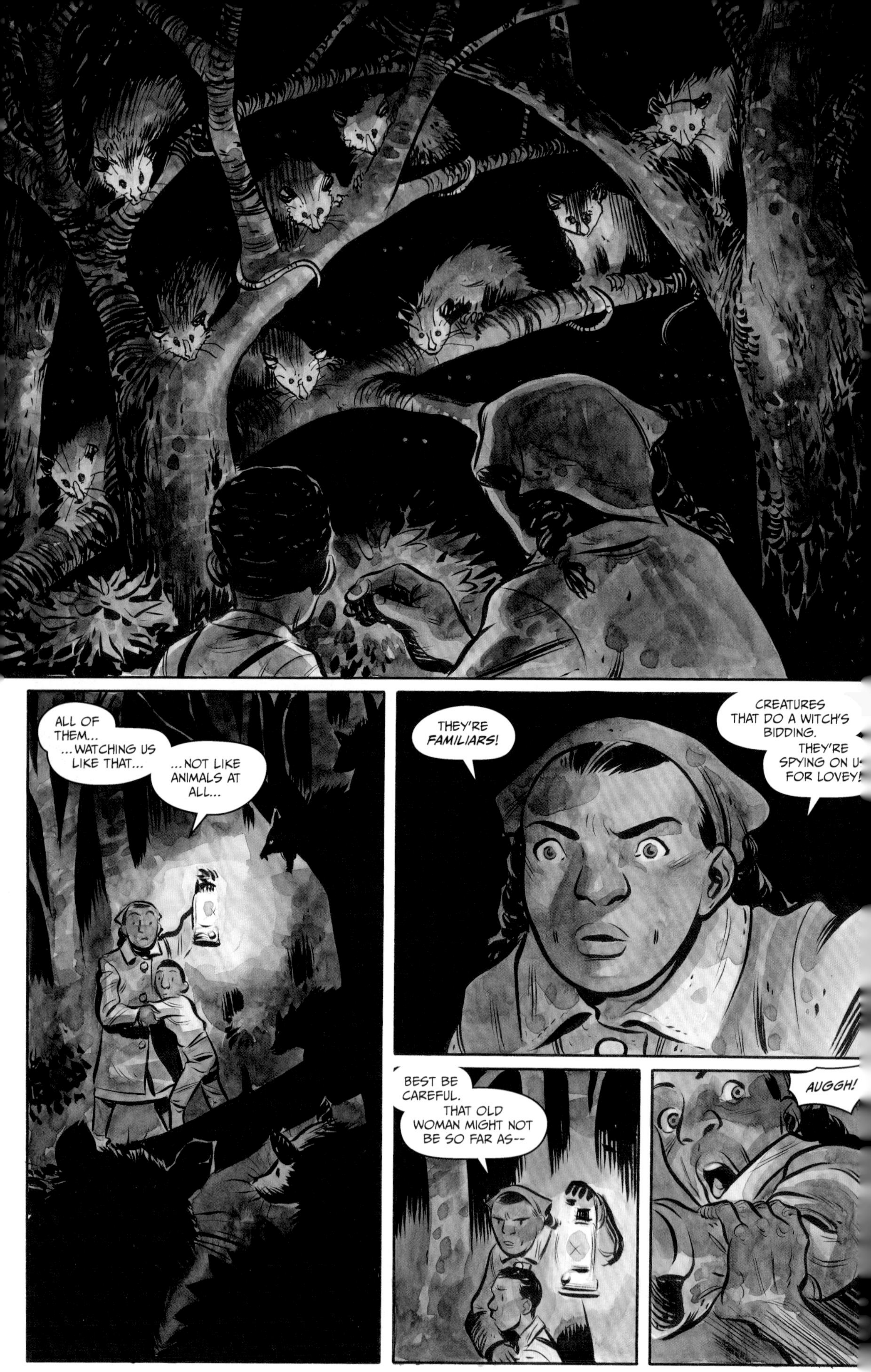
ALL OF THEM... ...WATCHING US LIKE THAT...
...NOT LIKE ANIMALS AT ALL...
THEY'RE *FAMILIARS!*
CREATURES THAT DO A WITCH'S BIDDING.
THEY'RE SPYING ON US FOR LOVEY!
BEST BE CAREFUL.
THAT OLD WOMAN MIGHT NOT BE SO FAR AS--
AUGGH!

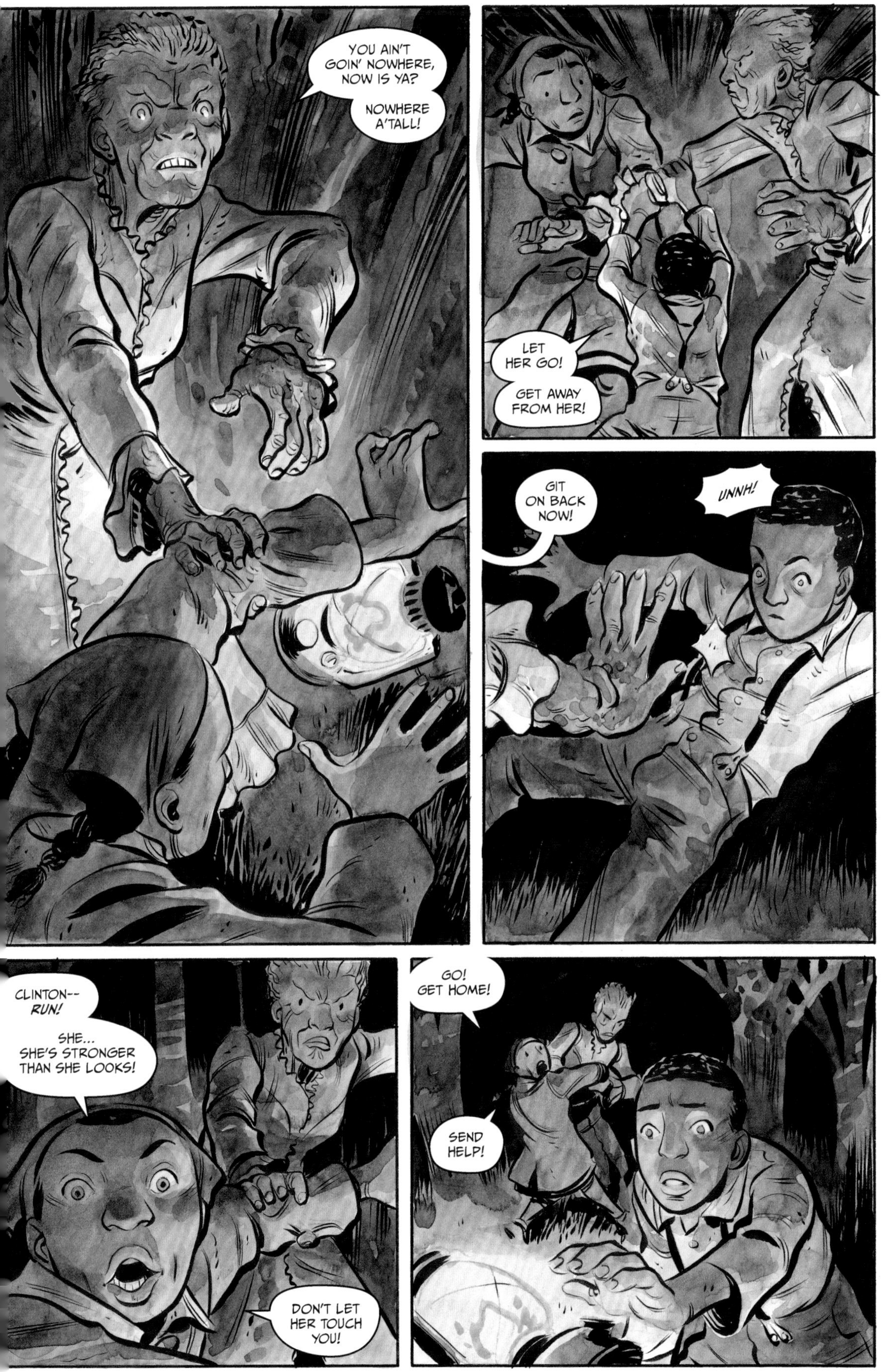
YOU AIN'T GOIN' NOWHERE, NOW IS YA?
NOWHERE A'TALL!
LET HER GO!
GET AWAY FROM HER!
GIT ON BACK NOW!
UNNH!
CLINTON-- RUN!
SHE... SHE'S STRONGER THAN SHE LOOKS!
DON'T LET HER TOUCH YOU!
GO! GET HOME!
SEND HELP!

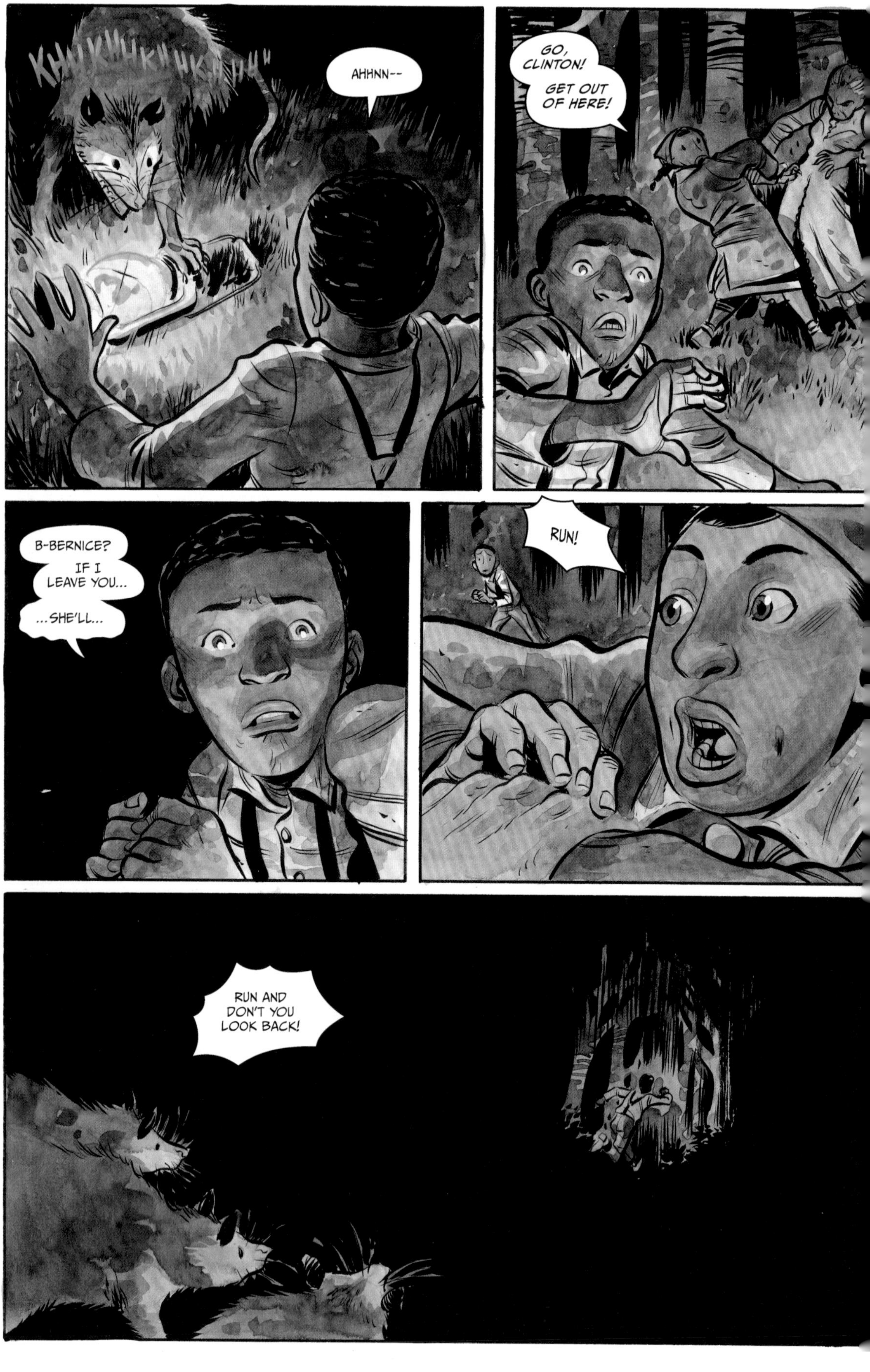
AHHNN--
GO, CLINTON!
GET OUT OF HERE!
B-BERNICE?
IF I LEAVE YOU...
...SHE'LL...
RUN!
RUN AND DON'T YOU LOOK BACK!

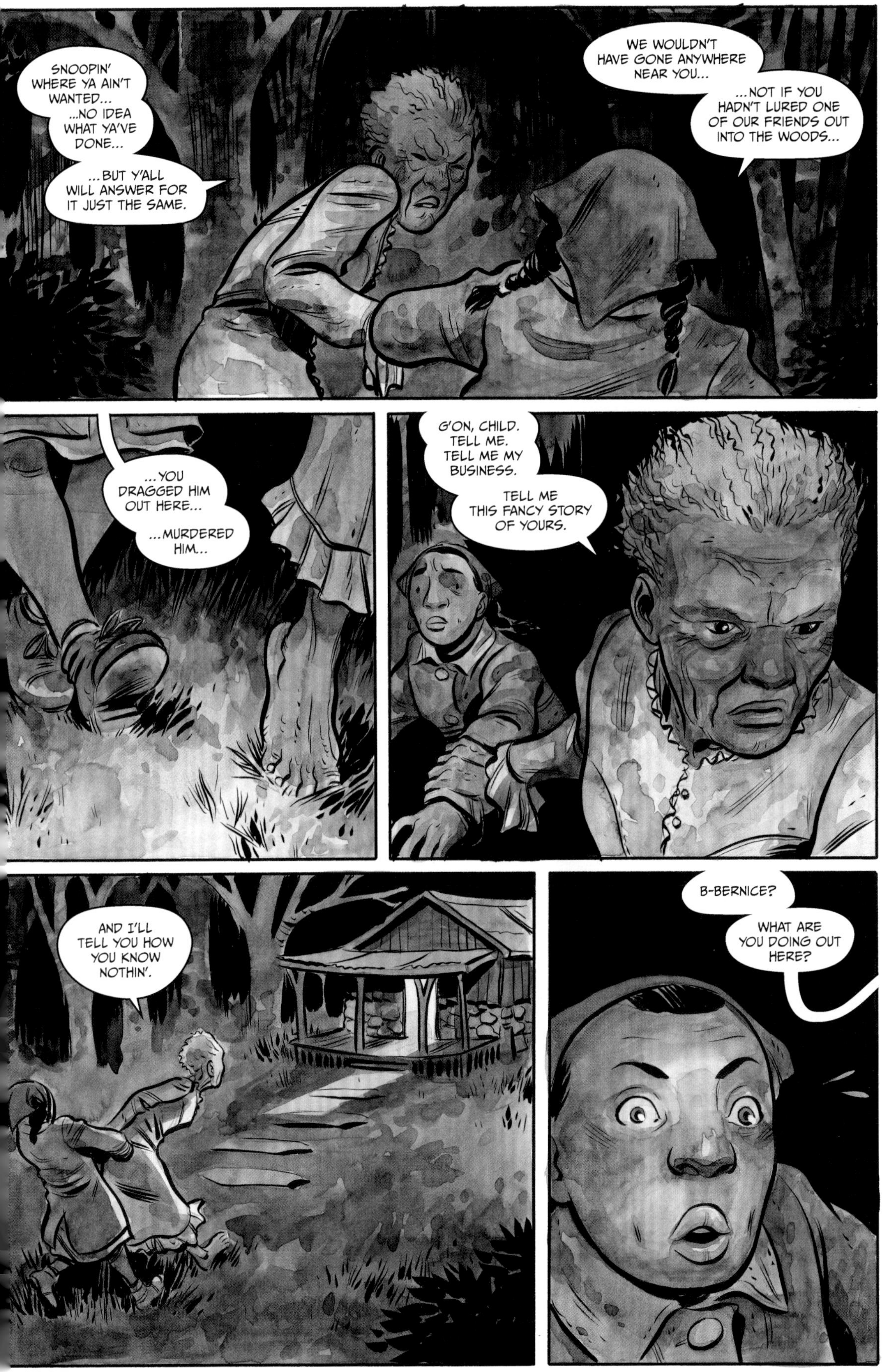
SNOOPIN' WHERE YA AIN'T WANTED...
...NO IDEA WHAT YA'VE DONE...
...BUT Y'ALL WILL ANSWER FOR IT JUST THE SAME.
WE WOULDN'T HAVE GONE ANYWHERE NEAR YOU...
...NOT IF YOU HADN'T LURED ONE OF OUR FRIENDS OUT INTO THE WOODS...
...YOU DRAGGED HIM OUT HERE...
...MURDERED HIM...
G'ON, CHILD. TELL ME. TELL ME MY BUSINESS.
TELL ME THIS FANCY STORY OF YOURS.
AND I'LL TELL YOU HOW YOU KNOW NOTHIN'.
B-BERNICE?
WHAT ARE YOU DOING OUT HERE?

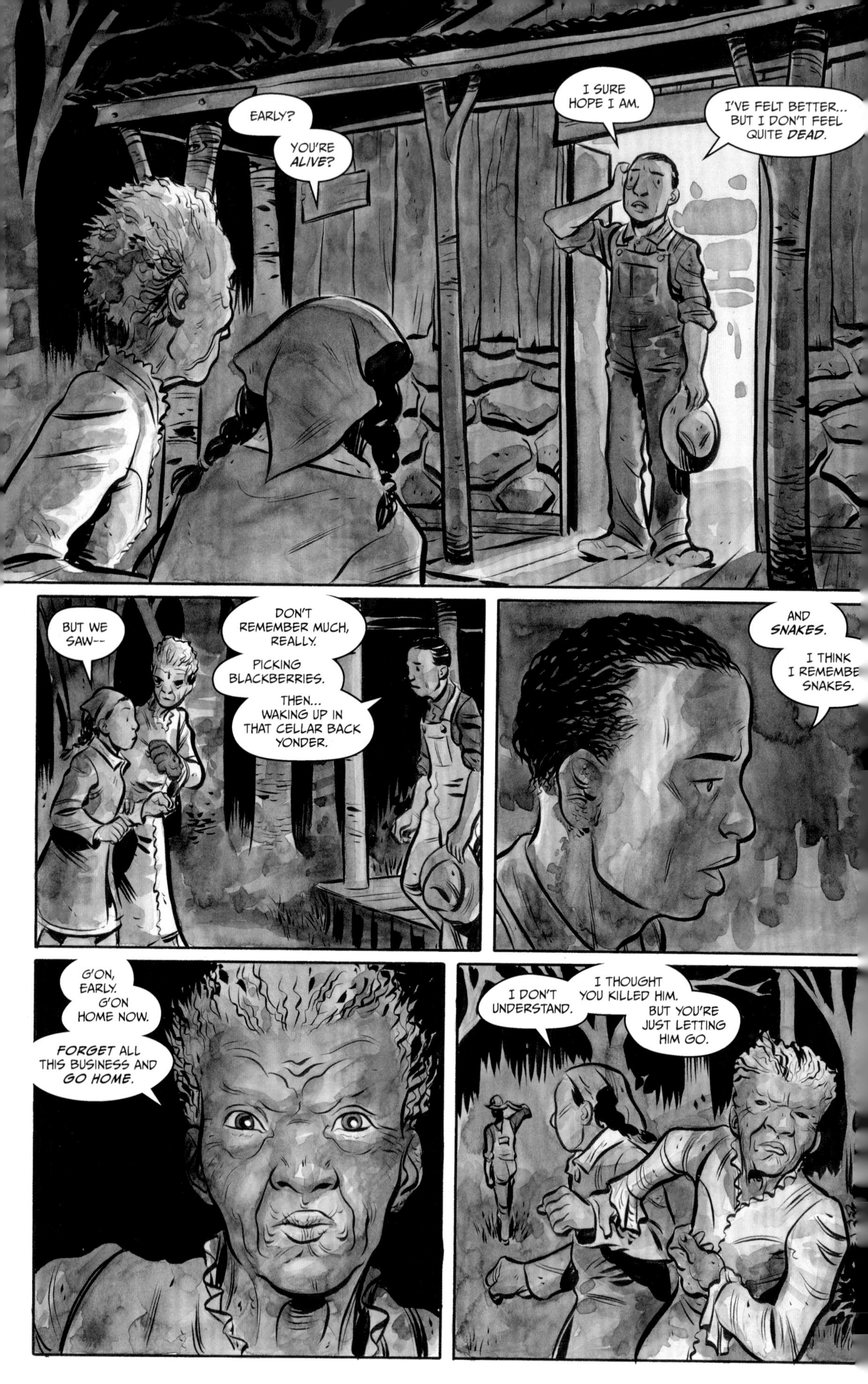
EARLY?
YOU'RE ALIVE?
I SURE HOPE I AM.
I'VE FELT BETTER... BUT I DON'T FEEL QUITE DEAD.
BUT WE SAW--
DON'T REMEMBER MUCH, REALLY.
PICKING BLACKBERRIES.
THEN... WAKING UP IN THAT CELLAR BACK YONDER.
AND SNAKES.
I THINK I REMEMBE SNAKES.
G'ON, EARLY. G'ON HOME NOW.
FORGET ALL THIS BUSINESS AND GO HOME.
I DON'T UNDERSTAND.
I THOUGHT YOU KILLED HIM.
BUT YOU'RE JUST LETTING HIM GO.

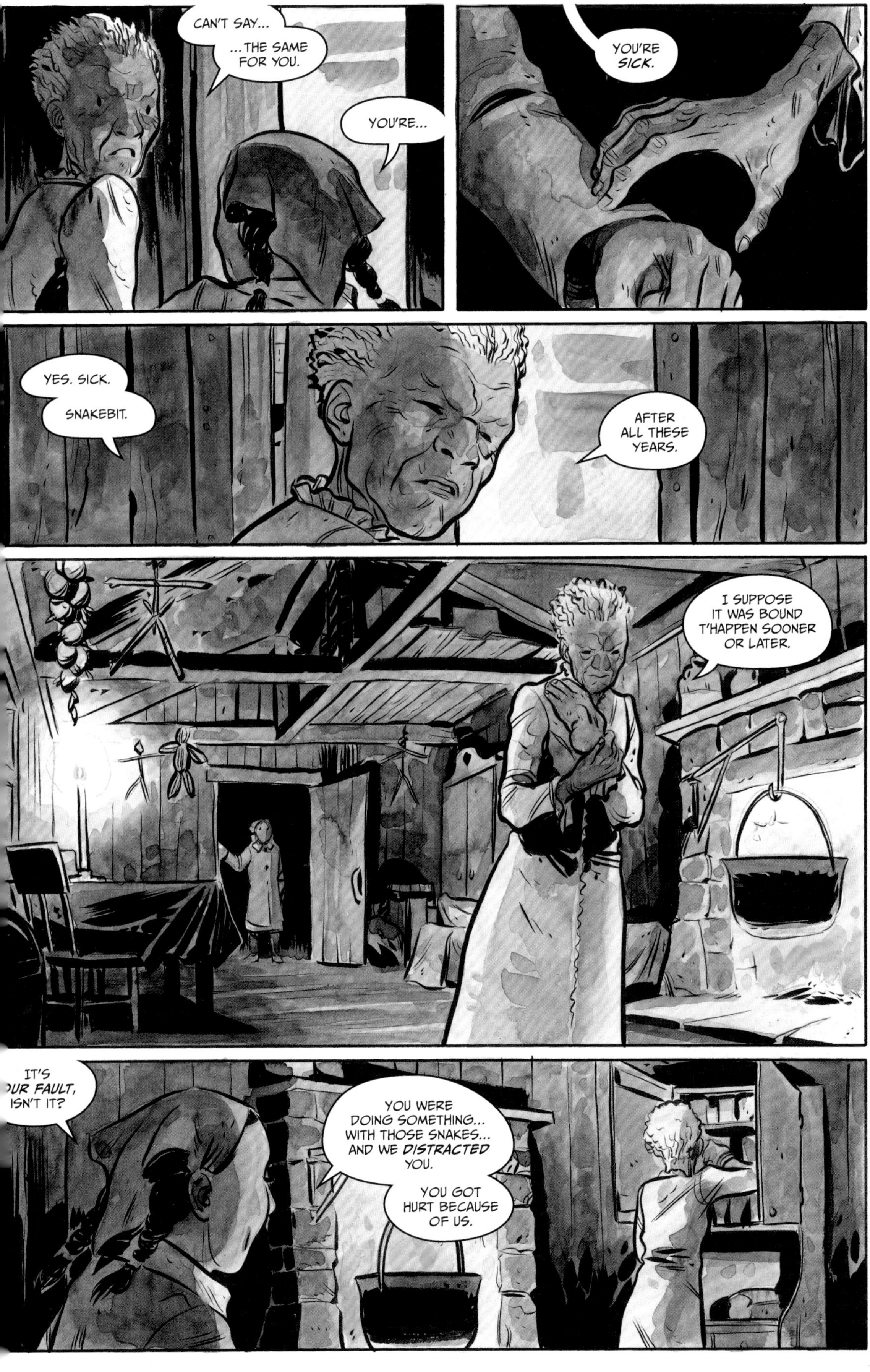
CAN'T SAY...
...THE SAME FOR YOU.
YOU'RE...
YOU'RE SICK.
YES. SICK.
SNAKEBIT.
AFTER ALL THESE YEARS.
I SUPPOSE IT WAS BOUND T'HAPPEN SOONER OR LATER.
IT'S OUR FAULT, ISN'T IT?
YOU WERE DOING SOMETHING... WITH THOSE SNAKES... AND WE DISTRACTED YOU.
YOU GOT HURT BECAUSE OF US.

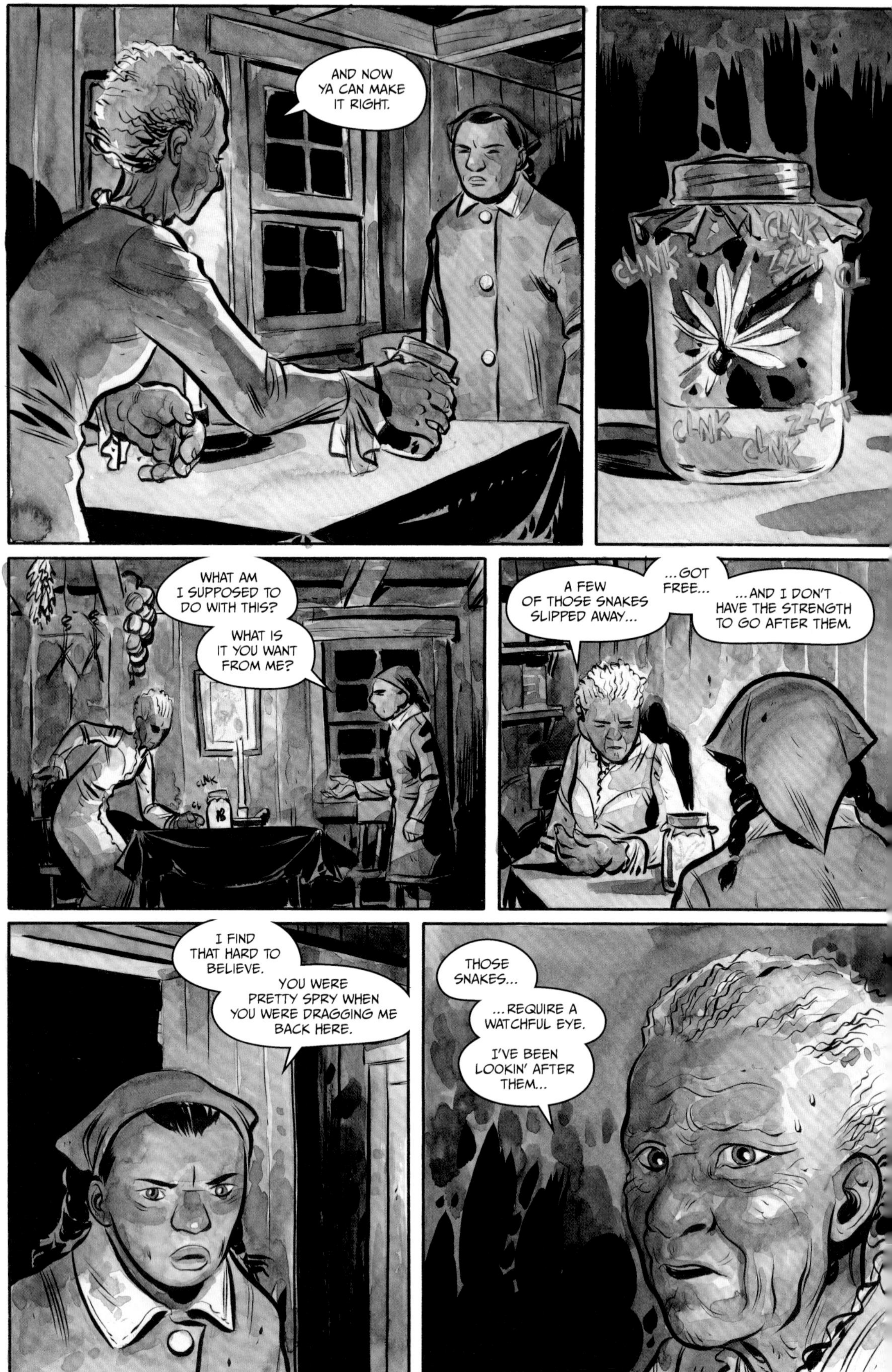
AND NOW YA CAN MAKE IT RIGHT.
CLINK
CLINK
ZZUT
CL
CLINK
ZZZT
CLINK
WHAT AM I SUPPOSED TO DO WITH THIS?
WHAT IS IT YOU WANT FROM ME?
CLINK
CL
A FEW OF THOSE SNAKES SLIPPED AWAY...
...GOT FREE...
...AND I DON'T HAVE THE STRENGTH TO GO AFTER THEM.
I FIND THAT HARD TO BELIEVE.
YOU WERE PRETTY SPRY WHEN YOU WERE DRAGGING ME BACK HERE.
THOSE SNAKES...
...REQUIRE A WATCHFUL EYE.
I'VE BEEN LOOKIN' AFTER THEM...

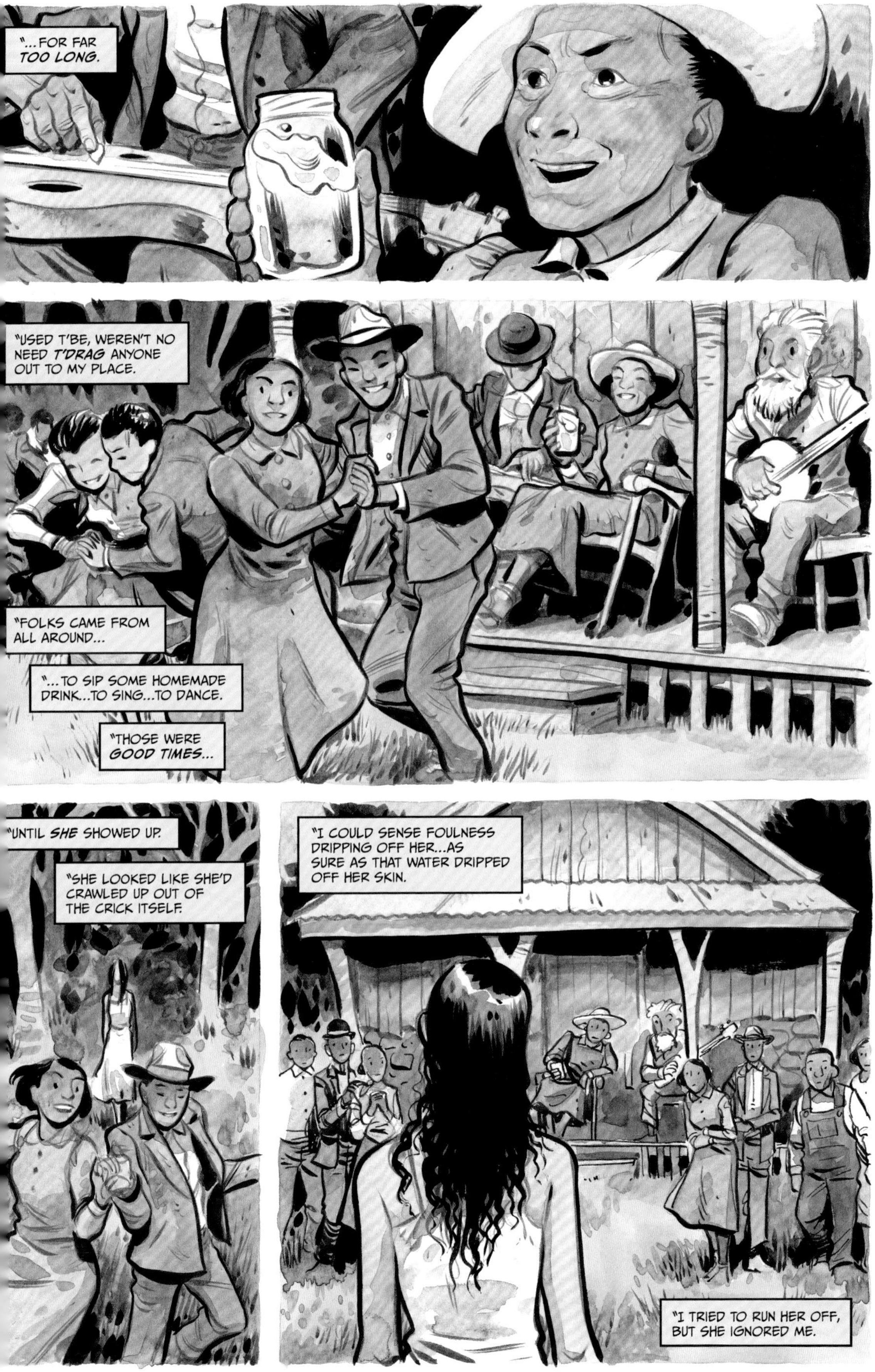
"...FOR FAR TOO LONG.
"USED T'BE, WEREN'T NO NEED T'DRAG ANYONE OUT TO MY PLACE.
"FOLKS CAME FROM ALL AROUND...
"...TO SIP SOME HOMEMADE DRINK...TO SING...TO DANCE.
"THOSE WERE GOOD TIMES...
"UNTIL SHE SHOWED UP.
"SHE LOOKED LIKE SHE'D CRAWLED UP OUT OF THE CRICK ITSELF.
"I COULD SENSE FOULNESS DRIPPING OFF HER...AS SURE AS THAT WATER DRIPPED OFF HER SKIN.
"I TRIED TO RUN HER OFF, BUT SHE IGNORED ME.

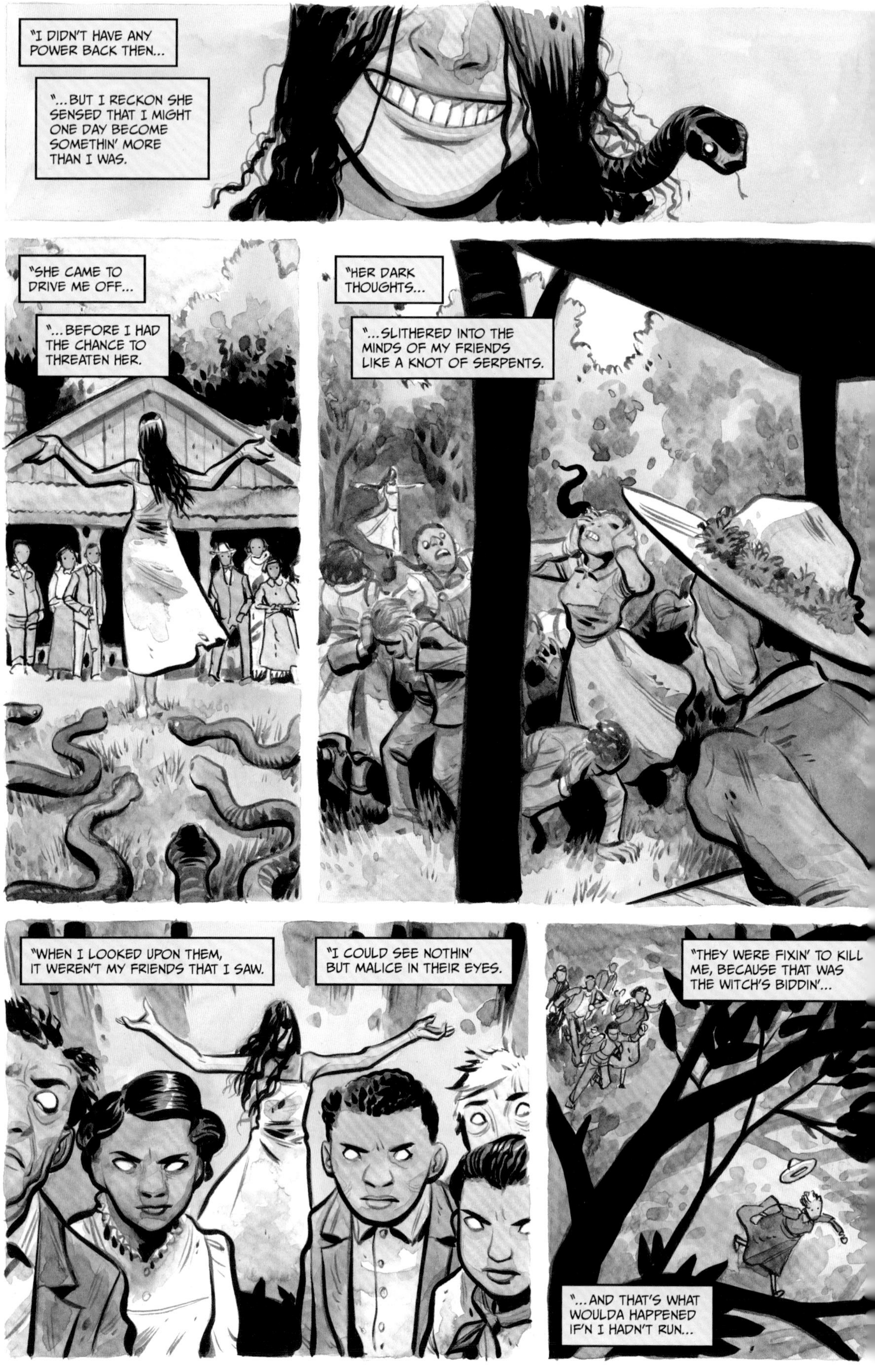
"I DIDN'T HAVE ANY POWER BACK THEN...
"...BUT I RECKON SHE SENSED THAT I MIGHT ONE DAY BECOME SOMETHIN' MORE THAN I WAS.
"SHE CAME TO DRIVE ME OFF...
"...BEFORE I HAD THE CHANCE TO THREATEN HER.
"HER DARK THOUGHTS...
"...SLITHERED INTO THE MINDS OF MY FRIENDS LIKE A KNOT OF SERPENTS.
"WHEN I LOOKED UPON THEM, IT WEREN'T MY FRIENDS THAT I SAW.
"I COULD SEE NOTHIN' BUT MALICE IN THEIR EYES.
"THEY WERE FIXIN' TO KILL ME, BECAUSE THAT WAS THE WITCH'S BIDDIN'...
"...AND THAT'S WHAT WOULDA HAPPENED IF'N I HADN'T RUN...

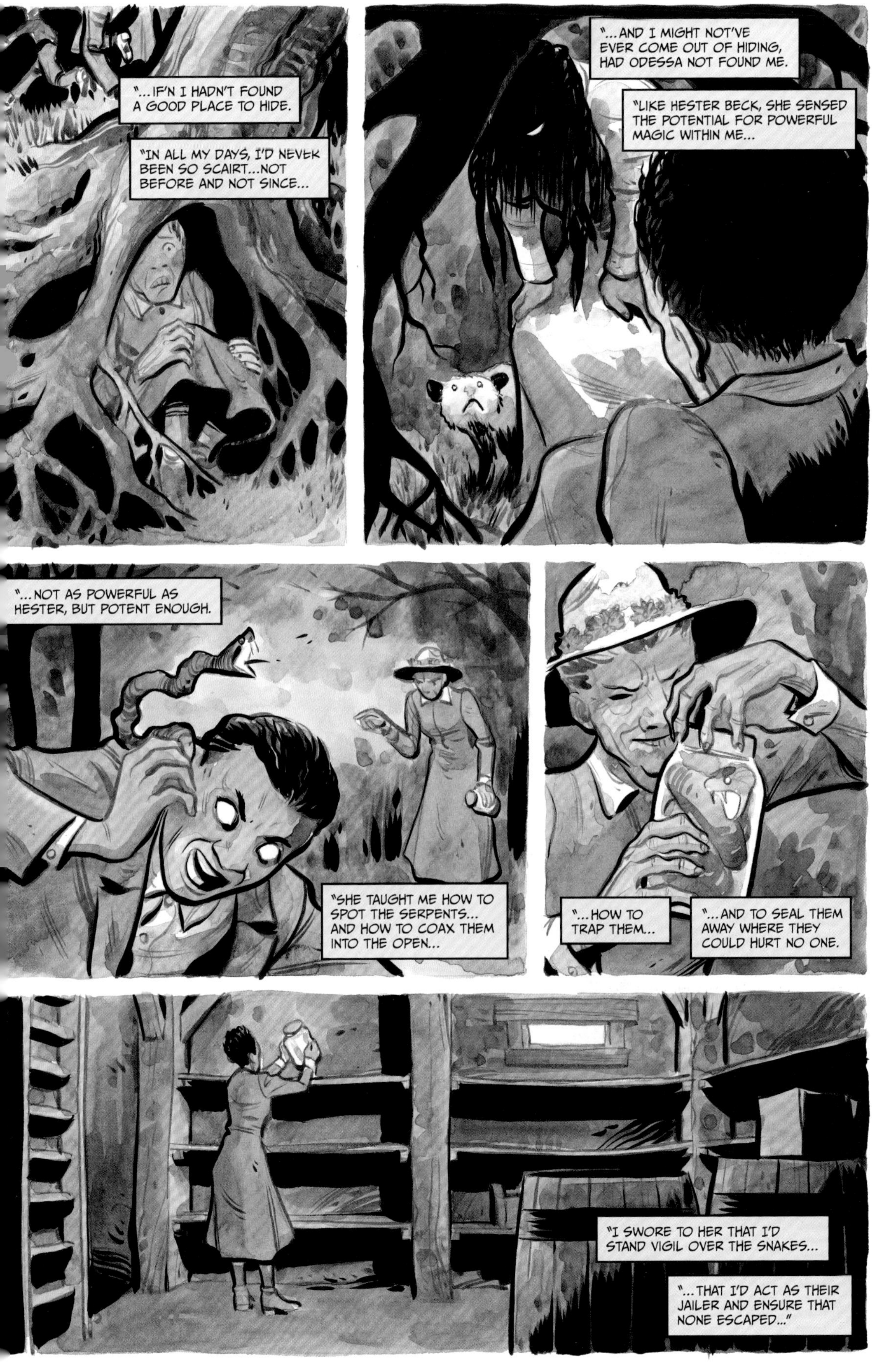
"...IF'N I HADN'T FOUND A GOOD PLACE TO HIDE.
"IN ALL MY DAYS, I'D NEVER BEEN SO SCAIRT...NOT BEFORE AND NOT SINCE...
"...AND I MIGHT NOT'VE EVER COME OUT OF HIDING, HAD ODESSA NOT FOUND ME.
"LIKE HESTER BECK, SHE SENSED THE POTENTIAL FOR POWERFUL MAGIC WITHIN ME...
"...NOT AS POWERFUL AS HESTER, BUT POTENT ENOUGH.
"SHE TAUGHT ME HOW TO SPOT THE SERPENTS... AND HOW TO COAX THEM INTO THE OPEN...
"...HOW TO TRAP THEM...
"...AND TO SEAL THEM AWAY WHERE THEY COULD HURT NO ONE.
"I SWORE TO HER THAT I'D STAND VIGIL OVER THE SNAKES...
"...THAT I'D ACT AS THEIR JAILER AND ENSURE THAT NONE ESCAPED..."

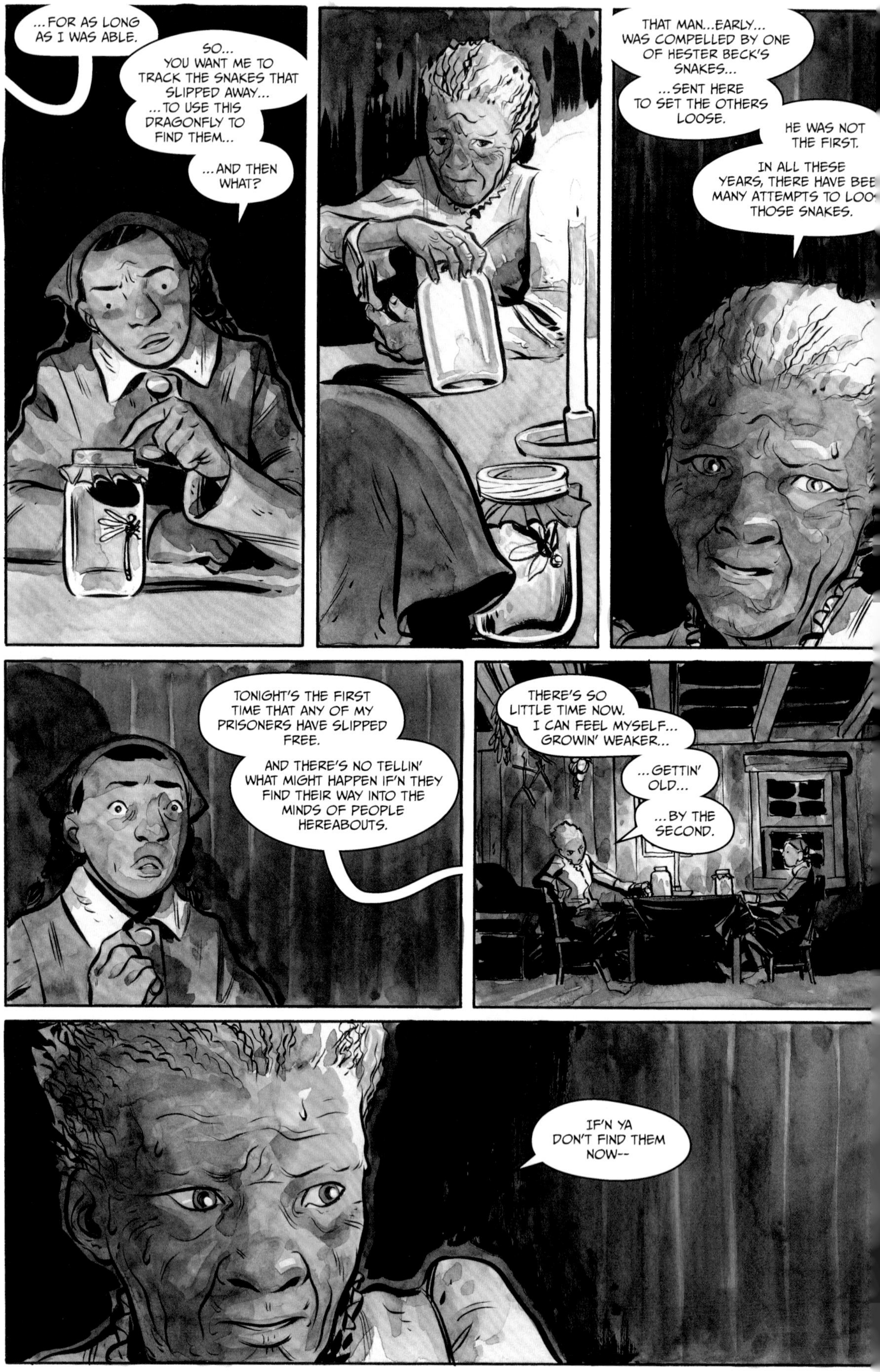
...FOR AS LONG AS I WAS ABLE.
SO... YOU WANT ME TO TRACK THE SNAKES THAT SLIPPED AWAY... ...TO USE THIS DRAGONFLY TO FIND THEM...
...AND THEN WHAT?
THAT MAN...EARLY... WAS COMPELLED BY ONE OF HESTER BECK'S SNAKES...
...SENT HERE TO SET THE OTHERS LOOSE.
HE WAS NOT THE FIRST.
IN ALL THESE YEARS, THERE HAVE BEE MANY ATTEMPTS TO LOO THOSE SNAKES.
TONIGHT'S THE FIRST TIME THAT ANY OF MY PRISONERS HAVE SLIPPED FREE.
AND THERE'S NO TELLIN' WHAT MIGHT HAPPEN IF'N THEY FIND THEIR WAY INTO THE MINDS OF PEOPLE HEREABOUTS.
THERE'S SO LITTLE TIME NOW. I CAN FEEL MYSELF... GROWIN' WEAKER...
...GETTIN' OLD...
...BY THE SECOND.
IF'N YA DON'T FIND THEM NOW--

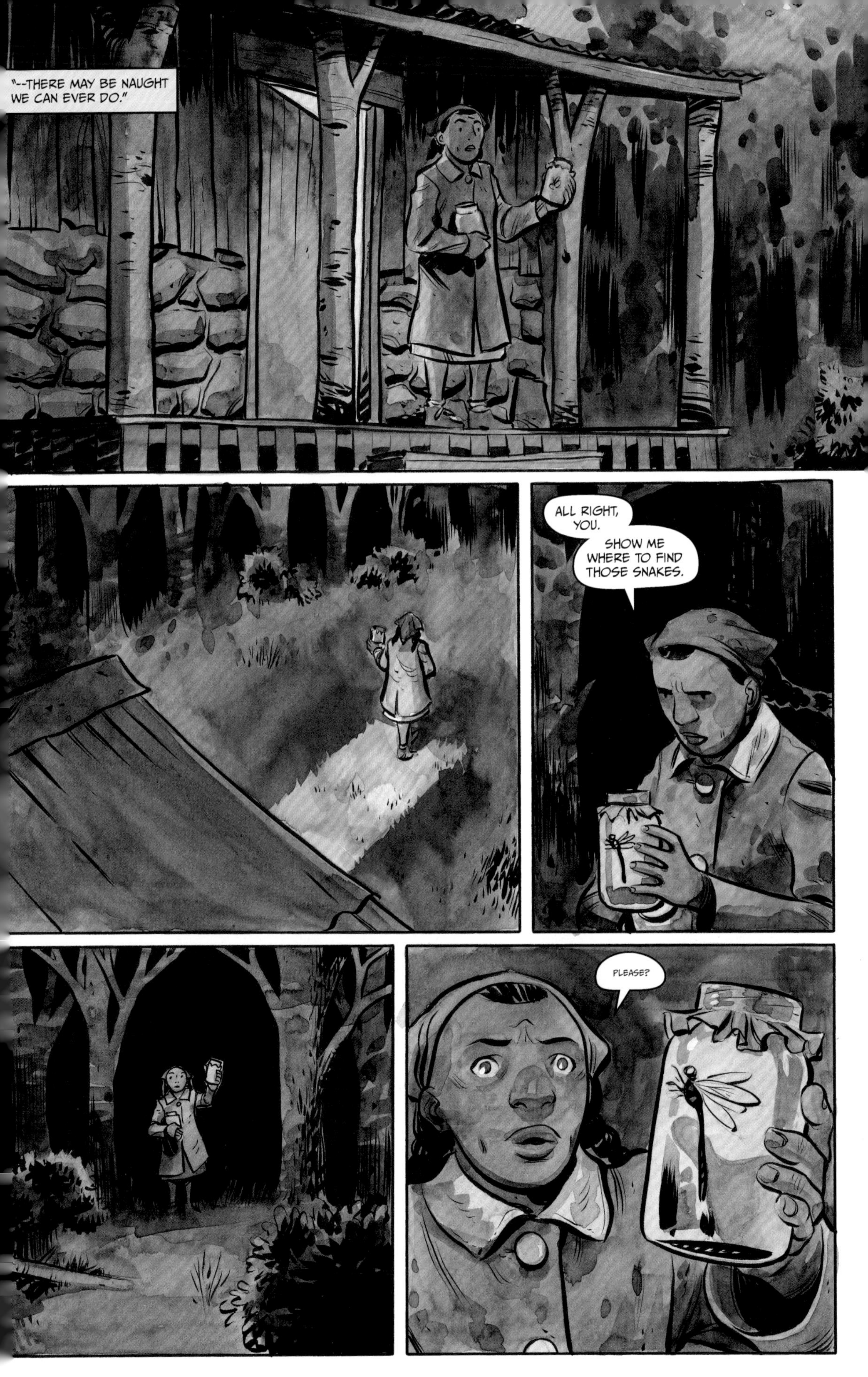
"--THERE MAY BE NAUGHT WE CAN EVER DO."
ALL RIGHT, YOU.
SHOW ME WHERE TO FIND THOSE SNAKES.
PLEASE?

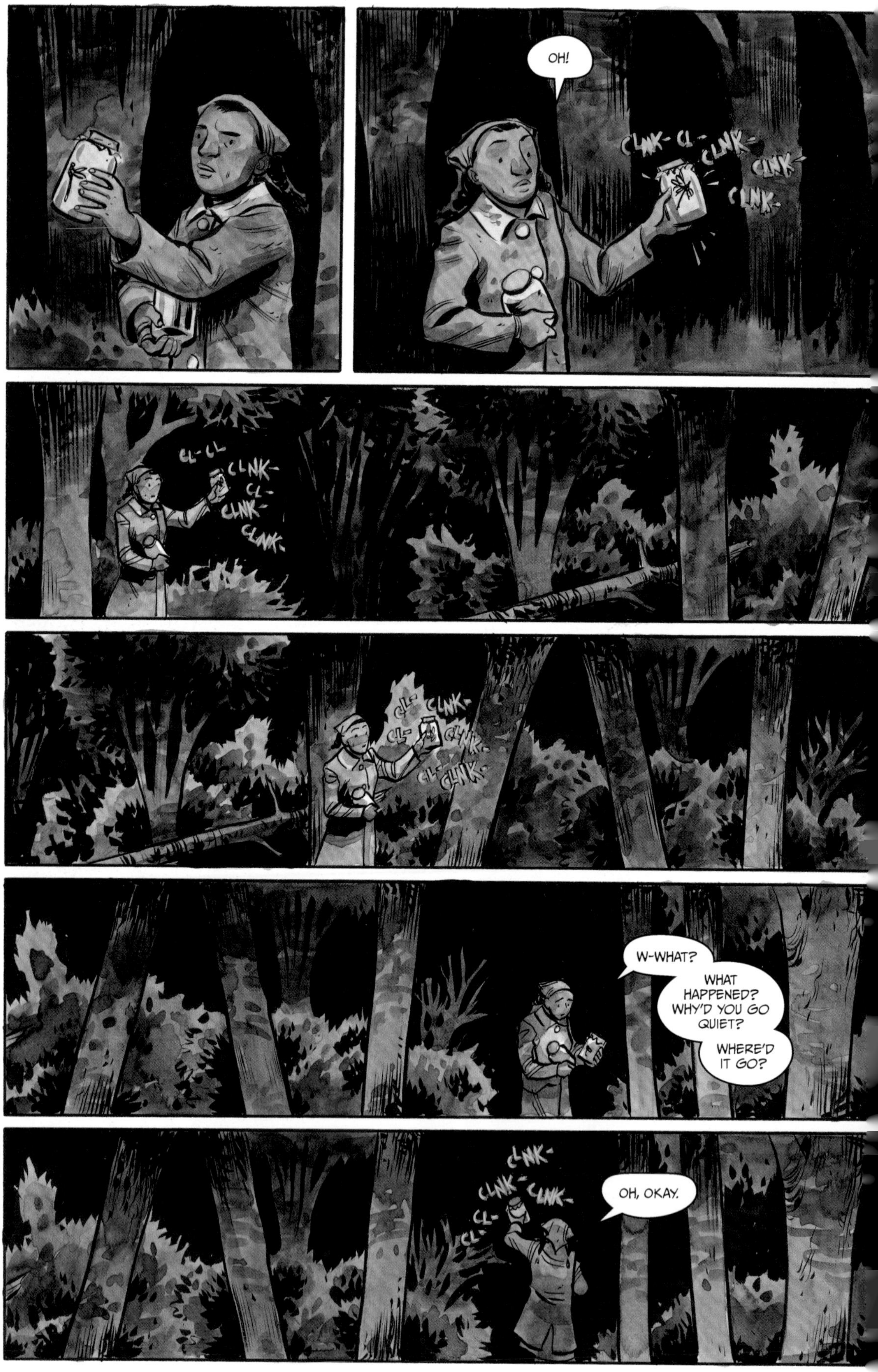
OH!
CLNK- CL- CLNK- CLNK- CLNK-
CL- CL CLNK- CL- CLNK- CLNK-
CL- CLNK- CL- CLNK- CL- CLNK-
W-WHAT?
WHAT HAPPENED? WHY'D YOU GO QUIET?
WHERE'D IT GO?
CLNK- CLNK- CLNK- CL- CL-
OH, OKAY.

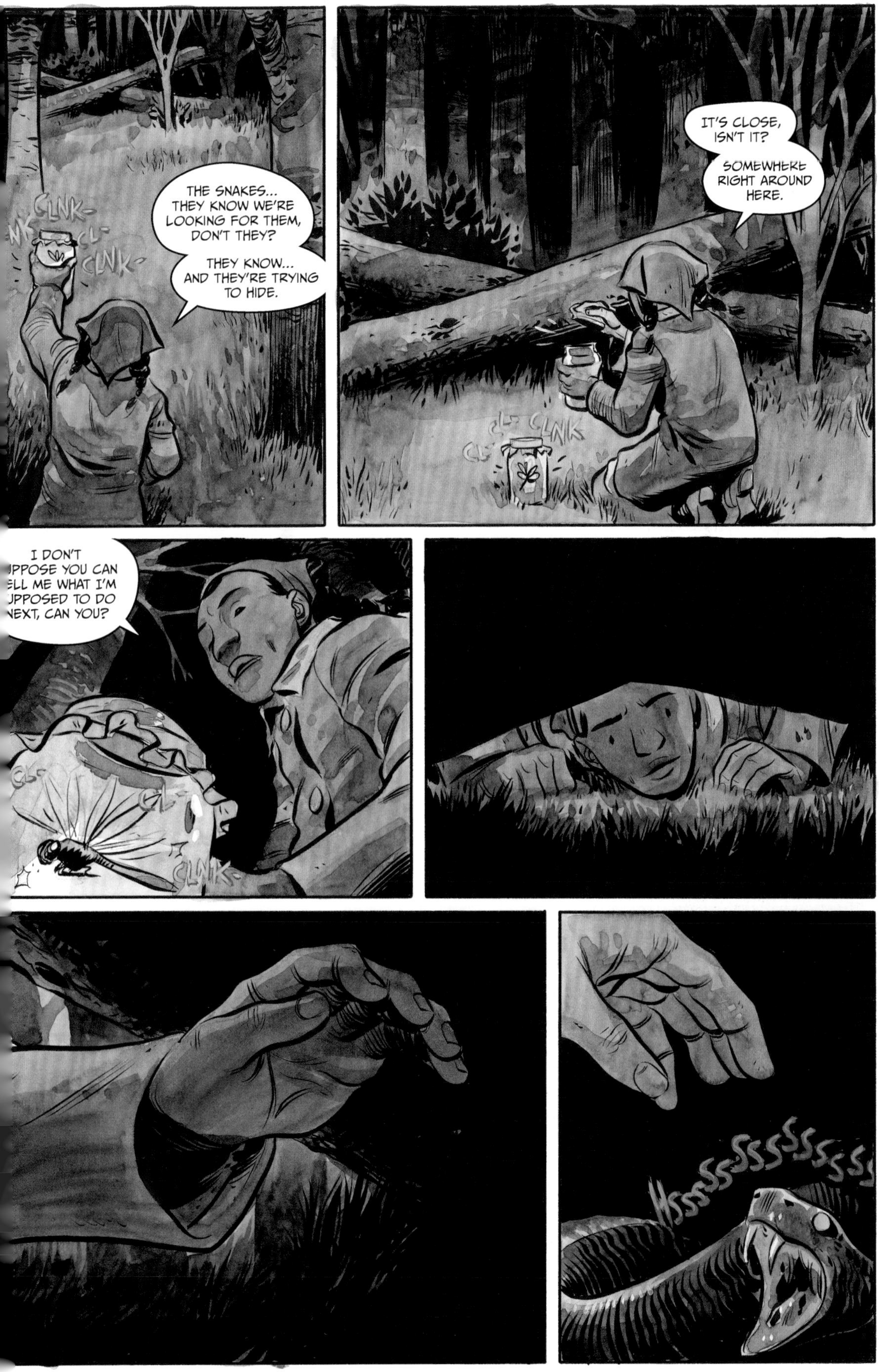
CLNK-
NK
CL-
CLNK-
THE SNAKES... THEY KNOW WE'RE LOOKING FOR THEM, DON'T THEY?
THEY KNOW... AND THEY'RE TRYING TO HIDE.
IT'S CLOSE, ISN'T IT?
SOMEWHERE RIGHT AROUND HERE.
CL- CLNK
CL-
I DON'T UPPOSE YOU CAN ELL ME WHAT I'M UPPOSED TO DO NEXT, CAN YOU?
CL-
CL-
CLNK-
HSSSSSSSSSSSS

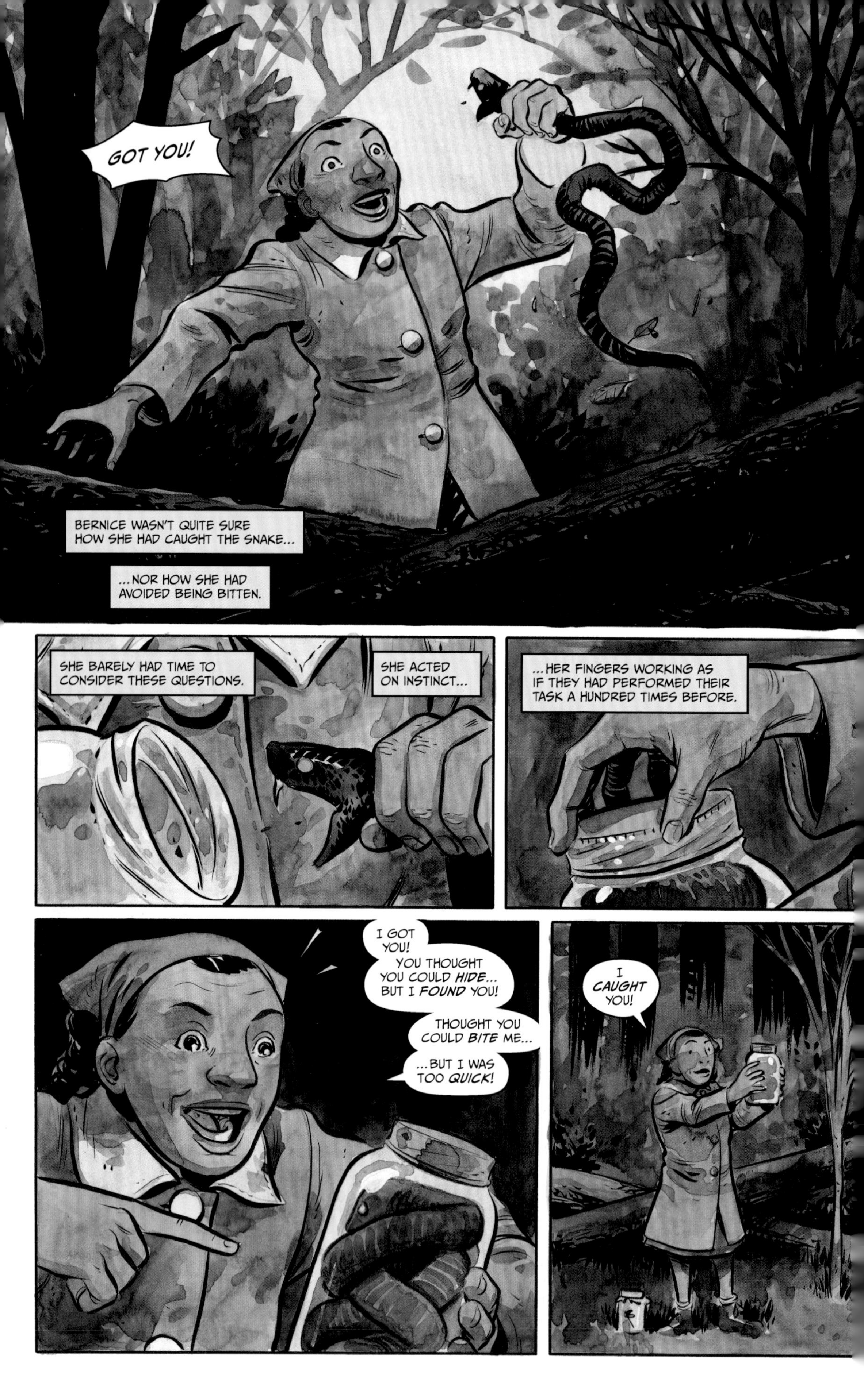
GOT YOU!
BERNICE WASN'T QUITE SURE HOW SHE HAD CAUGHT THE SNAKE...
...NOR HOW SHE HAD AVOIDED BEING BITTEN.
SHE BARELY HAD TIME TO CONSIDER THESE QUESTIONS.
SHE ACTED ON INSTINCT...
...HER FINGERS WORKING AS IF THEY HAD PERFORMED THEIR TASK A HUNDRED TIMES BEFORE.
I GOT YOU!
YOU THOUGHT YOU COULD HIDE... BUT I FOUND YOU!
THOUGHT YOU COULD BITE ME...
...BUT I WAS TOO QUICK!
I CAUGHT YOU!

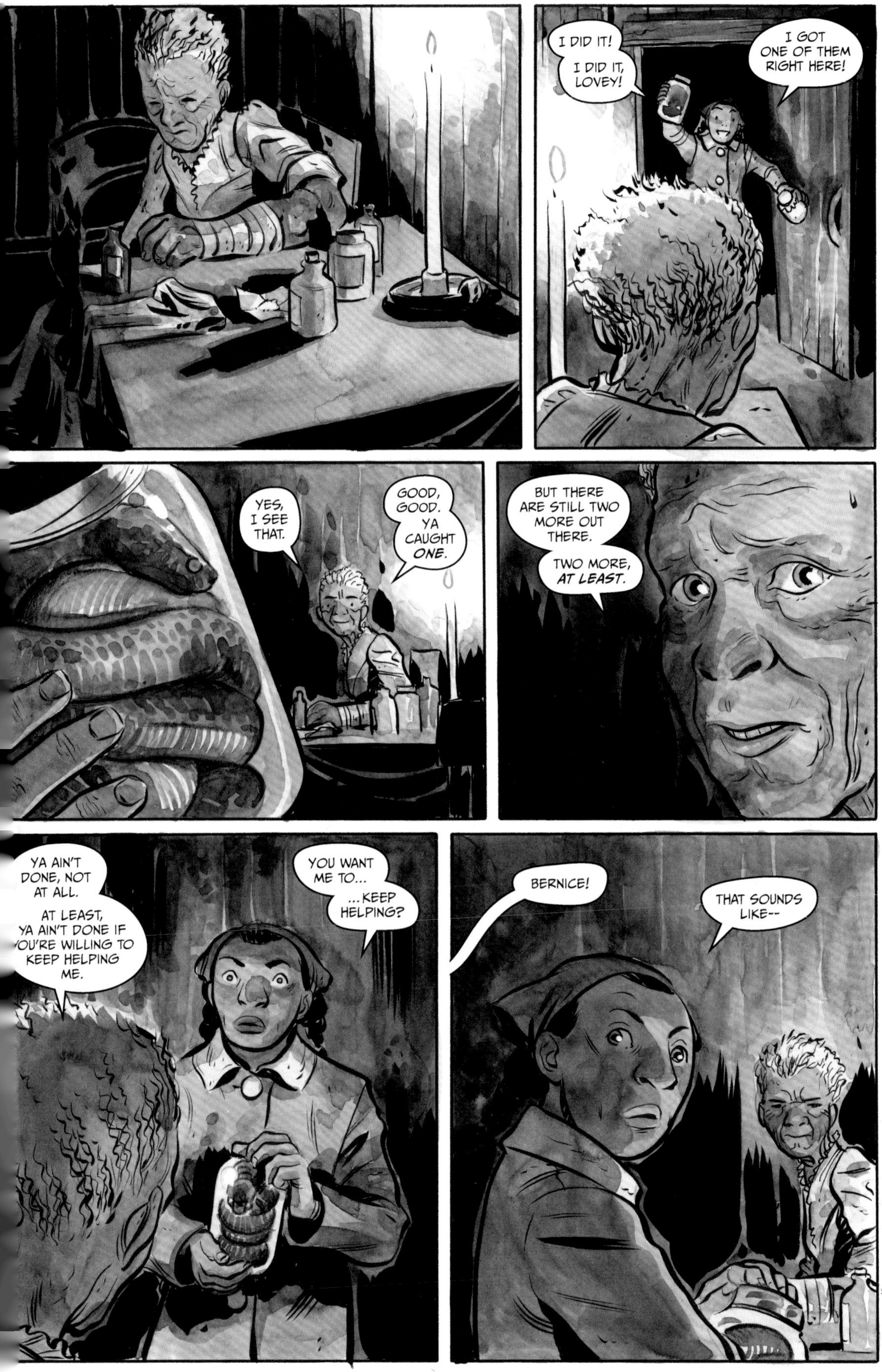
I DID IT!
I DID IT, LOVEY!
I GOT ONE OF THEM RIGHT HERE!
YES, I SEE THAT.
GOOD, GOOD. YA CAUGHT *ONE*.
BUT THERE ARE STILL TWO MORE OUT THERE.
TWO MORE, *AT LEAST*.
YA AIN'T DONE, NOT AT ALL.
AT LEAST, YA AIN'T DONE IF YOU'RE WILLING TO KEEP HELPING ME.
YOU WANT ME TO...
...KEEP HELPING?
BERNICE!
THAT SOUNDS LIKE--

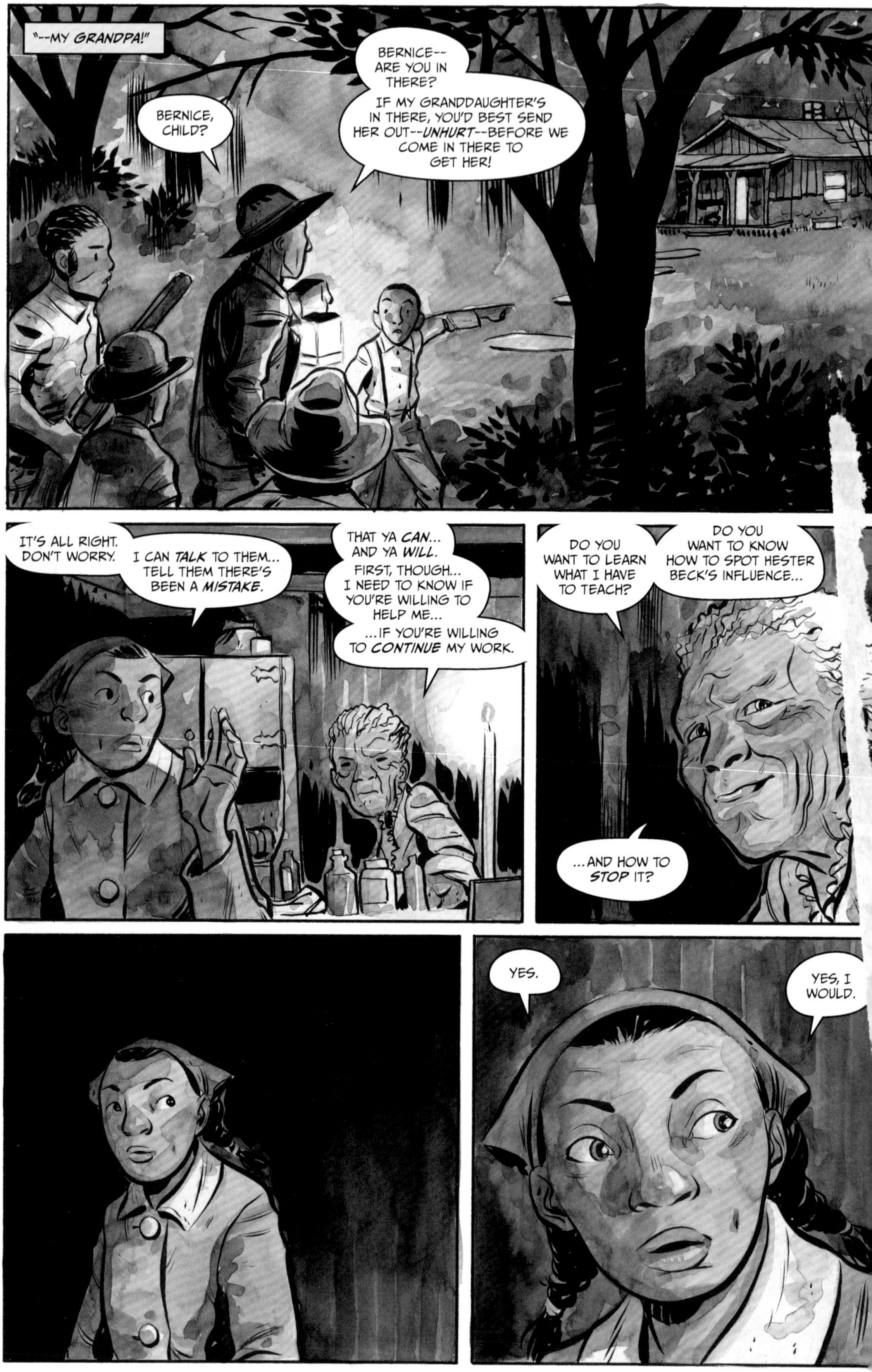
"--MY GRANDPA!"
BERNICE, CHILD?
BERNICE-- ARE YOU IN THERE?
IF MY GRANDDAUGHTER'S IN THERE, YOU'D BEST SEND HER OUT--UNHURT--BEFORE WE COME IN THERE TO GET HER!
IT'S ALL RIGHT. DON'T WORRY.
I CAN TALK TO THEM... TELL THEM THERE'S BEEN A MISTAKE.
THAT YA CAN... AND YA WILL.
FIRST, THOUGH... I NEED TO KNOW IF YOU'RE WILLING TO HELP ME...
...IF YOU'RE WILLING TO CONTINUE MY WORK.
DO YOU WANT TO LEARN WHAT I HAVE TO TEACH?
DO YOU WANT TO KNOW HOW TO SPOT HESTER BECK'S INFLUENCE...
...AND HOW TO STOP IT?
YES.
YES, I WOULD.

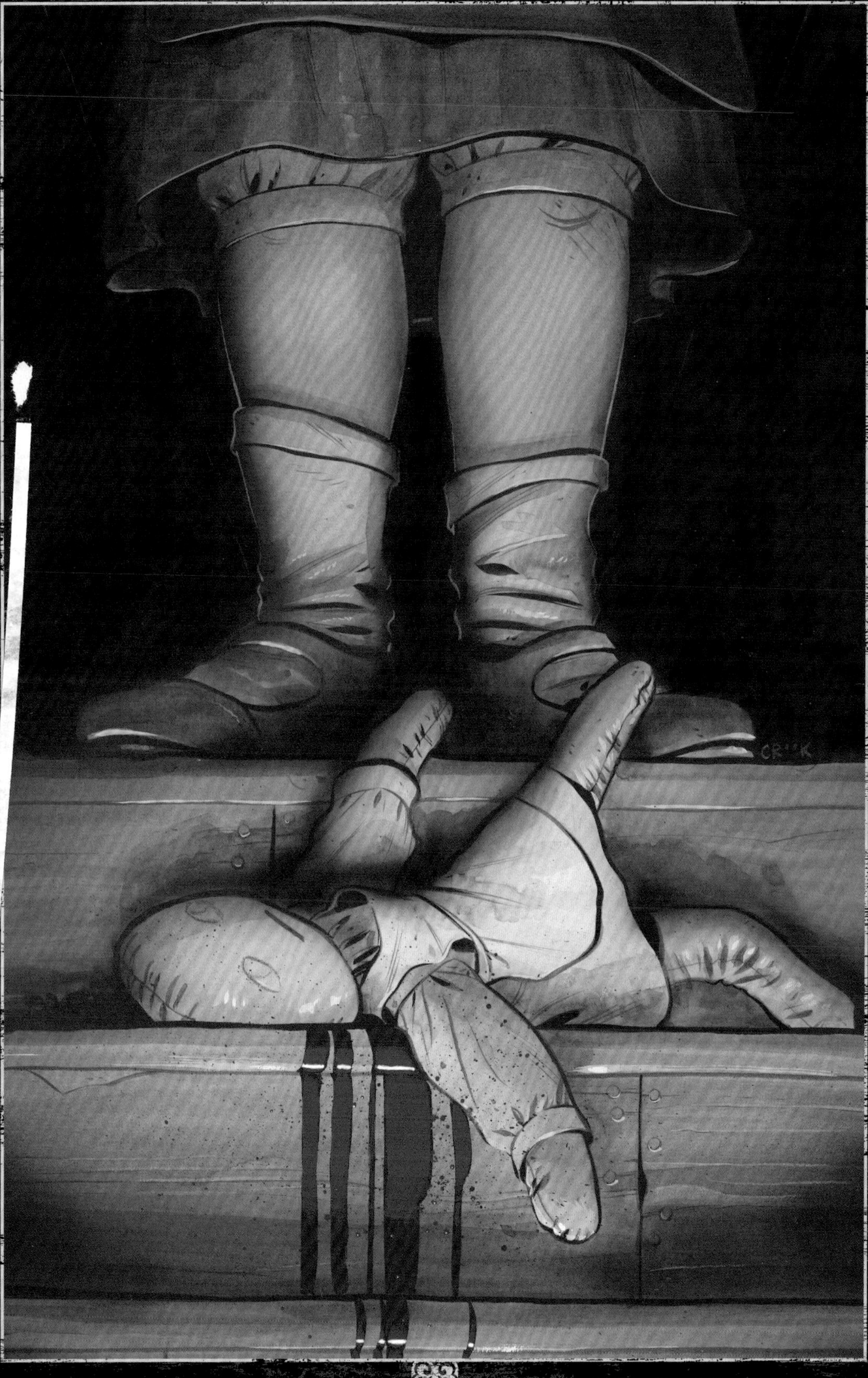

FOUR

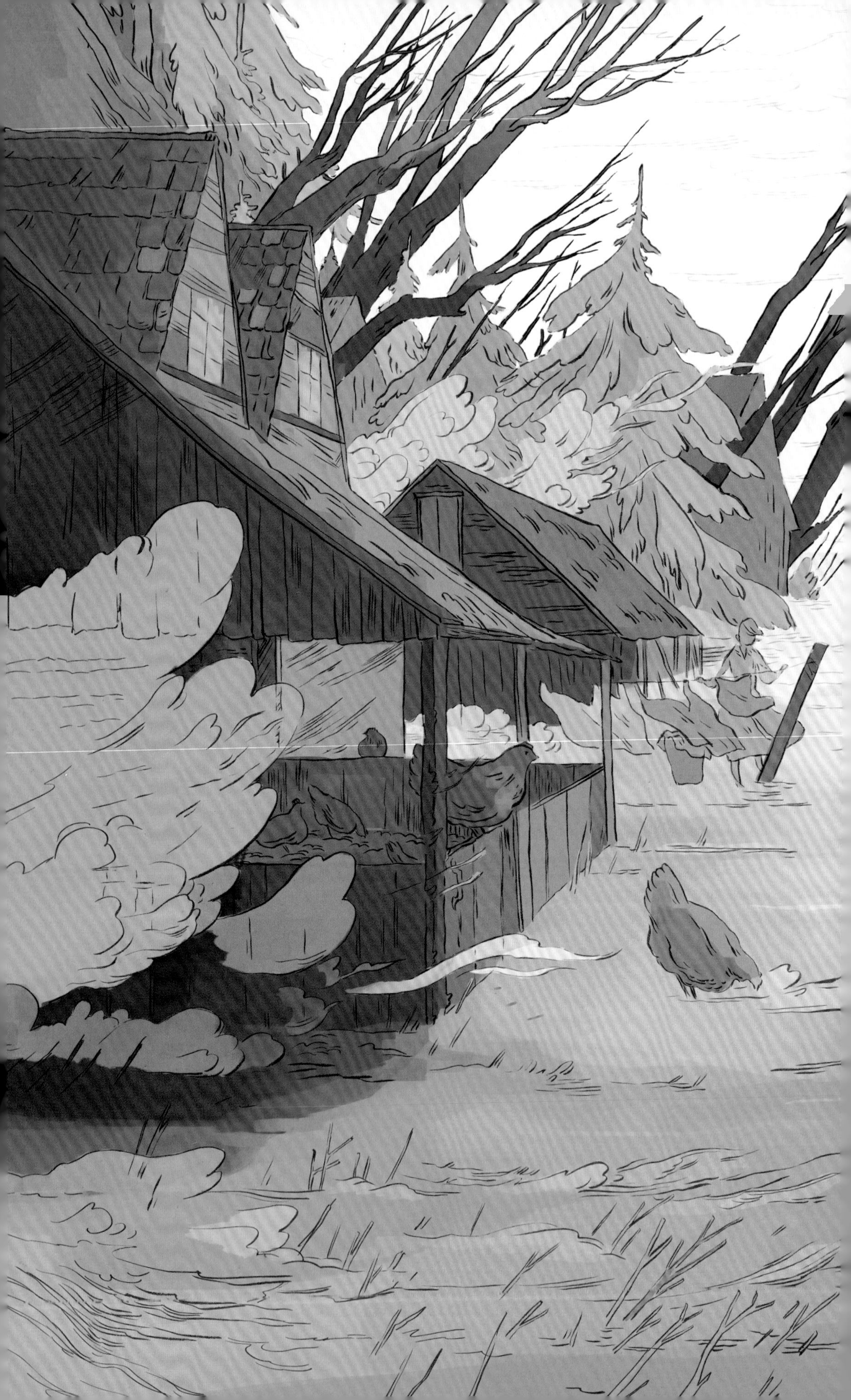

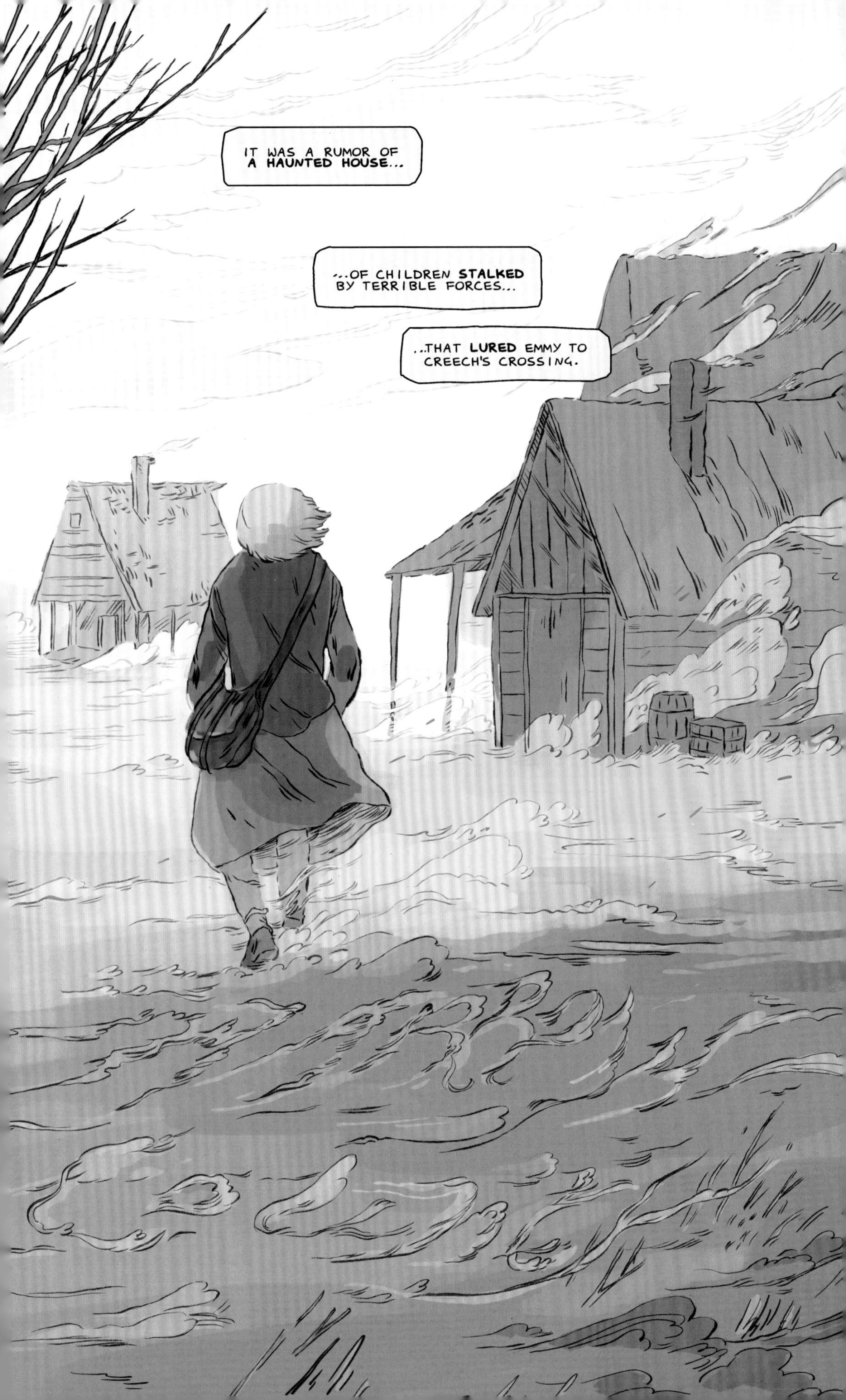
IT WAS A RUMOR OF A HAUNTED HOUSE...
...OF CHILDREN STALKED BY TERRIBLE FORCES...
...THAT LURED EMMY TO CREECH'S CROSSING.

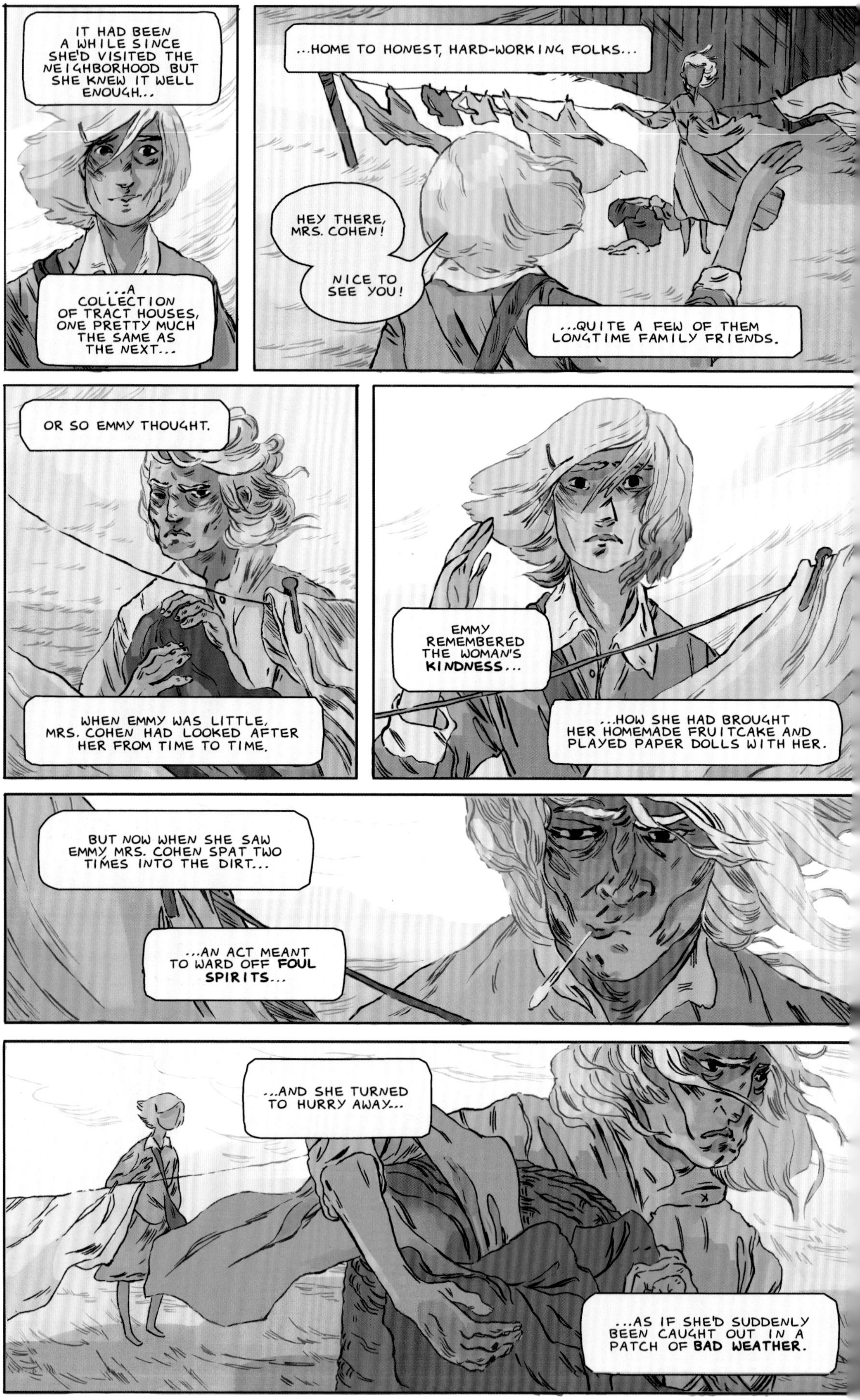
IT HAD BEEN A WHILE SINCE SHE'D VISITED THE NEIGHBORHOOD BUT SHE KNEW IT WELL ENOUGH...
...A COLLECTION OF TRACT HOUSES, ONE PRETTY MUCH THE SAME AS THE NEXT...
...HOME TO HONEST, HARD-WORKING FOLKS...
HEY THERE, MRS. COHEN!
NICE TO SEE YOU!
...QUITE A FEW OF THEM LONGTIME FAMILY FRIENDS.
OR SO EMMY THOUGHT.
WHEN EMMY WAS LITTLE, MRS. COHEN HAD LOOKED AFTER HER FROM TIME TO TIME.
EMMY REMEMBERED THE WOMAN'S **KINDNESS**...
...HOW SHE HAD BROUGHT HER HOMEMADE FRUITCAKE AND PLAYED PAPER DOLLS WITH HER.
BUT NOW WHEN SHE SAW EMMY, MRS. COHEN SPAT TWO TIMES INTO THE DIRT...
...AN ACT MEANT TO WARD OFF **FOUL SPIRITS**...
...AND SHE TURNED TO HURRY AWAY...
...AS IF SHE'D SUDDENLY BEEN CAUGHT OUT IN A PATCH OF **BAD WEATHER**.

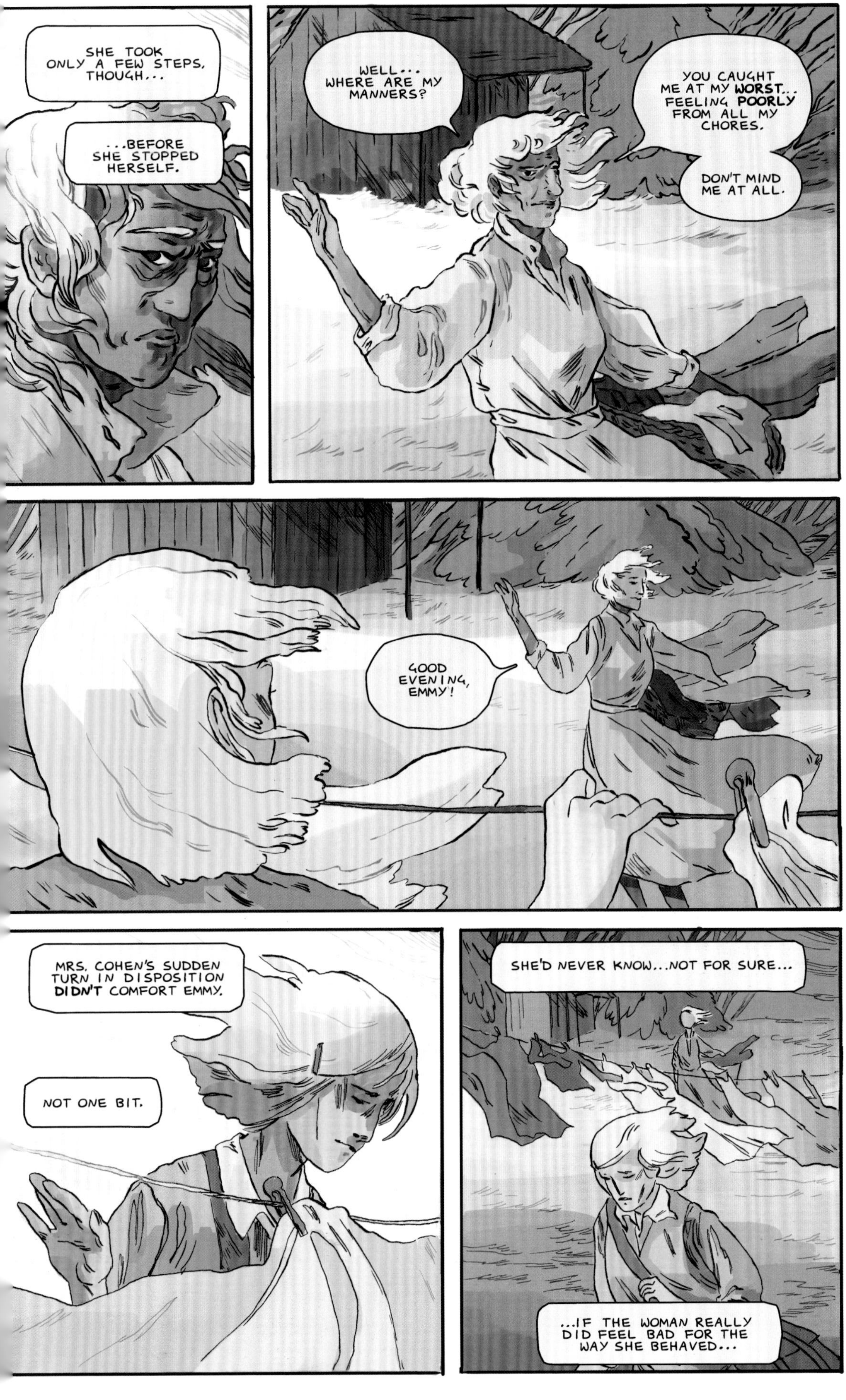
SHE TOOK ONLY A FEW STEPS, THOUGH...
...BEFORE SHE STOPPED HERSELF.
WELL... WHERE ARE MY MANNERS?
YOU CAUGHT ME AT MY **WORST**... FEELING **POORLY** FROM ALL MY CHORES.
DON'T MIND ME AT ALL.
GOOD EVENING, EMMY!
MRS. COHEN'S SUDDEN TURN IN DISPOSITION **DIDN'T** COMFORT EMMY.
NOT ONE BIT.
SHE'D NEVER KNOW...NOT FOR SURE...
...IF THE WOMAN REALLY DID FEEL BAD FOR THE WAY SHE BEHAVED...

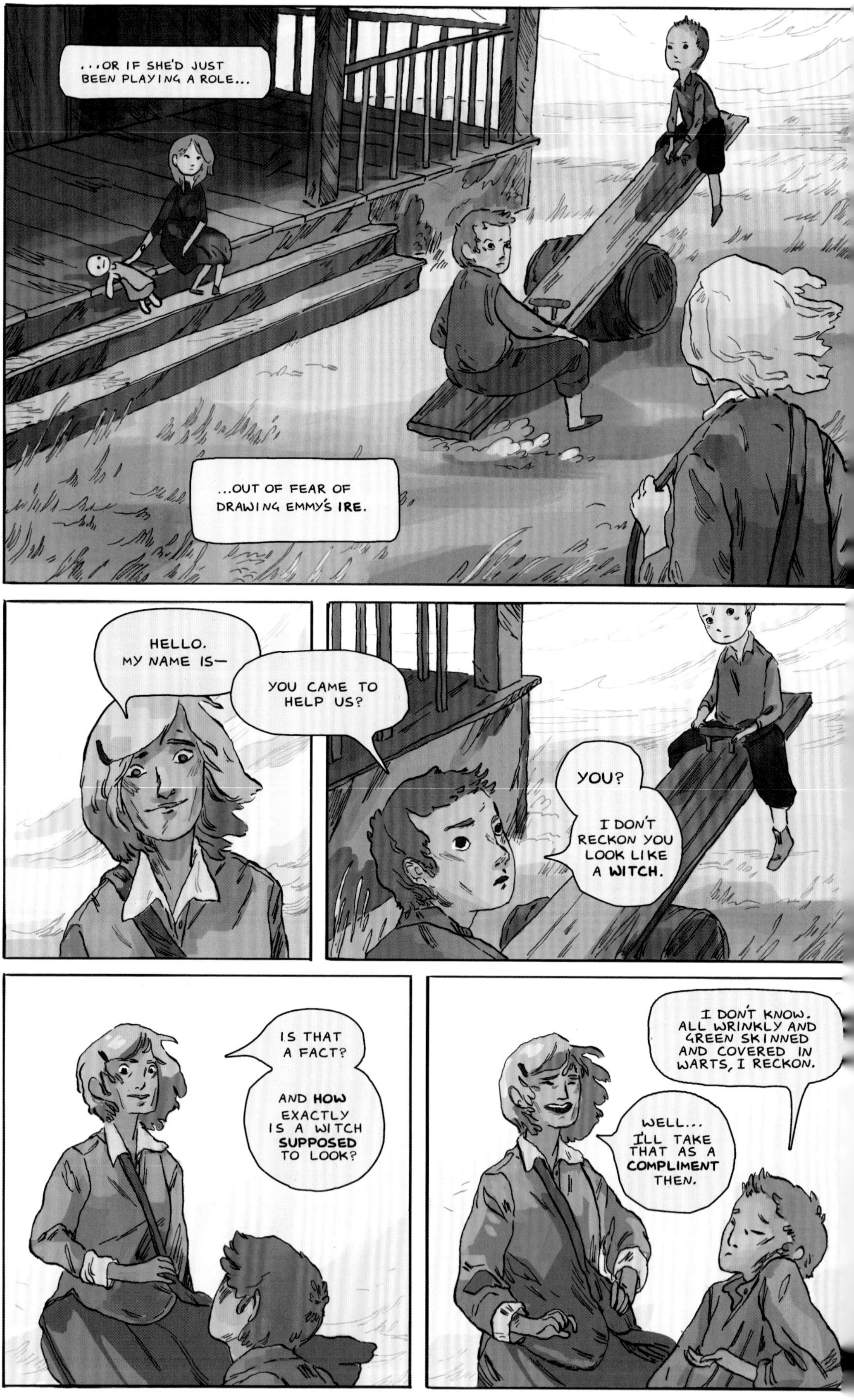
...OR IF SHE'D JUST BEEN PLAYING A ROLE...
...OUT OF FEAR OF DRAWING EMMY'S IRE.
HELLO. MY NAME IS—
YOU CAME TO HELP US?
YOU?
I DON'T RECKON YOU LOOK LIKE A WITCH.
IS THAT A FACT?
AND HOW EXACTLY IS A WITCH SUPPOSED TO LOOK?
I DON'T KNOW. ALL WRINKLY AND GREEN SKINNED AND COVERED IN WARTS, I RECKON.
WELL... I'LL TAKE THAT AS A COMPLIMENT THEN.

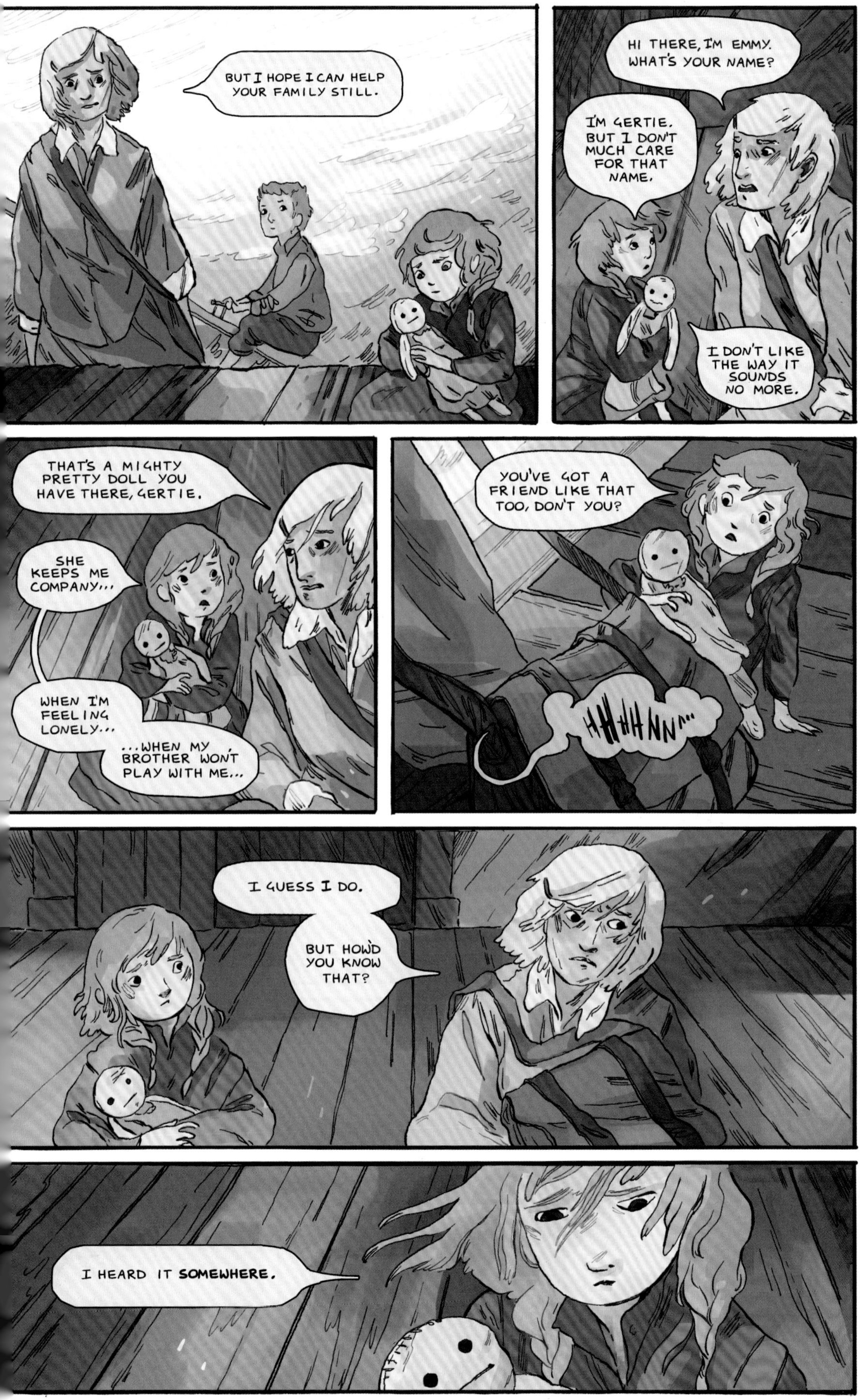
BUT I HOPE I CAN HELP YOUR FAMILY STILL.
HI THERE, I'M EMMY. WHAT'S YOUR NAME?
I'M GERTIE. BUT I DON'T MUCH CARE FOR THAT NAME.
I DON'T LIKE THE WAY IT SOUNDS NO MORE.
THAT'S A MIGHTY PRETTY DOLL YOU HAVE THERE, GERTIE.
SHE KEEPS ME COMPANY...
WHEN I'M FEELING LONELY...
...WHEN MY BROTHER WON'T PLAY WITH ME...
YOU'VE GOT A FRIEND LIKE THAT TOO, DON'T YOU?
HHHHNN
I GUESS I DO.
BUT HOW'D YOU KNOW THAT?
I HEARD IT SOMEWHERE.

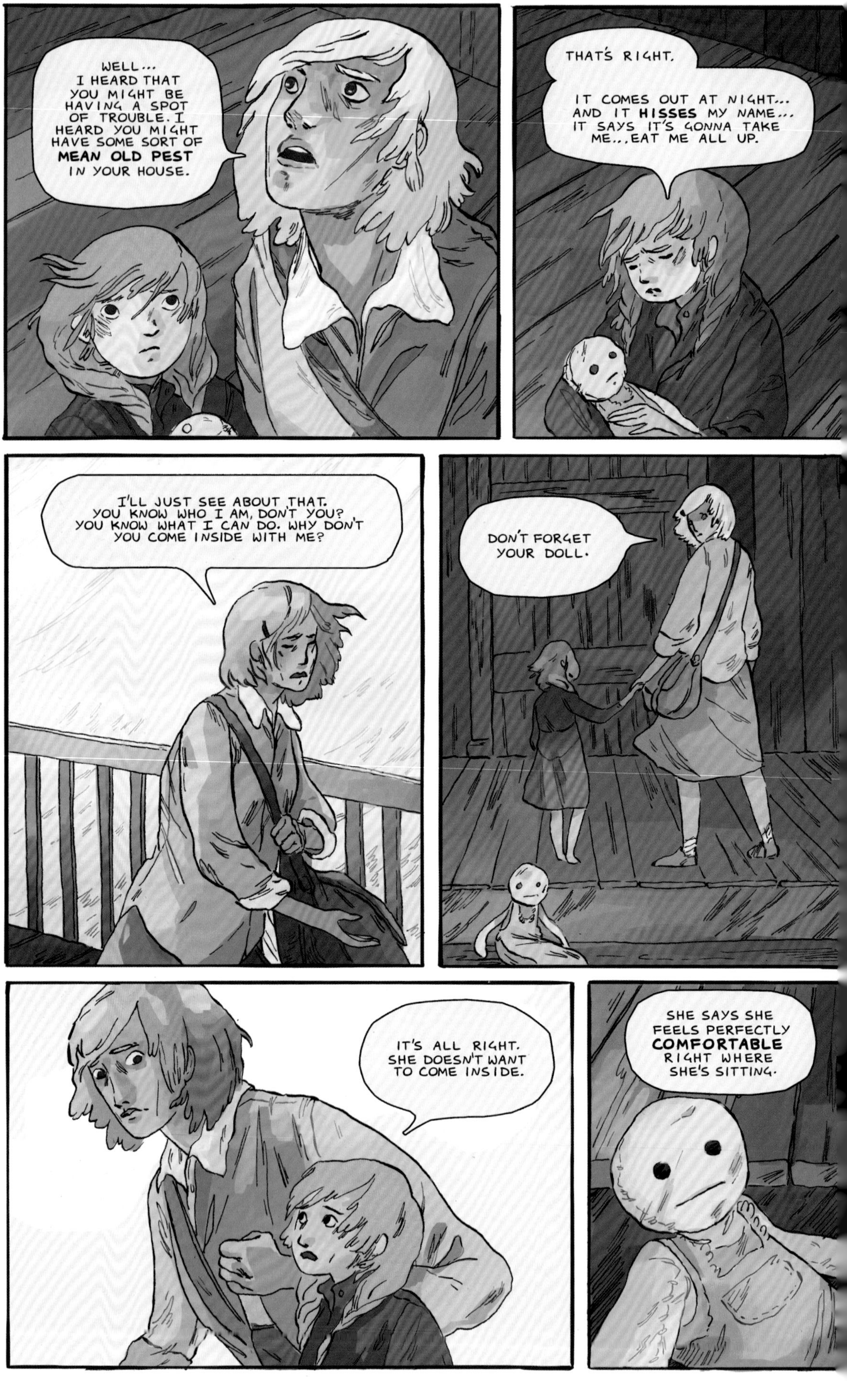
WELL... I HEARD THAT YOU MIGHT BE HAVING A SPOT OF TROUBLE. I HEARD YOU MIGHT HAVE SOME SORT OF **MEAN OLD PEST** IN YOUR HOUSE.
THAT'S RIGHT.
IT COMES OUT AT NIGHT... AND IT **HISSES** MY NAME... IT SAYS IT'S GONNA TAKE ME... EAT ME ALL UP.
I'LL JUST SEE ABOUT THAT. YOU KNOW WHO I AM, DON'T YOU? YOU KNOW WHAT I CAN DO. WHY DON'T YOU COME INSIDE WITH ME?
DON'T FORGET YOUR DOLL.
IT'S ALL RIGHT. SHE DOESN'T WANT TO COME INSIDE.
SHE SAYS SHE FEELS PERFECTLY **COMFORTABLE** RIGHT WHERE SHE'S SITTING.

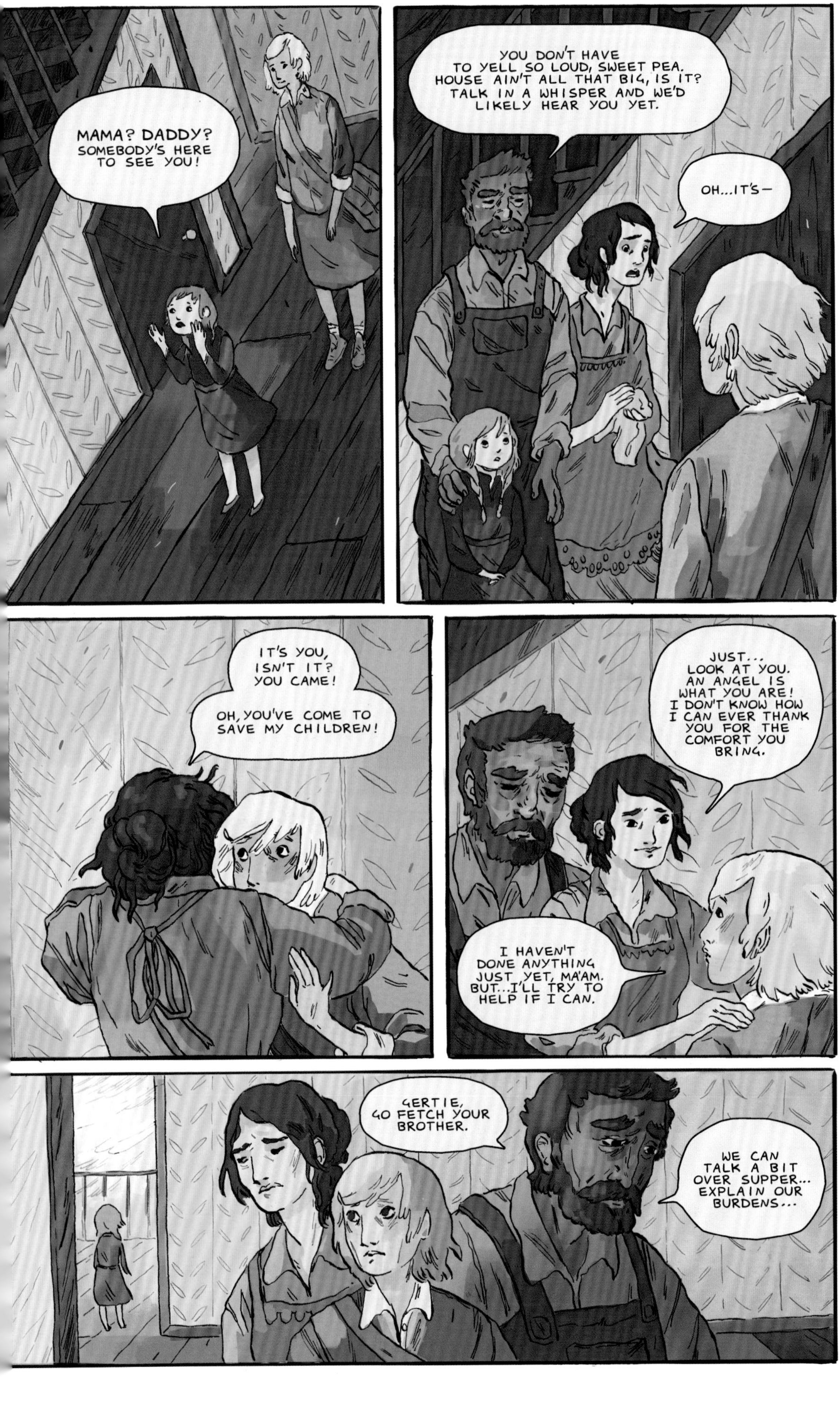
MAMA? DADDY? SOMEBODY'S HERE TO SEE YOU!
YOU DON'T HAVE TO YELL SO LOUD, SWEET PEA. HOUSE AIN'T ALL THAT BIG, IS IT? TALK IN A WHISPER AND WE'D LIKELY HEAR YOU YET.
OH...IT'S—
IT'S YOU, ISN'T IT? YOU CAME!
OH, YOU'VE COME TO SAVE MY CHILDREN!
JUST... LOOK AT YOU. AN ANGEL IS WHAT YOU ARE! I DON'T KNOW HOW I CAN EVER THANK YOU FOR THE COMFORT YOU BRING.
I HAVEN'T DONE ANYTHING JUST YET, MA'AM. BUT...I'LL TRY TO HELP IF I CAN.
GERTIE, GO FETCH YOUR BROTHER.
WE CAN TALK A BIT OVER SUPPER... EXPLAIN OUR BURDENS...

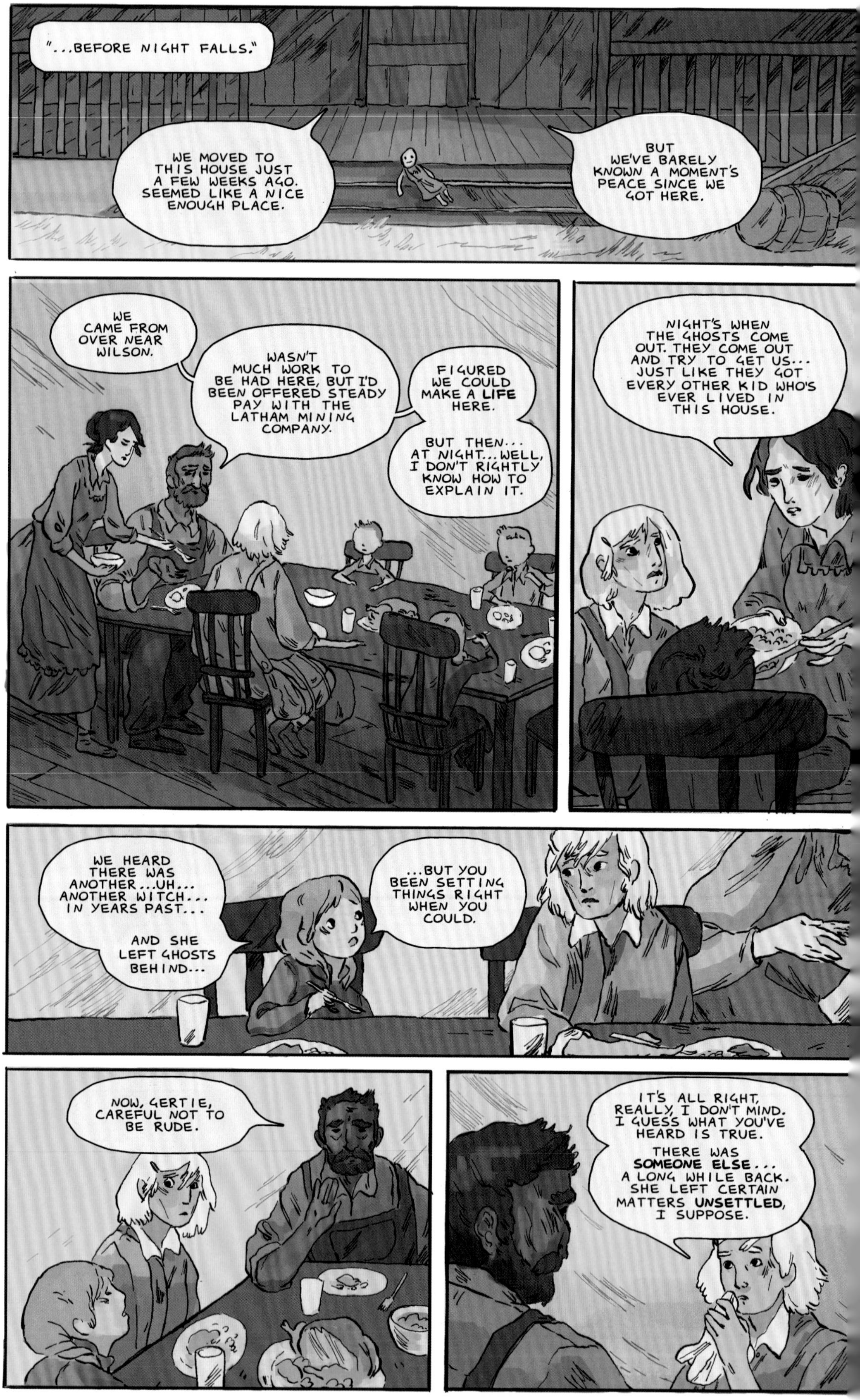
"...BEFORE NIGHT FALLS."
WE MOVED TO THIS HOUSE JUST A FEW WEEKS AGO. SEEMED LIKE A NICE ENOUGH PLACE.
BUT WE'VE BARELY KNOWN A MOMENT'S PEACE SINCE WE GOT HERE.
WE CAME FROM OVER NEAR WILSON.
WASN'T MUCH WORK TO BE HAD HERE, BUT I'D BEEN OFFERED STEADY PAY WITH THE LATHAM MINING COMPANY.
FIGURED WE COULD MAKE A **LIFE** HERE.
BUT THEN... AT NIGHT... WELL, I DON'T RIGHTLY KNOW HOW TO EXPLAIN IT.
NIGHT'S WHEN THE GHOSTS COME OUT. THEY COME OUT AND TRY TO GET US... JUST LIKE THEY GOT EVERY OTHER KID WHO'S EVER LIVED IN THIS HOUSE.
WE HEARD THERE WAS ANOTHER... UH... ANOTHER WITCH... IN YEARS PAST...
AND SHE LEFT GHOSTS BEHIND...
...BUT YOU BEEN SETTING THINGS RIGHT WHEN YOU COULD.
NOW, GERTIE, CAREFUL NOT TO BE RUDE.
IT'S ALL RIGHT, REALLY, I DON'T MIND. I GUESS WHAT YOU'VE HEARD IS TRUE.
THERE WAS **SOMEONE ELSE**... A LONG WHILE BACK. SHE LEFT CERTAIN MATTERS **UNSETTLED**, I SUPPOSE.

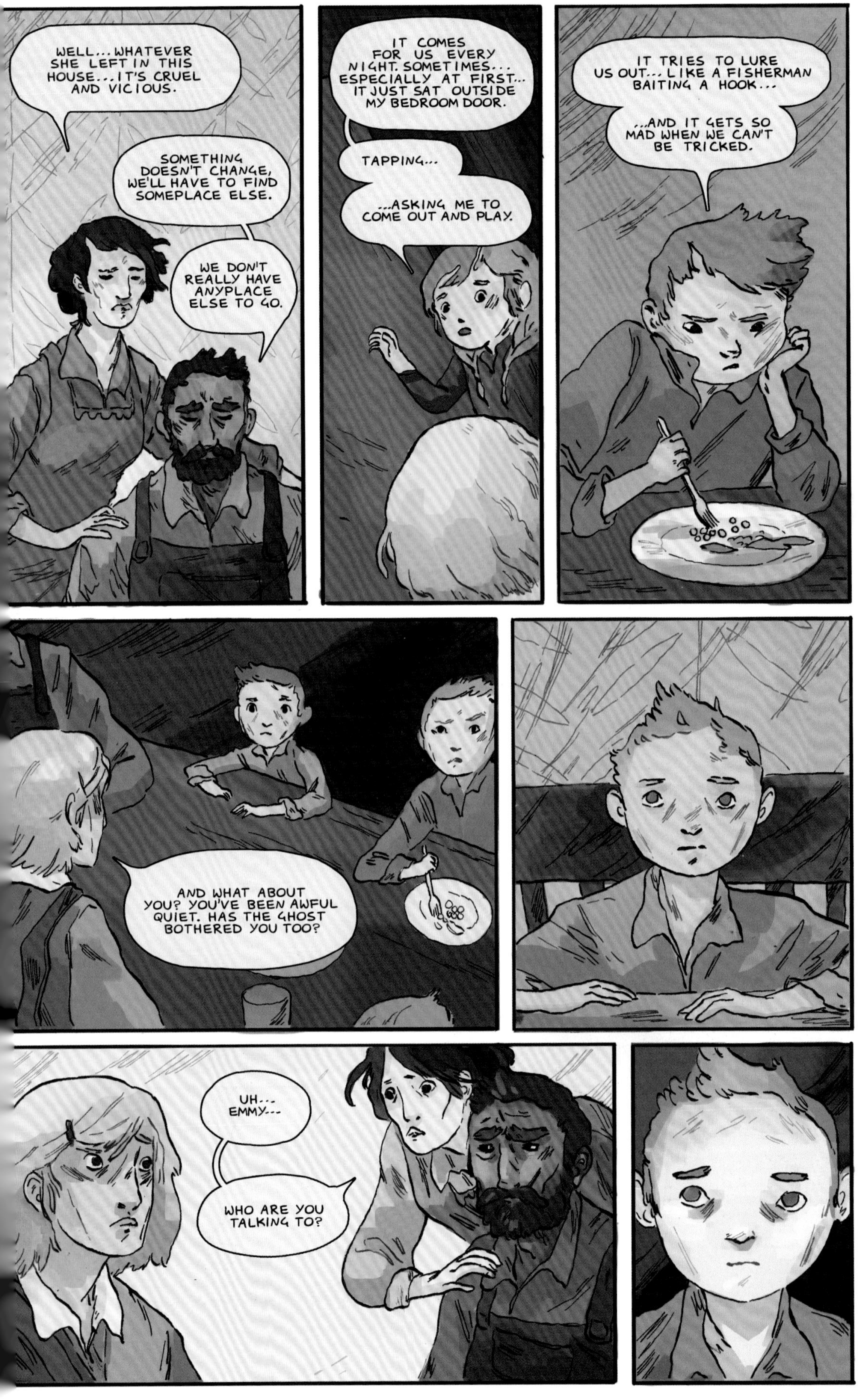
WELL... WHATEVER SHE LEFT IN THIS HOUSE... IT'S CRUEL AND VICIOUS.
SOMETHING DOESN'T CHANGE, WE'LL HAVE TO FIND SOMEPLACE ELSE.
WE DON'T REALLY HAVE ANYPLACE ELSE TO GO.
IT COMES FOR US EVERY NIGHT. SOMETIMES... ESPECIALLY AT FIRST... IT JUST SAT OUTSIDE MY BEDROOM DOOR.
TAPPING...
...ASKING ME TO COME OUT AND PLAY.
IT TRIES TO LURE US OUT... LIKE A FISHERMAN BAITING A HOOK...
...AND IT GETS SO MAD WHEN WE CAN'T BE TRICKED.
AND WHAT ABOUT YOU? YOU'VE BEEN AWFUL QUIET. HAS THE GHOST BOTHERED YOU TOO?
UH... EMMY...
WHO ARE YOU TALKING TO?

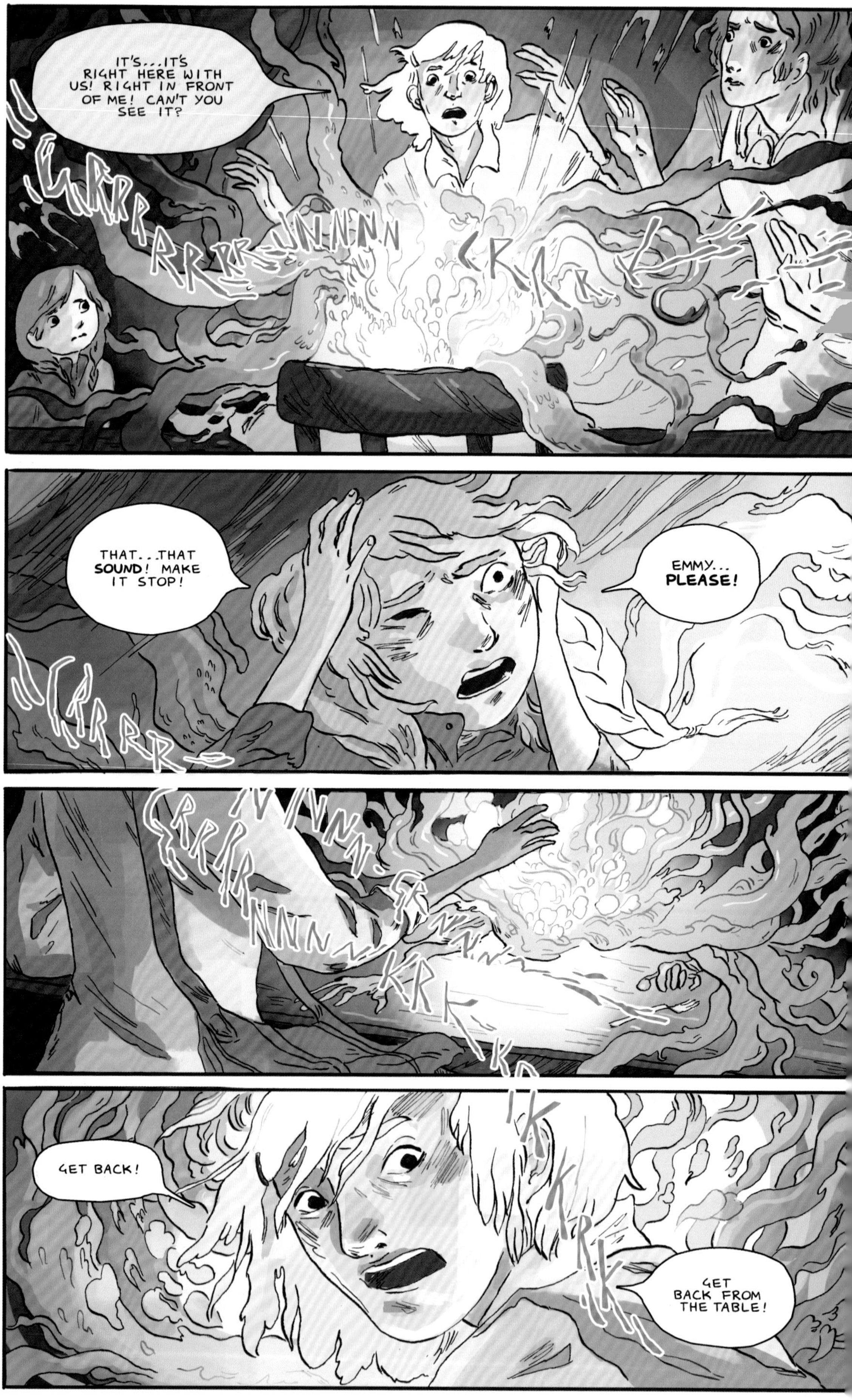
IT'S...IT'S RIGHT HERE WITH US! RIGHT IN FRONT OF ME! CAN'T YOU SEE IT?
GRRRRRRRR-NNNNN CRRRK
THAT...THAT **SOUND**! MAKE IT STOP!
EMMY... **PLEASE!**
GRRRR-
GRRRRNNNNN-NNNN-GRNNN-KRK
GET BACK!
GET BACK FROM THE TABLE!

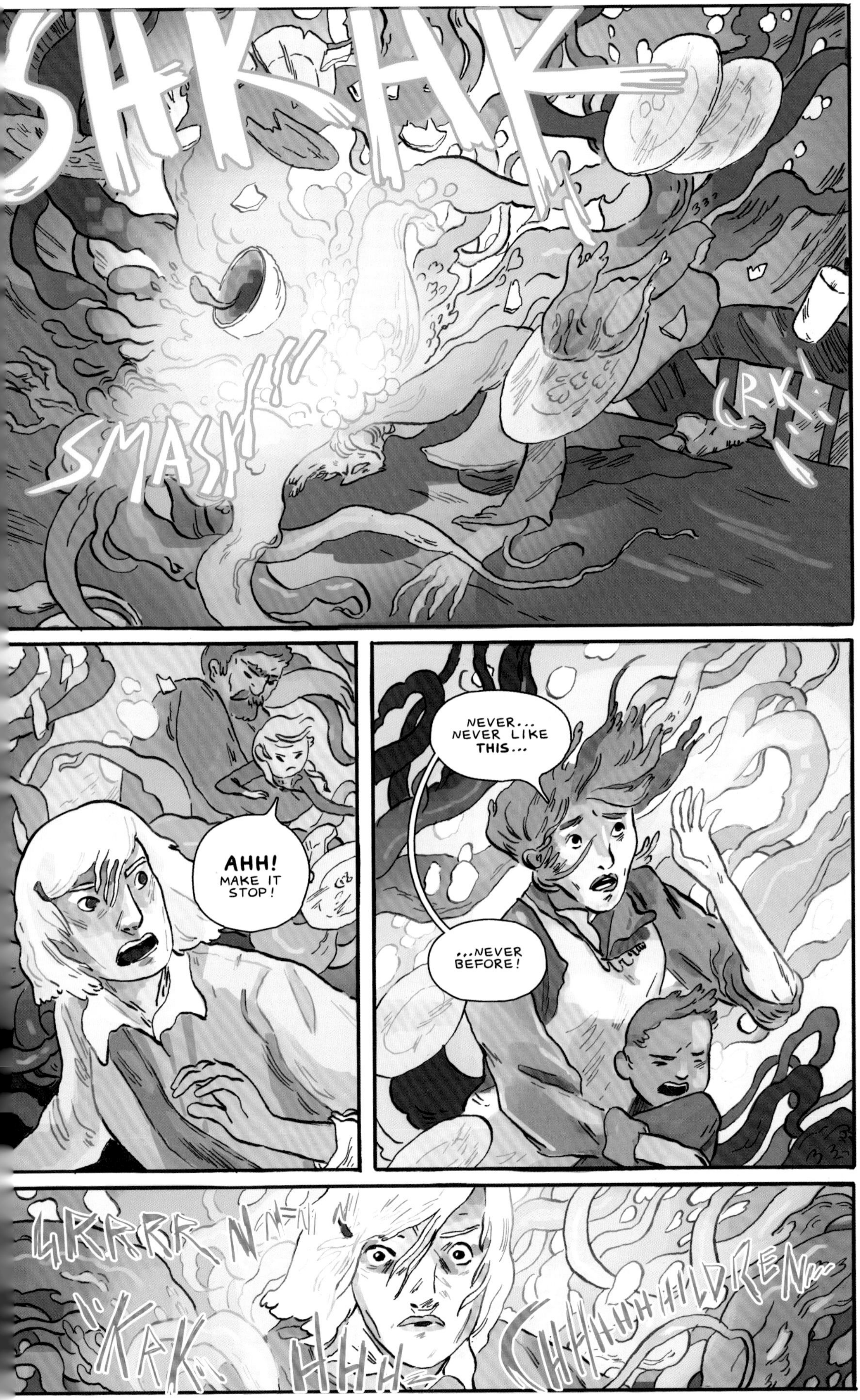
SHKHK
SMASH!!
CRK!
AHH! MAKE IT STOP!
NEVER... NEVER LIKE THIS...
...NEVER BEFORE!
GRRRR NNNN
KAK.. HHH..
CHHHHHHILDREN...

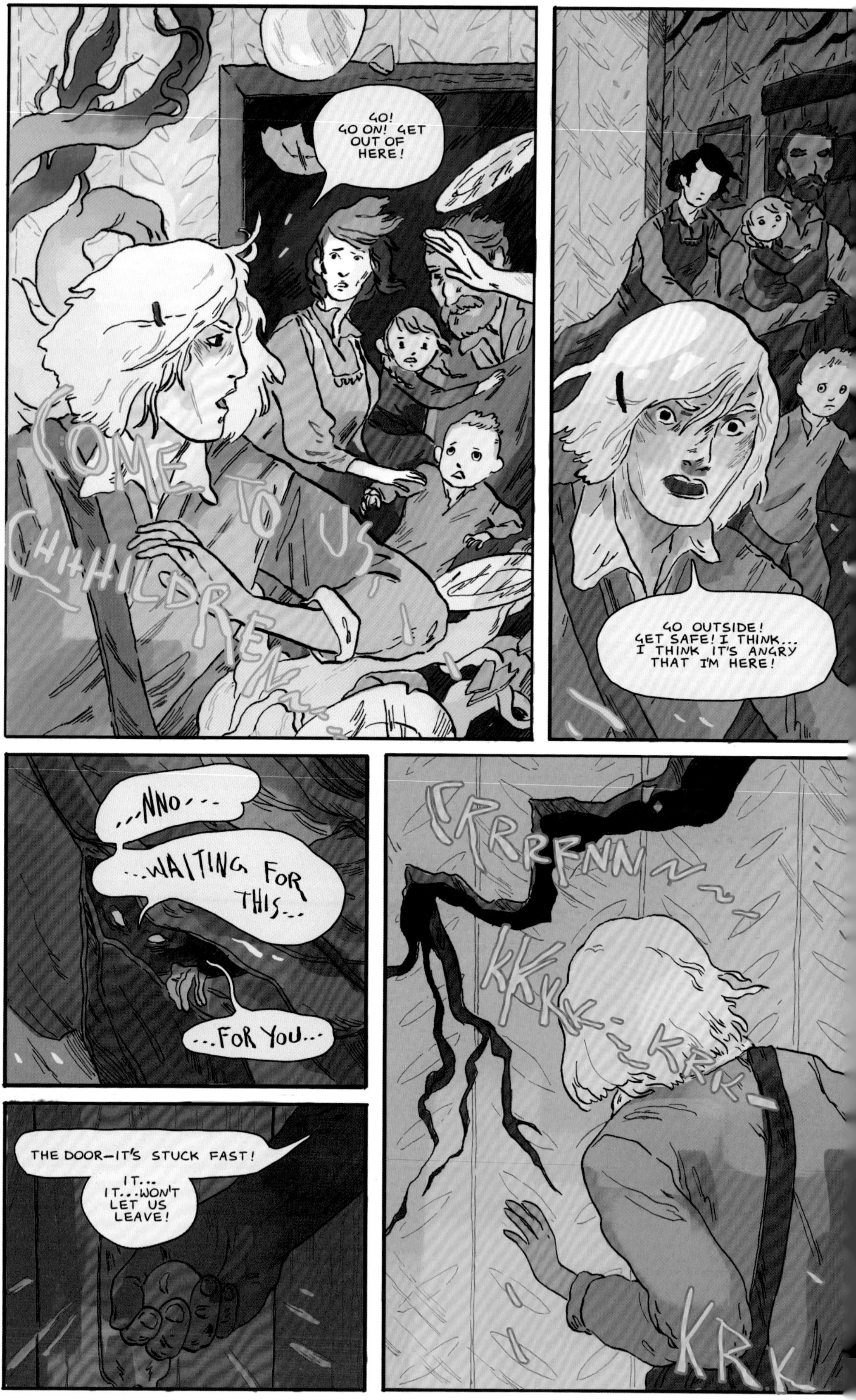
GO! GO ON! GET OUT OF HERE!
COME TO US CHIHILDREN...
GO OUTSIDE! GET SAFE! I THINK... I THINK IT'S ANGRY THAT I'M HERE!
...NNO...
...WAITING FOR THIS...
...FOR YOU...
CRRRRNNN~~
KKKKK-KRK-
KRK
THE DOOR—IT'S STUCK FAST!
IT... IT...WON'T LET US LEAVE!

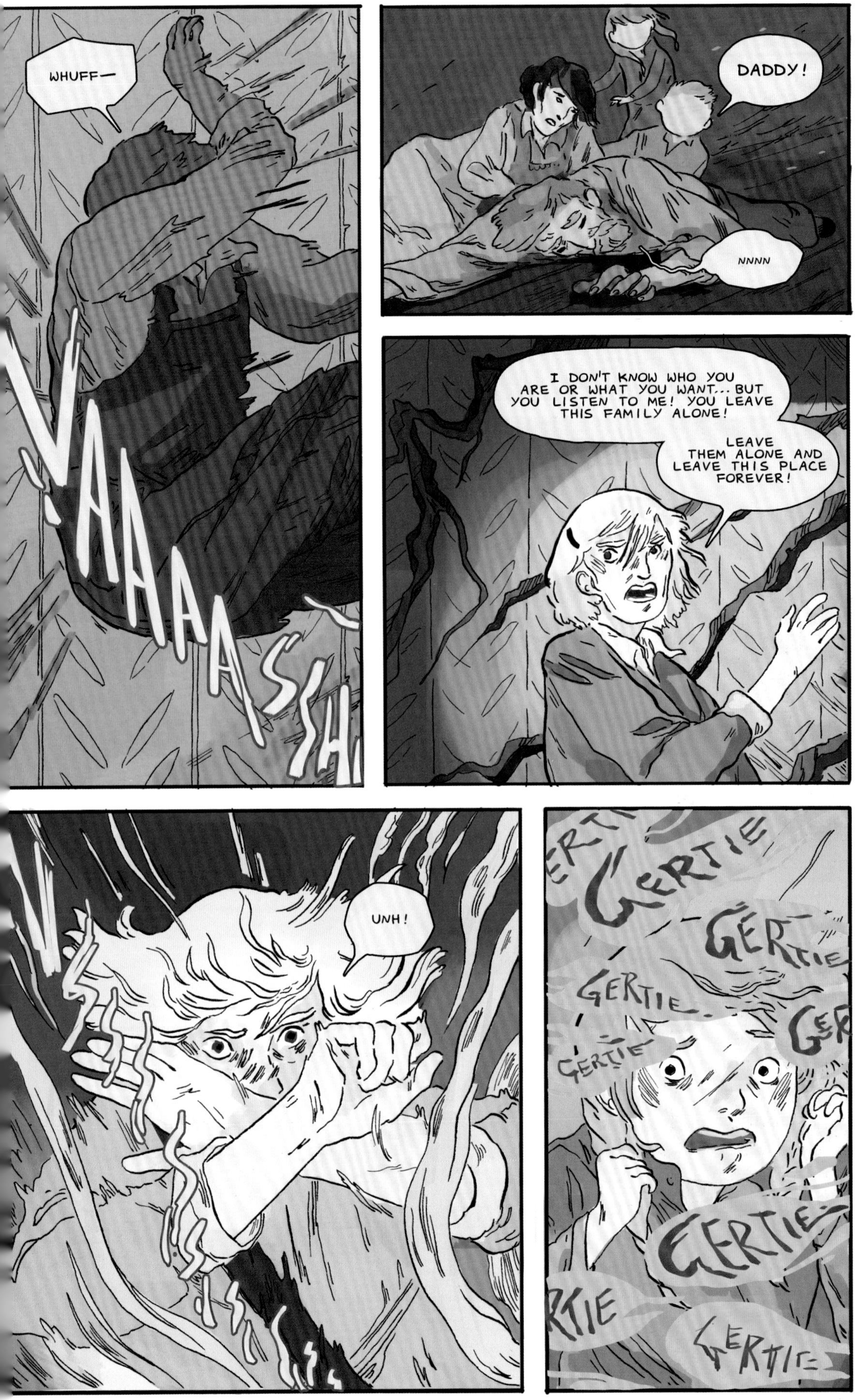
WHUFF—
DADDY!
NNNN
I DON'T KNOW WHO YOU ARE OR WHAT YOU WANT... BUT YOU LISTEN TO ME! YOU LEAVE THIS FAMILY ALONE!
LEAVE THEM ALONE AND LEAVE THIS PLACE FOREVER!
UNH!
GERTIE
GERTIE
GERTIE
GERTIE
GERTIE
GERTIE

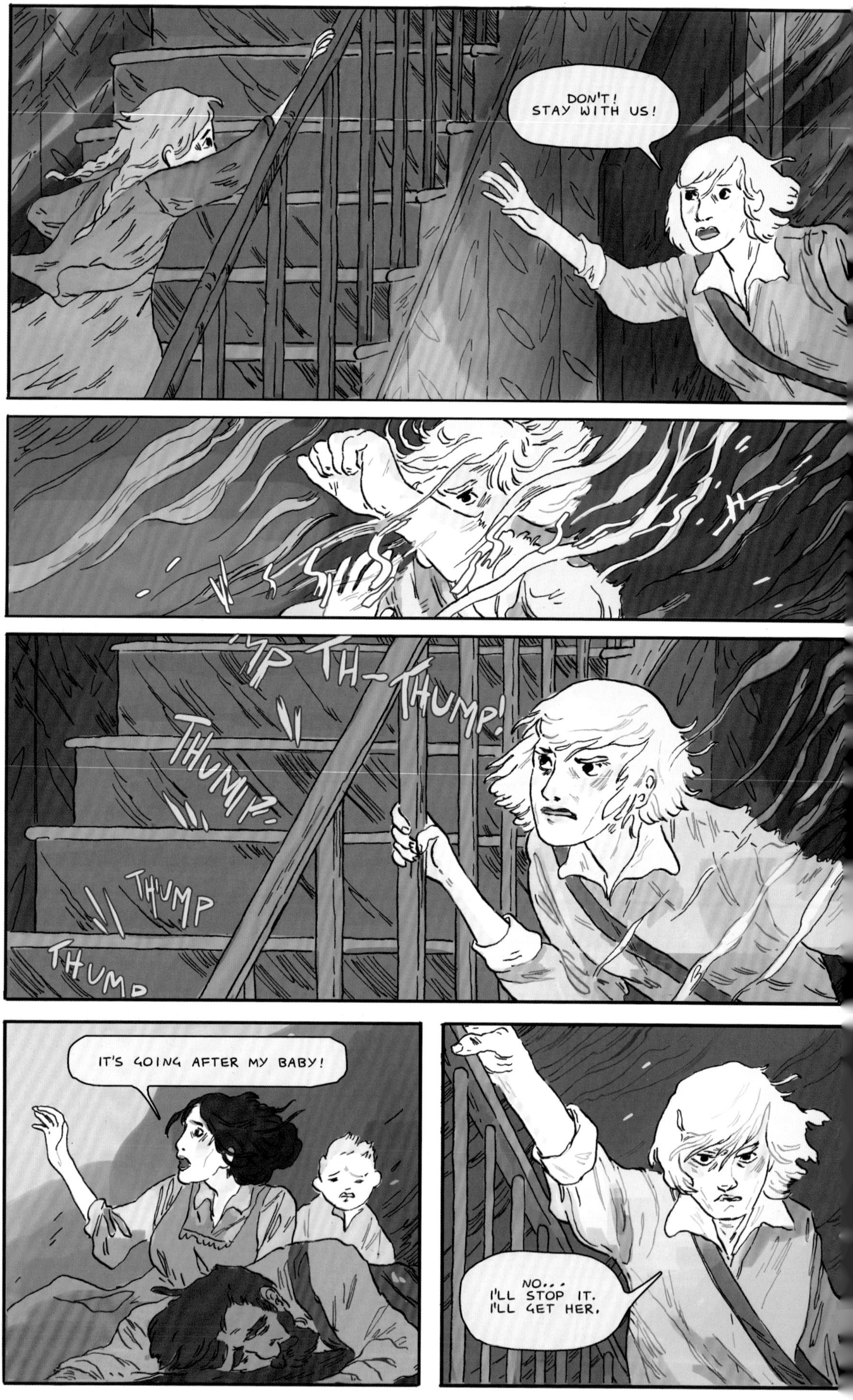
DON'T!
STAY WITH US!
-MP TH-THUMP!
THUMP!
THUMP
THUMP
IT'S GOING AFTER MY BABY!
NO...
I'LL STOP IT.
I'LL GET HER.

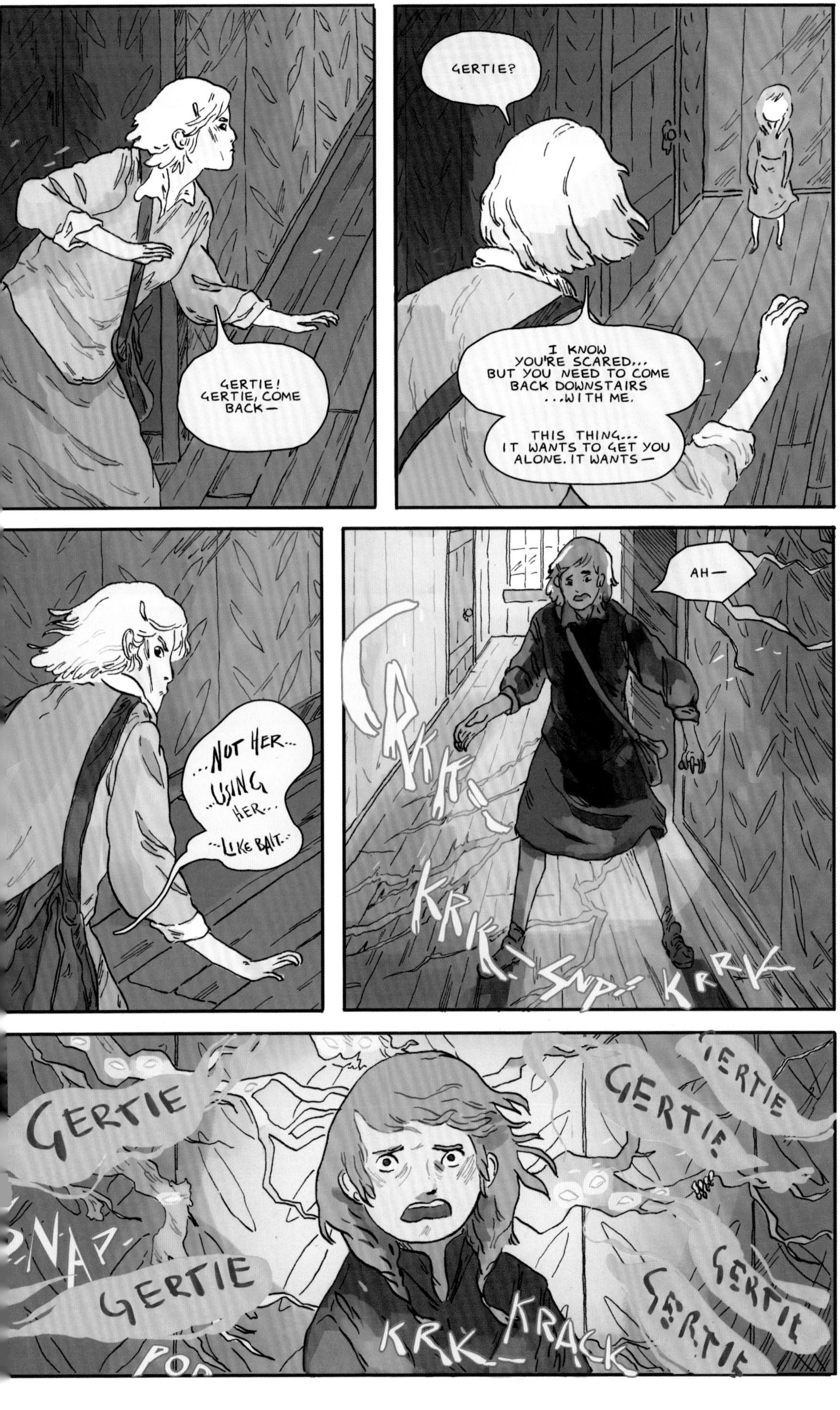
GERTIE! GERTIE, COME BACK—
GERTIE?
I KNOW YOU'RE SCARED... BUT YOU NEED TO COME BACK DOWNSTAIRS ...WITH ME.
THIS THING... IT WANTS TO GET YOU ALONE. IT WANTS—
...NOT HER... USING HER... LIKE BAIT.
AH—
KRKK
KRK
SNP
KRRK
GERTIE
GERTIE
GERTIE
GERTIE
GERTIE
GERTIE
GERTIE
KRK
KRACK

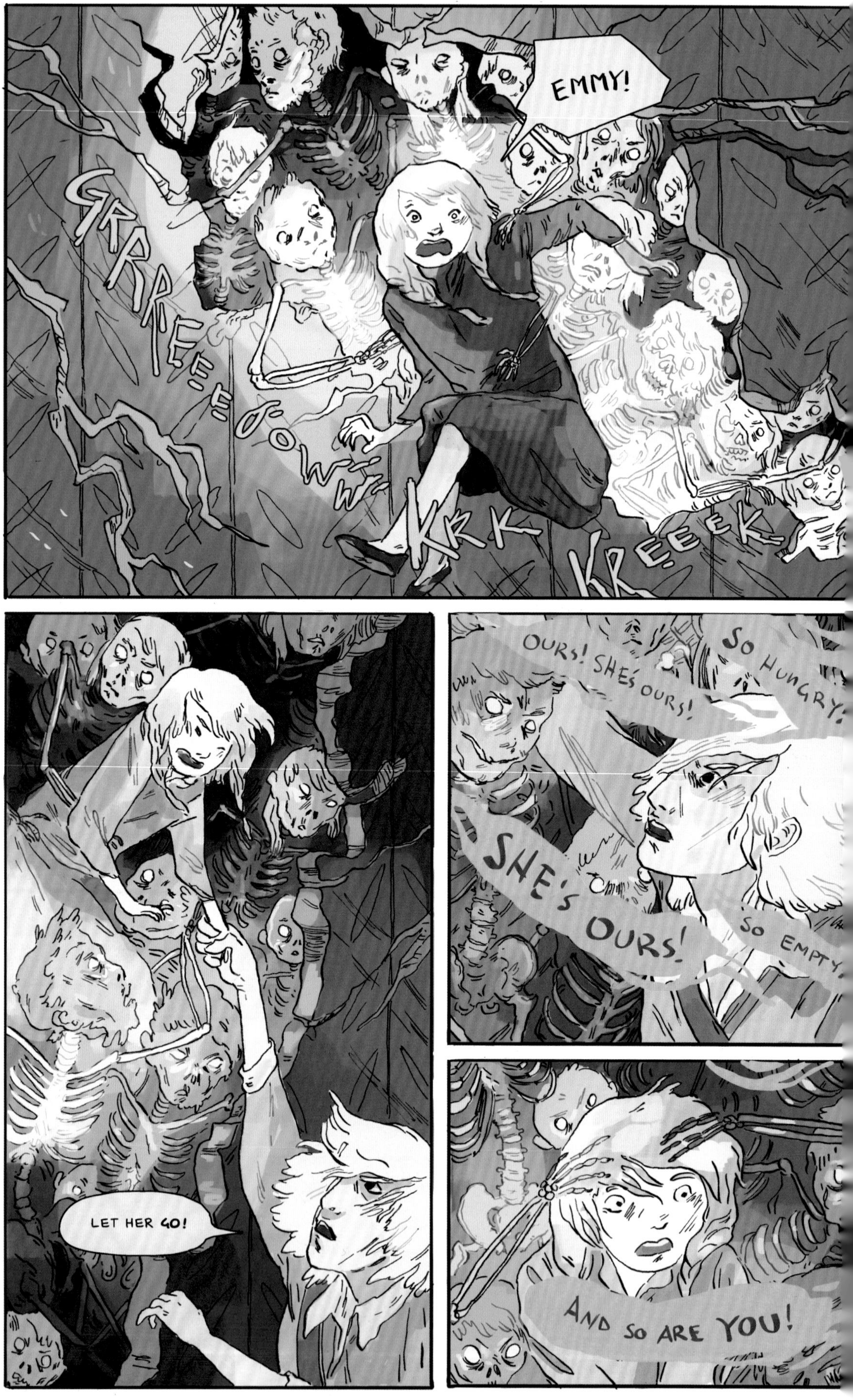
EMMY!
GRRREEEOOWW
KRK
KREEEK
OURS! SHE'S OURS!
SO HUNGRY!
SHE'S OURS!
SO EMPTY
LET HER GO!
AND SO ARE YOU!

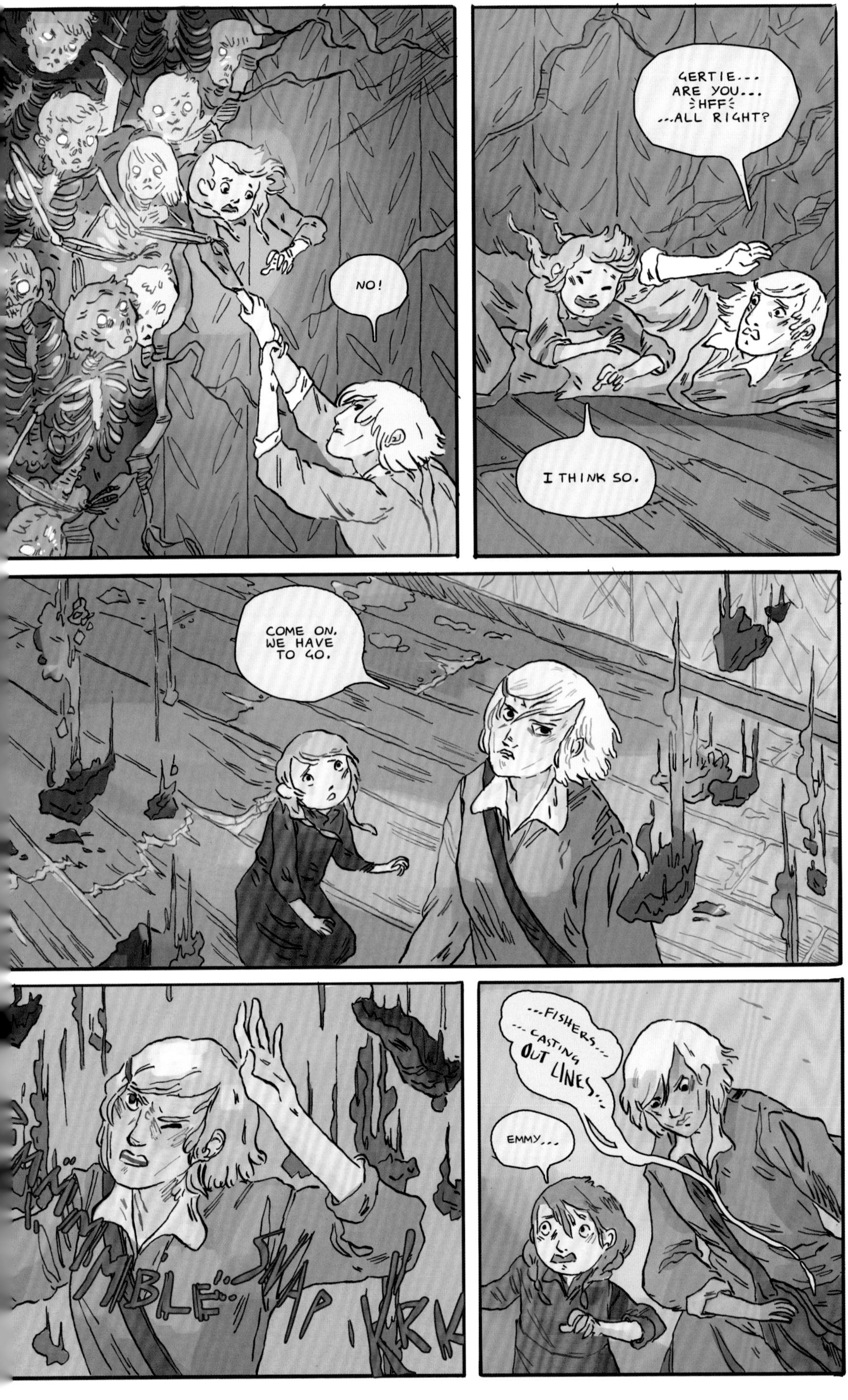
NO!
GERTIE... ARE YOU... HFF ...ALL RIGHT?
I THINK SO.
COME ON. WE HAVE TO GO.
MMMMMBLE..
SNAP
KRK
...FISHERS... ...CASTING OUT LINES...
EMMY...

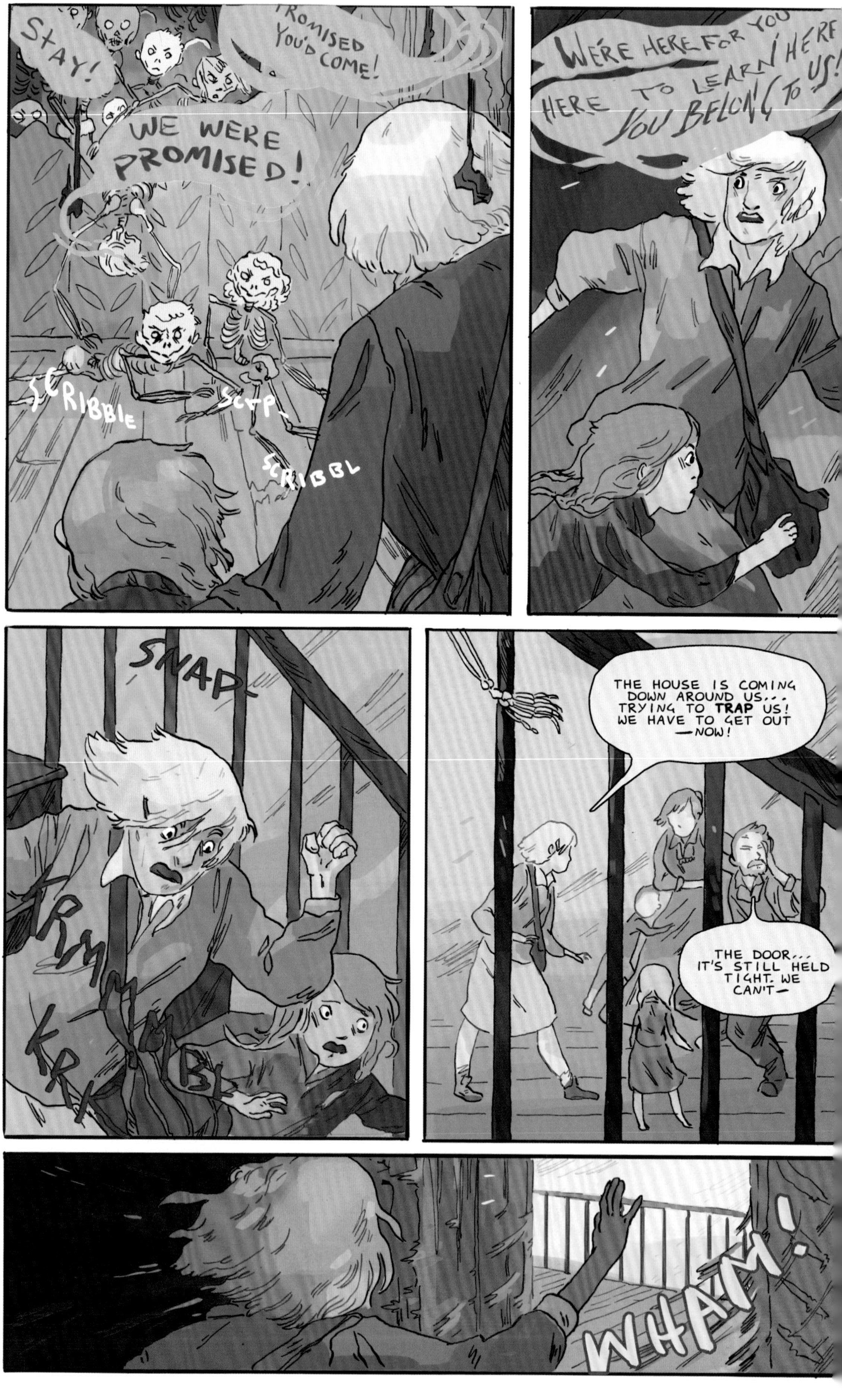
STAY!
ROMISED YOU'D COME!
WE WERE PROMISED!
SCRIBBLE
SCRP
SCRIBBL
WE'RE HERE FOR YOU
HERE TO LEARN HERE
YOU BELONG TO US!
SNAP
KRK
KRUMMMBL
THE HOUSE IS COMING DOWN AROUND US... TRYING TO **TRAP** US! WE HAVE TO GET OUT —NOW!
THE DOOR... IT'S STILL HELD TIGHT. WE CAN'T—
WHAM!

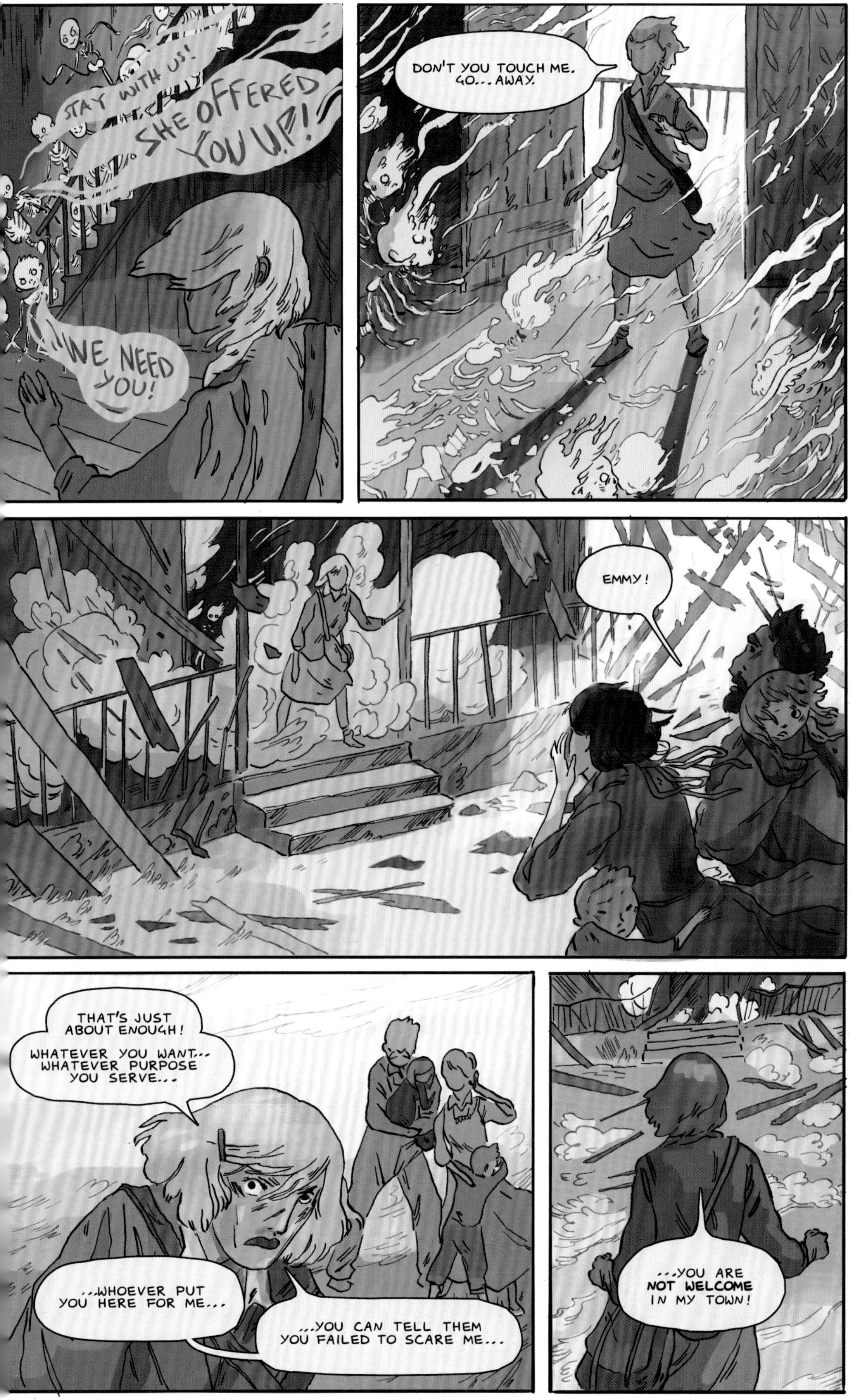
STAY WITH US!
SHE OFFERED YOU UP!
WE NEED YOU!
DON'T YOU TOUCH ME. GO... AWAY.
EMMY!
THAT'S JUST ABOUT ENOUGH!
WHATEVER YOU WANT... WHATEVER PURPOSE YOU SERVE...
...WHOEVER PUT YOU HERE FOR ME...
...YOU CAN TELL THEM YOU FAILED TO SCARE ME...
...YOU ARE **NOT WELCOME** IN MY TOWN!

SMASH - GRRRN - KR!

THE HOUSE REARED UP LIKE A **TWISTED SPIDER.**

THE GROAN OF THE TWISTING, CRACKING TIMBERS WAS LIKE A **ROAR.**

GRUUUUUJOUUAAAK

IT WAS A TRAP SPRINGING SHUT...

...AND ANGRY THAT ITS PREY HAD SLIPPED AWAY.

THE HOUSE SLITHERED AWAY...

...RETREATED UNDERGROUND IN ITS DEFEAT.

EMMY WONDERED IF SHE HAD SEEN THE LAST OF IT.

SHE KNEW THAT **VILE THINGS** COULD HIDE FOR A LONG WHILE BENEATH THE DIRT.

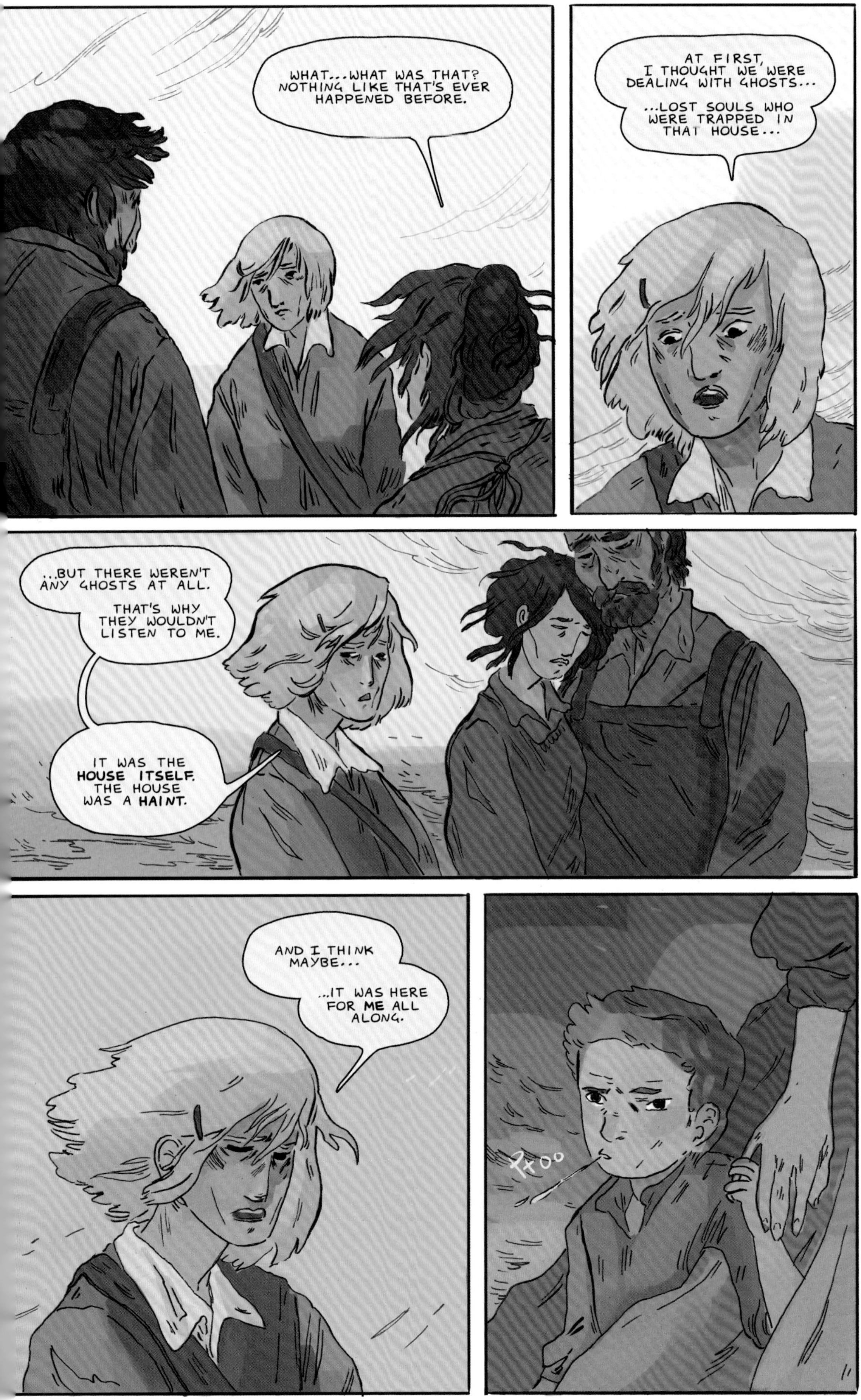
WHAT...WHAT WAS THAT? NOTHING LIKE THAT'S EVER HAPPENED BEFORE.
AT FIRST, I THOUGHT WE WERE DEALING WITH GHOSTS...
...LOST SOULS WHO WERE TRAPPED IN THAT HOUSE...
...BUT THERE WEREN'T ANY GHOSTS AT ALL.
THAT'S WHY THEY WOULDN'T LISTEN TO ME.
IT WAS THE **HOUSE ITSELF**. THE HOUSE WAS A **HAINT**.
AND I THINK MAYBE...
...IT WAS HERE FOR **ME** ALL ALONG.
PTOO

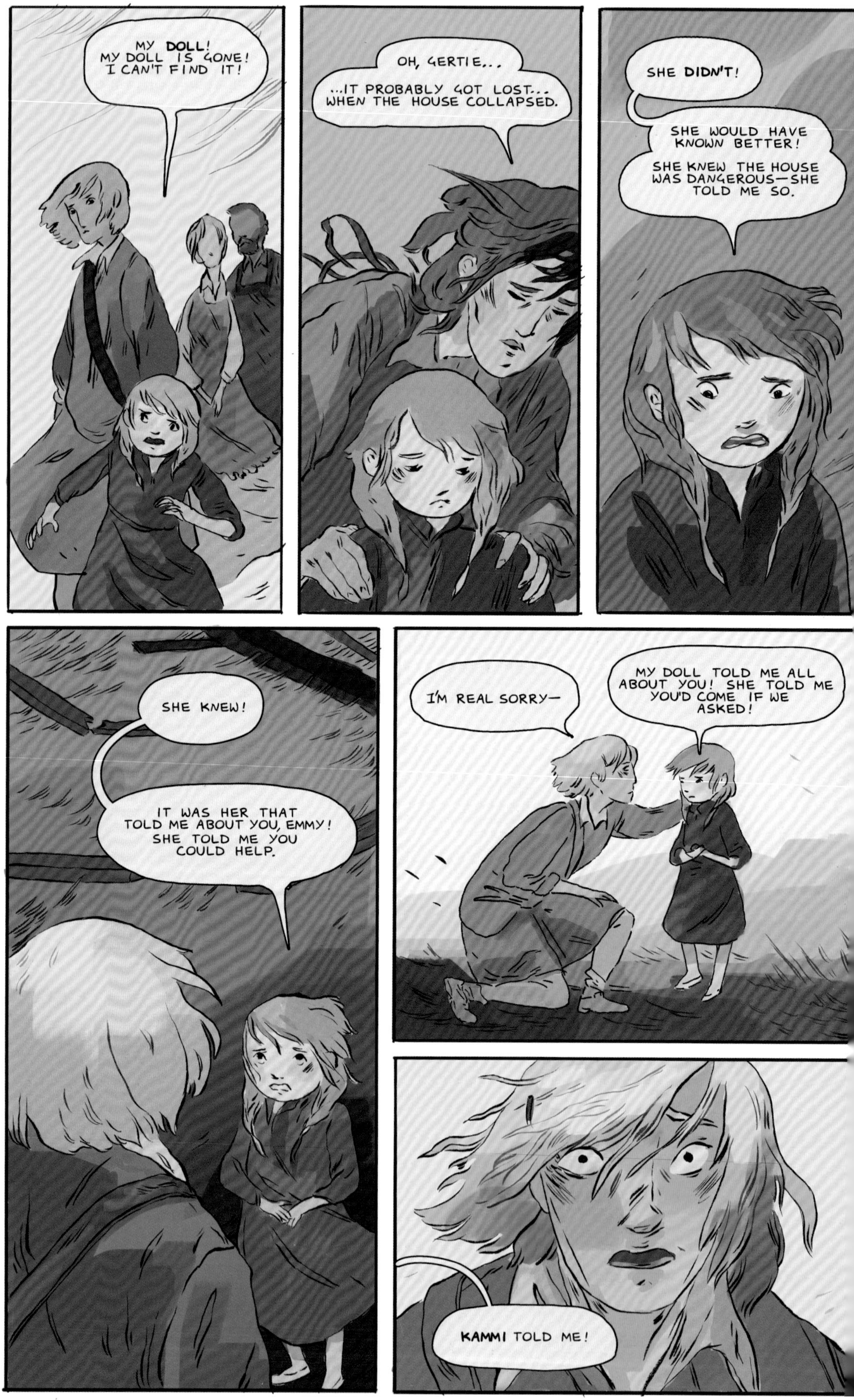
MY **DOLL**! MY DOLL IS GONE! I CAN'T FIND IT!
OH, GERTIE...
...IT PROBABLY GOT LOST... WHEN THE HOUSE COLLAPSED.
SHE **DIDN'T**!
SHE WOULD HAVE KNOWN BETTER!
SHE KNEW THE HOUSE WAS DANGEROUS—SHE TOLD ME SO.
SHE KNEW!
IT WAS HER THAT TOLD ME ABOUT YOU, EMMY! SHE TOLD ME YOU COULD HELP.
I'M REAL SORRY—
MY DOLL TOLD ME ALL ABOUT YOU! SHE TOLD ME YOU'D COME IF WE ASKED!
KAMMI TOLD ME!

HARROW
►SKETCHBOOK◄
COUNTY

**NOTES BY
TYLER CROOK, CARLA SPEED McNEIL,
and HANNAH CHRISTENSON**

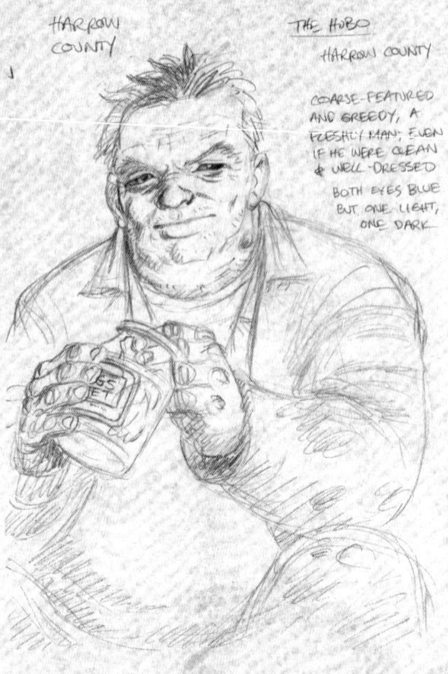
HARROW COUNTY
THE HOBO
HARROW COUNTY
COARSE-FEATURED AND GREEDY, A FLESHY MAN; EVEN IF HE WERE CLEAN & WELL-DRESSED
BOTH EYES BLUE BUT ONE LIGHT, ONE DARK

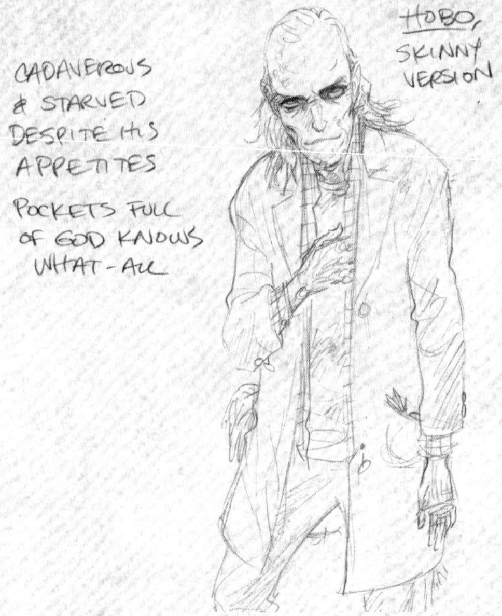
CADAVEROUS & STARVED DESPITE HIS APPETITES
POCKETS FULL OF GOD KNOWS WHAT-ALL
HOBO, SKINNY VERSION

CARLA SPEED McNEIL: **The sizable-gent design for the hobo is based on Oliver Platt. I love Oliver Platt. One of these days I'm gonna find a character who's right for him to "play." He also embodies a wino who scared the whiz out of me when I was about eleven, so there's that. After I submitted that first idea, Cullen and Tyler told me they wanted a walking coat hanger whose features should suggest a connection to some spoiler-spoiler-spoilery stuff, so I redesigned him to be a skeletal-wraith sort of person. His eyes are his most interesting feature to draw, since they're so deep set. They're a pair of butterfly-shaped ellipses that make him look vicious and cringing at the same time.**

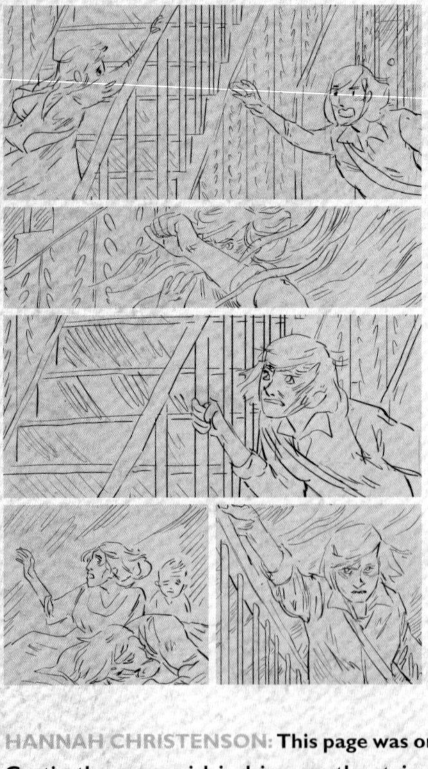

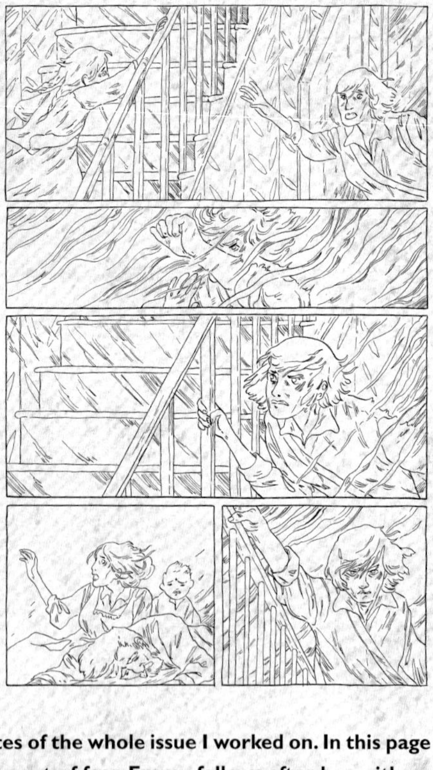

HANNAH CHRISTENSON: **This page was one of my favorites of the whole issue I worked on. In this page Gertie, the young girl, is driven up the stairs and into danger out of fear. Emmy follows after her with an expression of stone-cold determination. I sketched the layout for the pages of this issue over a midtone gray to help make the word balloons (not pictured) stand out, so as to better design the panels with them in mind. This made everything clear and easy to work with when I moved on to penciling and inking.**

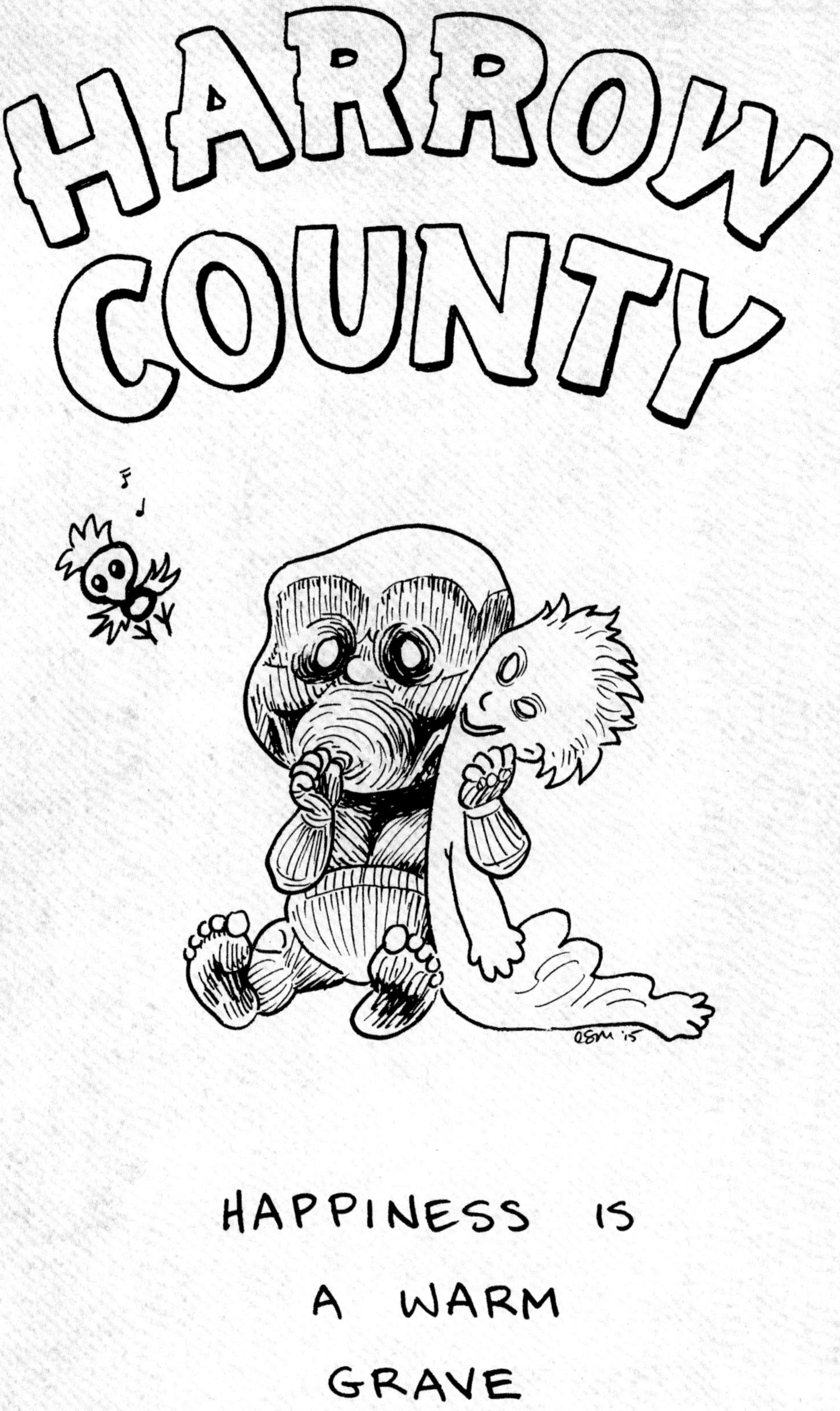
HARROW COUNTY
HAPPINESS IS A WARM GRAVE

CARLA SPEED McNEIL: There was something about the way the boy carefully rolled up the skin and carried it around that made me think of Charles Schulz's Linus. We hadn't seen him do that before. We also never saw Linus's blanket talk to him, but I've no doubt that it would have if they lived in Harrow County.

TYLER CROOK: This is the current lock screen on my phone.

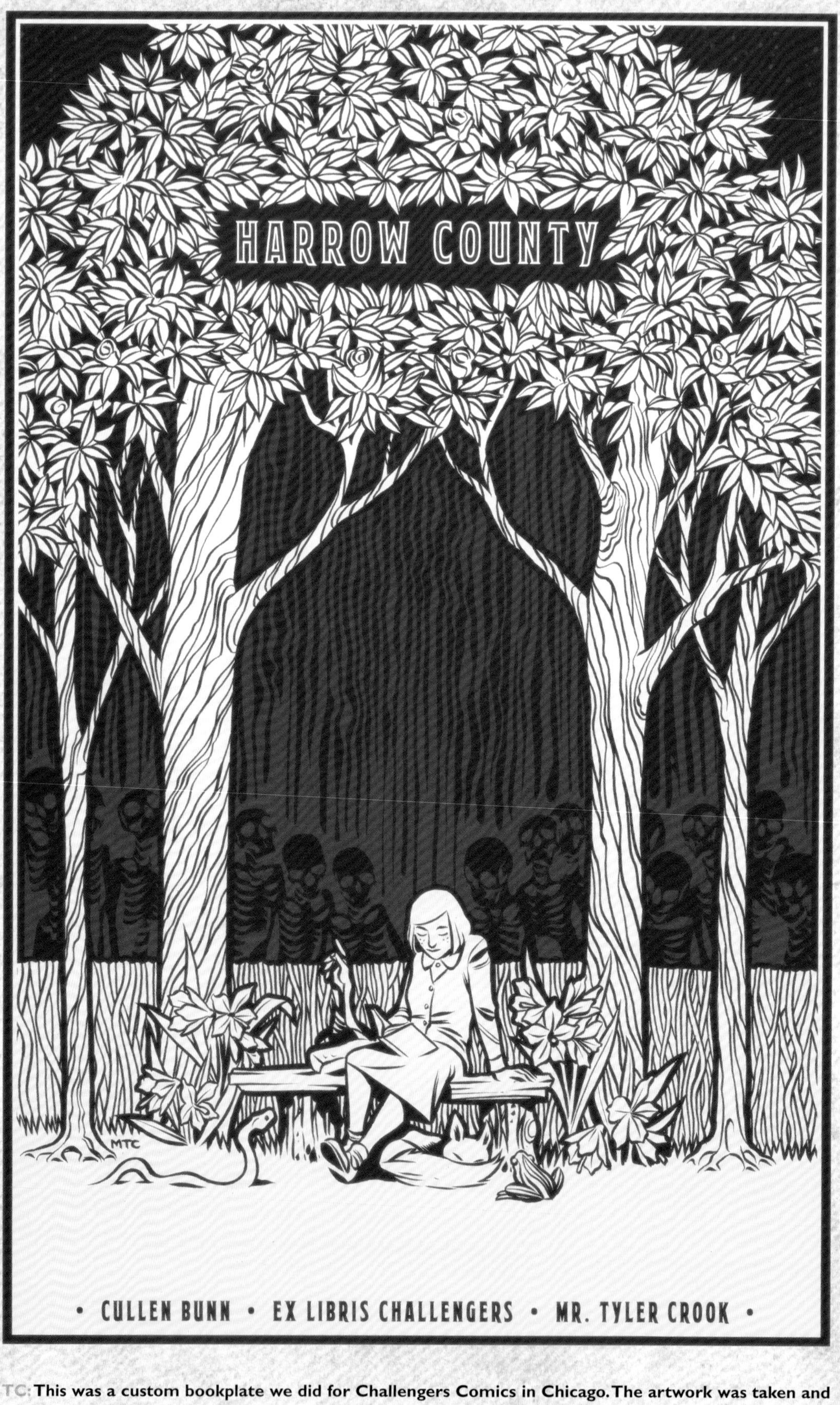
HARROW COUNTY
• CULLEN BUNN • EX LIBRIS CHALLENGERS • MR. TYLER CROOK •
MTC

TC: This was a custom bookplate we did for Challengers Comics in Chicago. The artwork was taken and adapted from a screenprinted poster that we did when the series first started.

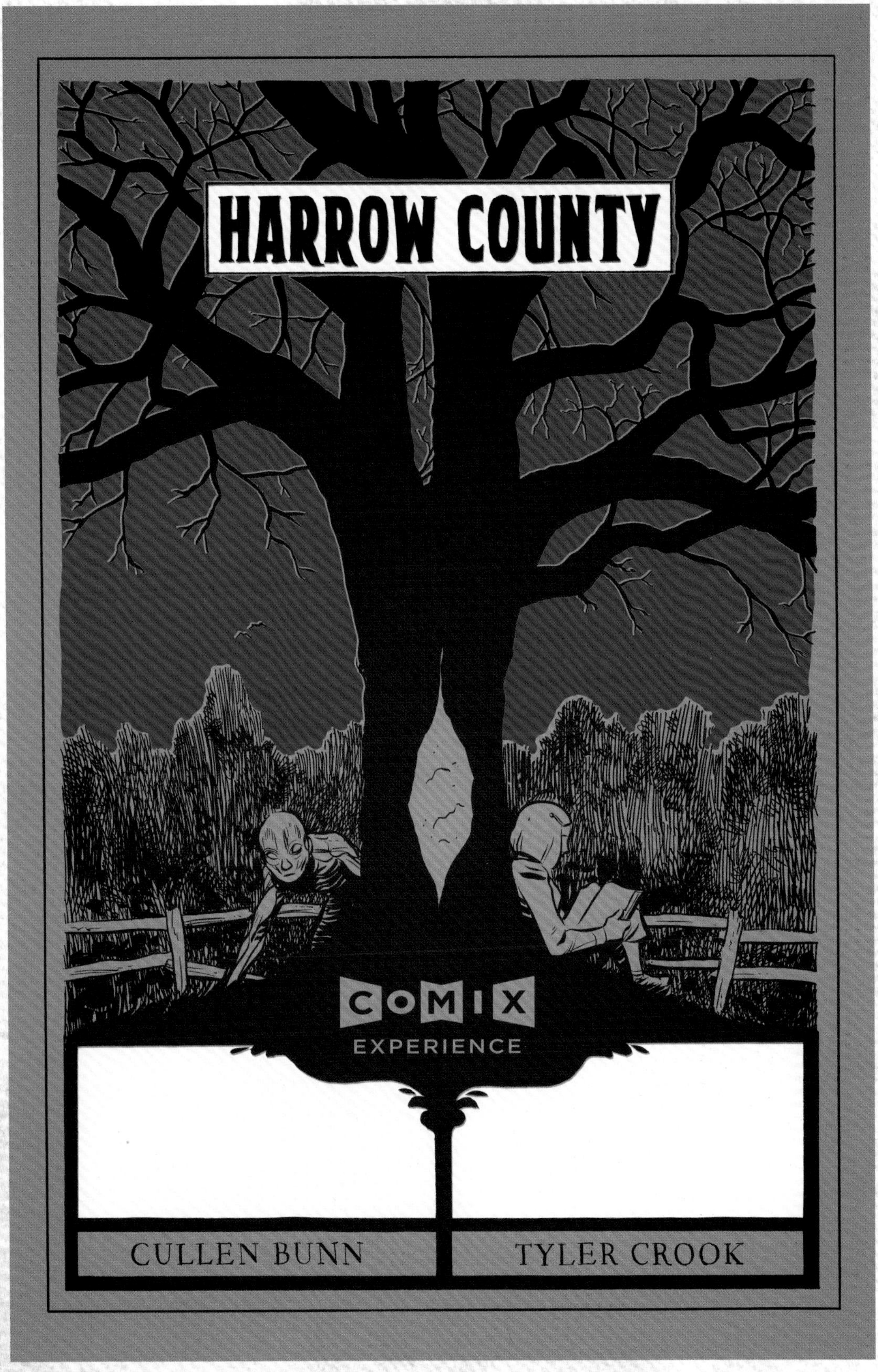
HARROW COUNTY
COMIX
EXPERIENCE
CULLEN BUNN
TYLER CROOK

TC: This bookplate was done for Comix Experience in San Francisco. I was trying to evoke book cover designs from the thirties and forties. It worked out okay, I guess. I like the poopy colors and the misregistered colors.

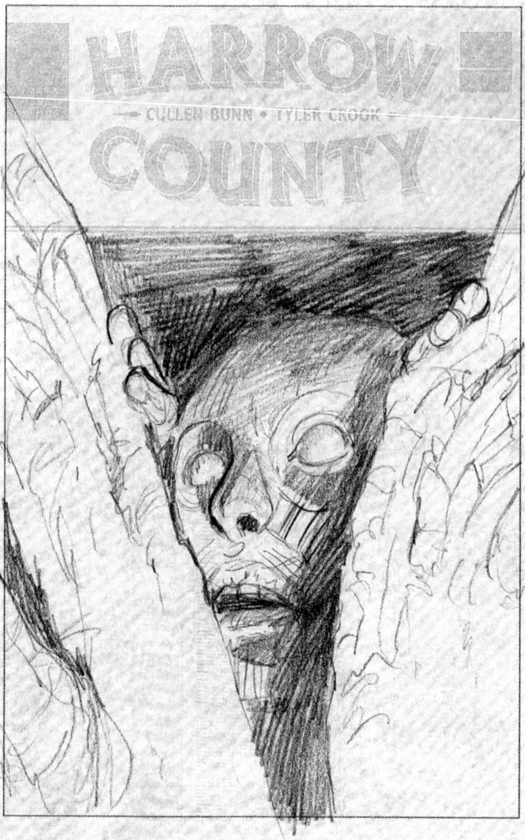
HARROW
CULLEN BUNN • TYLER CROOK
COUNTY

TC: This was a cover that I first pitched for issue #2. The sketch felt so haunting that I kept coming back to it. When we finally did a special Skinless Boy issue, I knew this would finally get used. There is a creepy sense of light in the sketch that I just love.

TC: The first pass I did on the pencils didn't include the leaves. I did a quick color mockup, and it somehow felt flat and awkward. So our editor, Daniel Chabon, recommended that I add some leaves, and he was totally right.

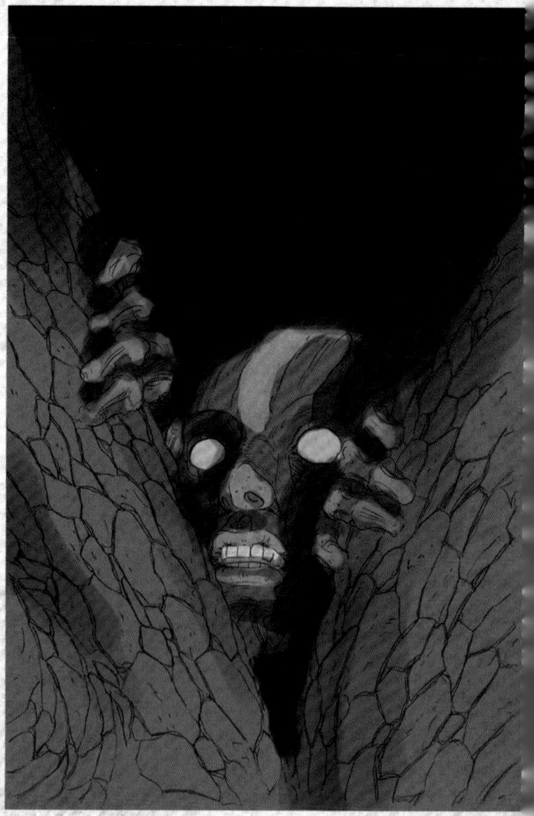

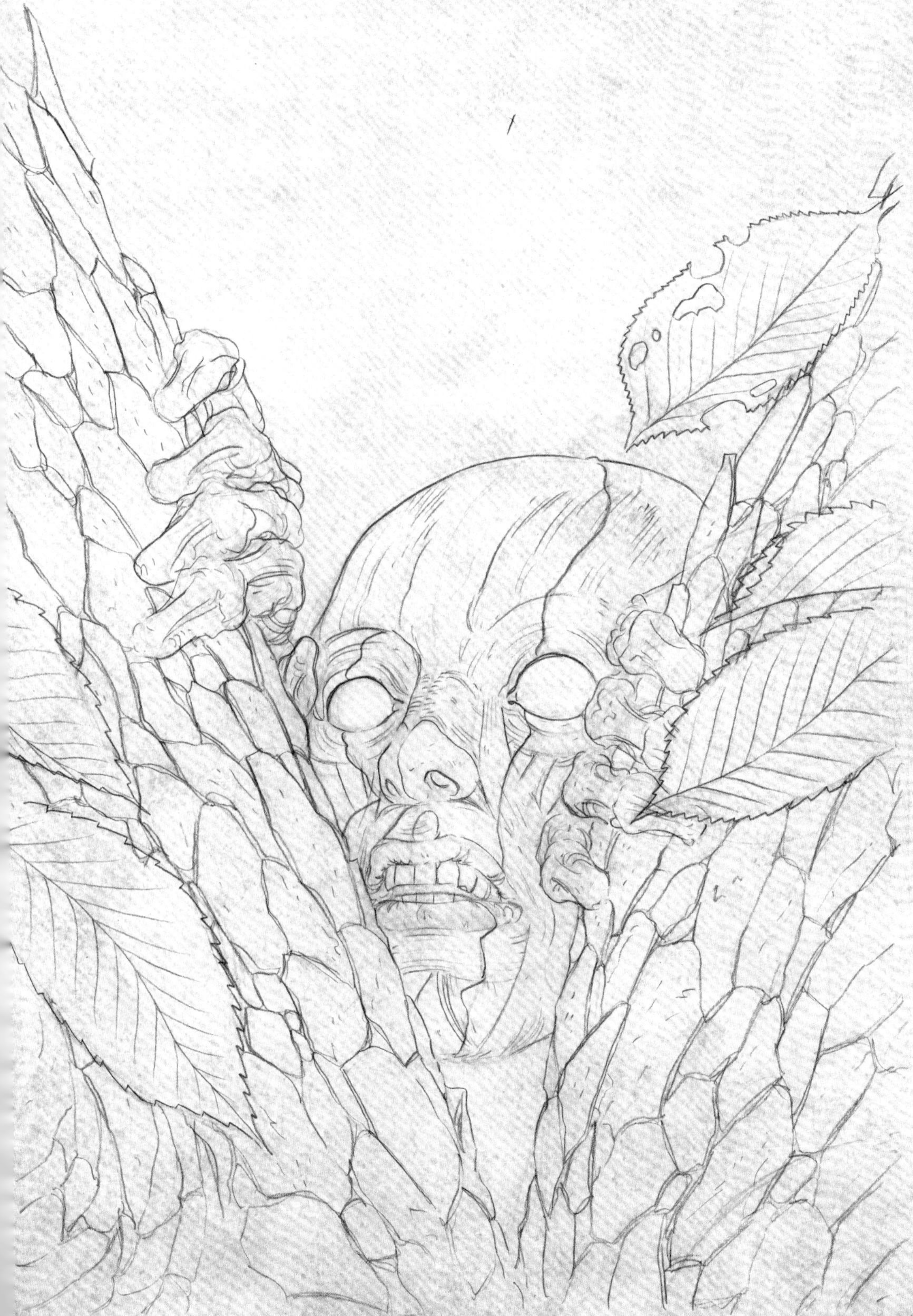

TC: This is what my final pencils looked like for the cover. A few days ago I was looking at the leaves on the right side of the image and realized that I drew the veins running backward. If anyone needs me, I'll be under my desk weeping.

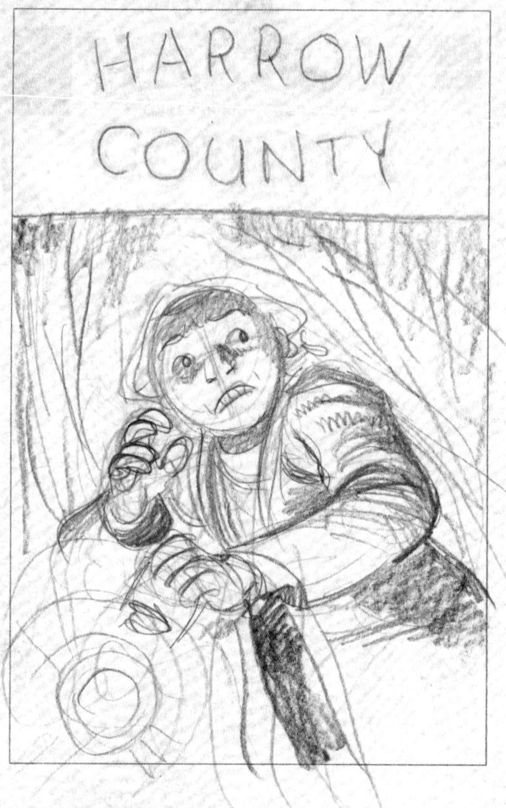
HARROW
COUNTY

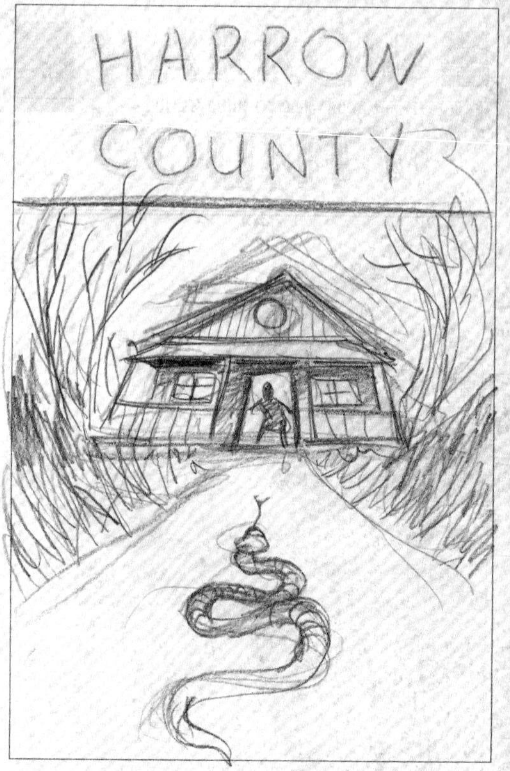
HARROW
COUNTY

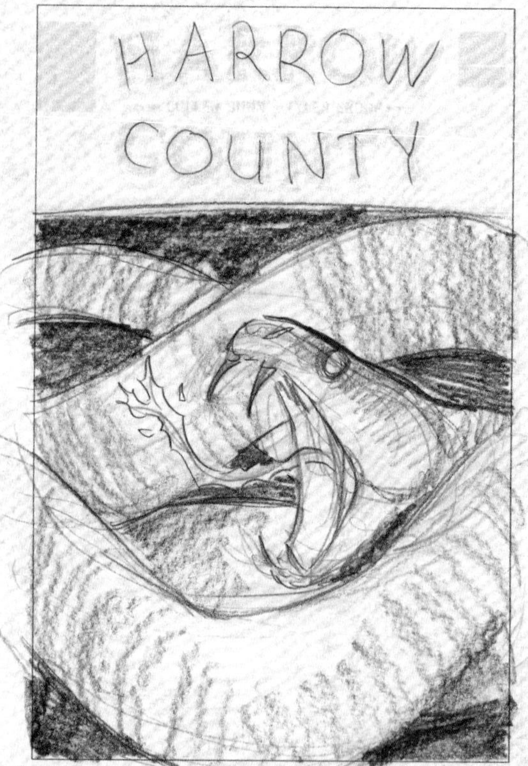
HARROW
COUNTY
TONGUE IS FIRE!!

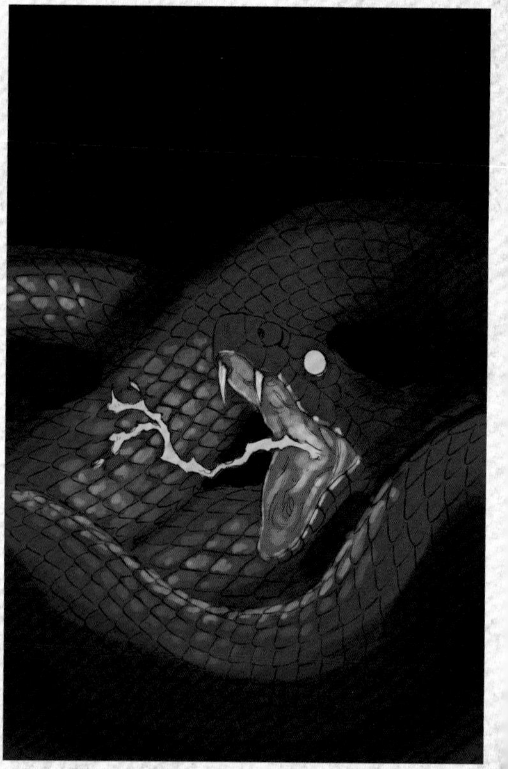

TC: **I think my best covers are the ones where I find a single element and give it a tight focus. You can see how the snake has an immediacy that the other two sketches lack. The fiery tongue is a little silly, but it makes for some cool lighting, so I don't mind it.**

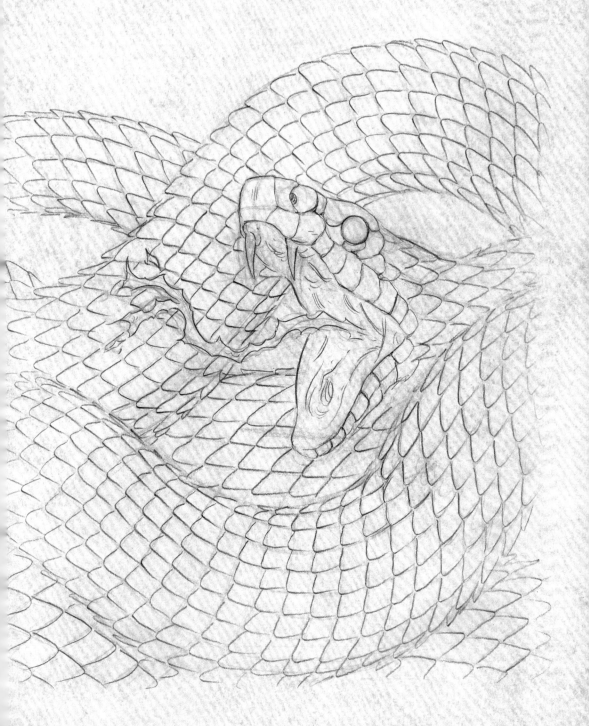

TC: This is one of those drawings where you spend 90 percent of the time just working out the scales. But if I'd skimped on the scales, I don't think the cover would have worked as well.

TC: **These sketches were initially intended for issue #11, but we decided that the cover featuring Bernice should be on the first issue of her story arc. My first ideas kind of revolved around snakes falling on people. Because, you know, that's scary as hell.**

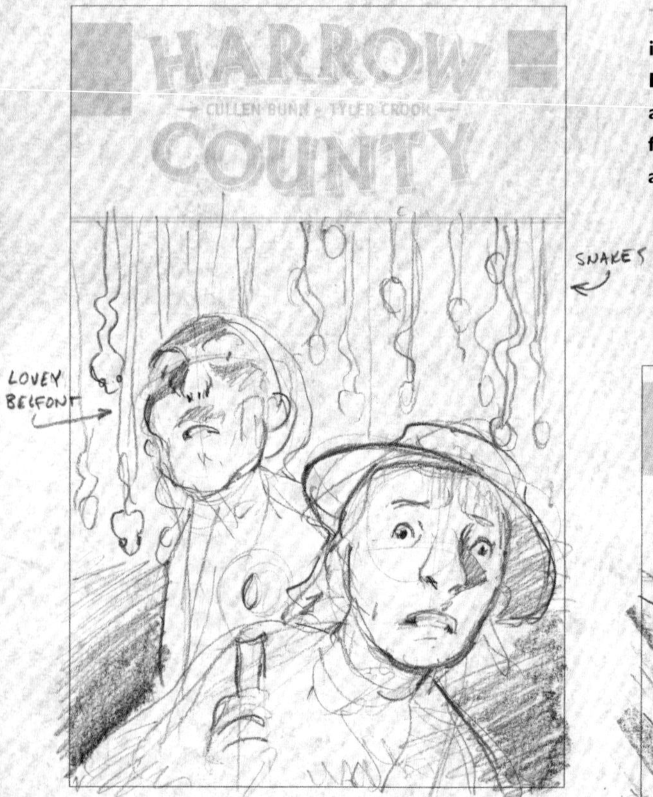
HARROW
CULLEN BUNN • TYLER CROOK
COUNTY
SNAKES
LOVEY BELFONT

#11 (A)

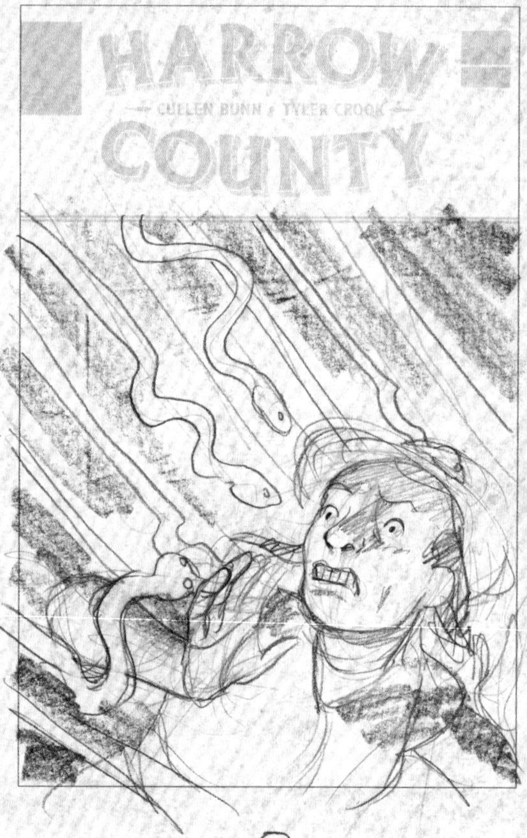
HARROW
CULLEN BUNN • TYLER CROOK
COUNTY

#11 (B)

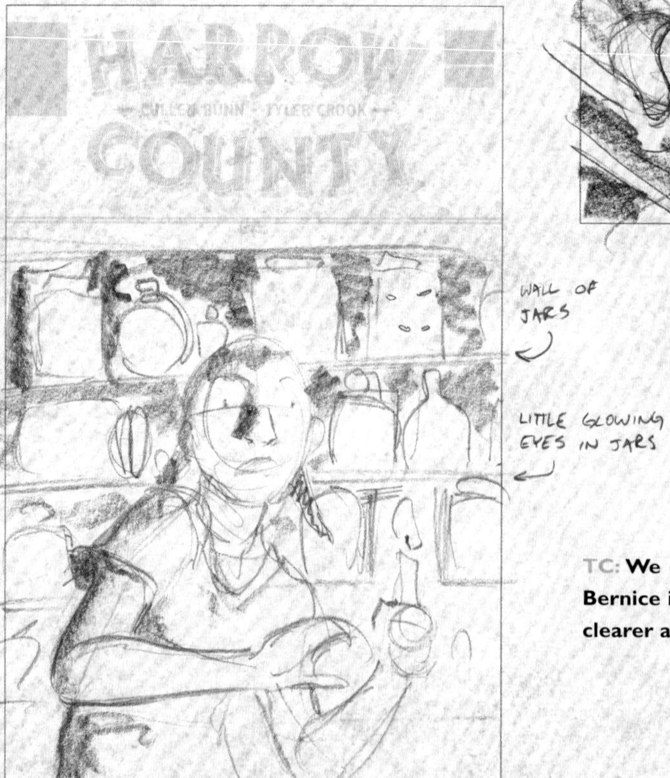
HARROW
CULLEN BUNN • TYLER CROOK
COUNTY
WALL OF JARS
LITTLE GLOWING EYES IN JARS

#11 (C)

TC: **We ended up going with the simple shot of Bernice in front of the wall of jars because it was clearer and had a greater sense of mood.**

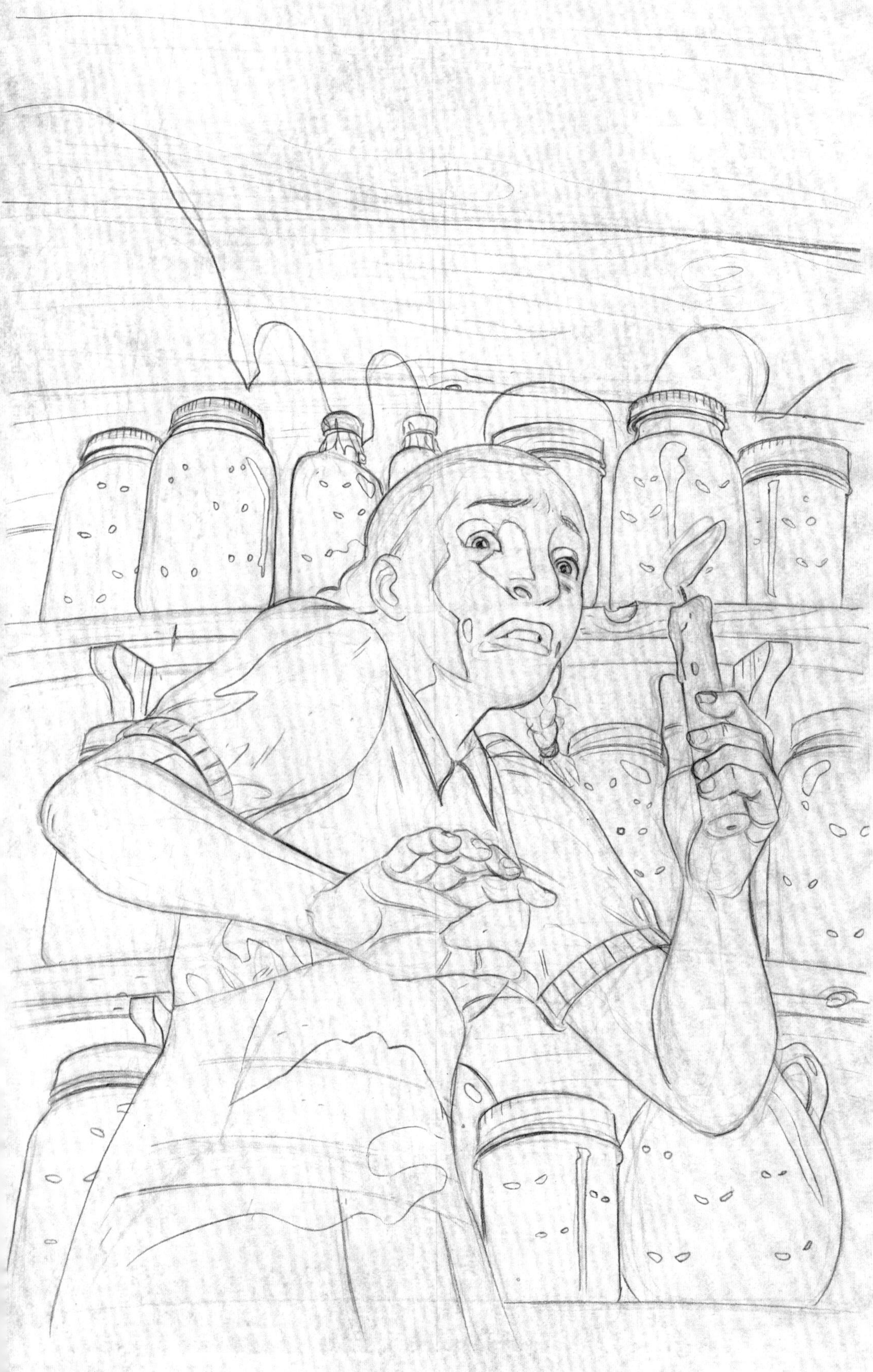

TC: . . . **And here's the final pencils!**

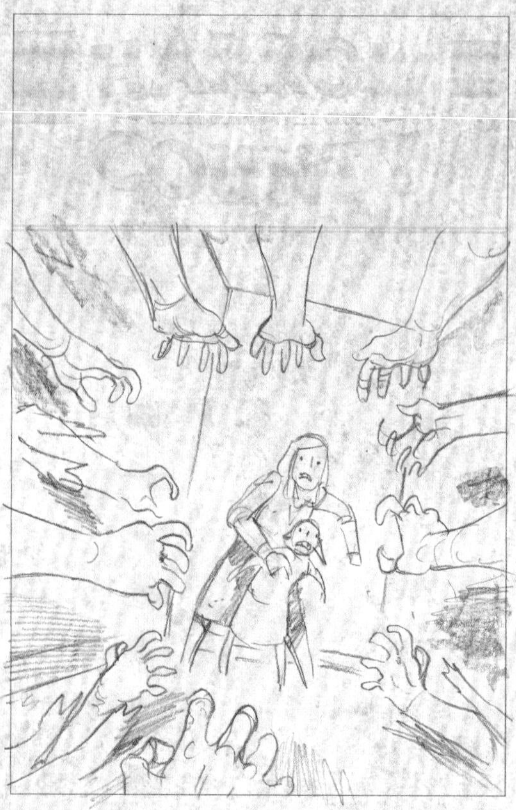

A

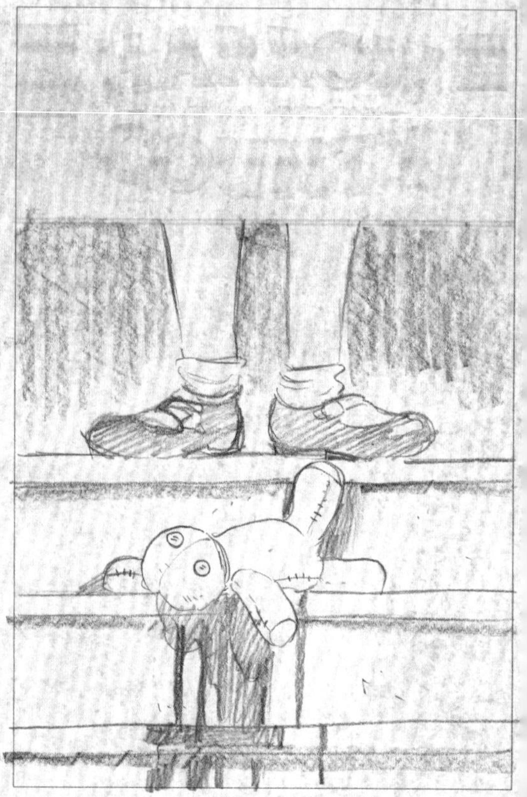

B
DOLL IS
BLEEDING

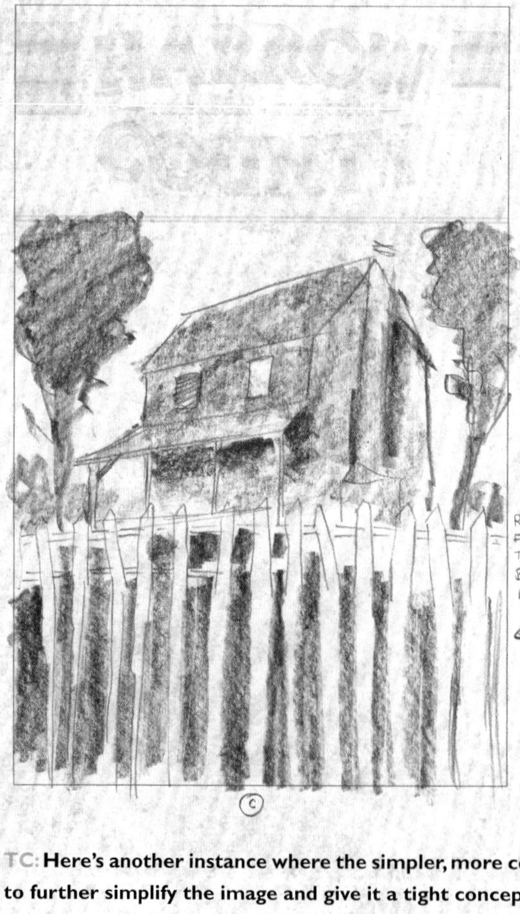

RED
WINDOW
RED PICKET
FENCE THAT
TURNS INTO
BLOOD
DRIPS
C

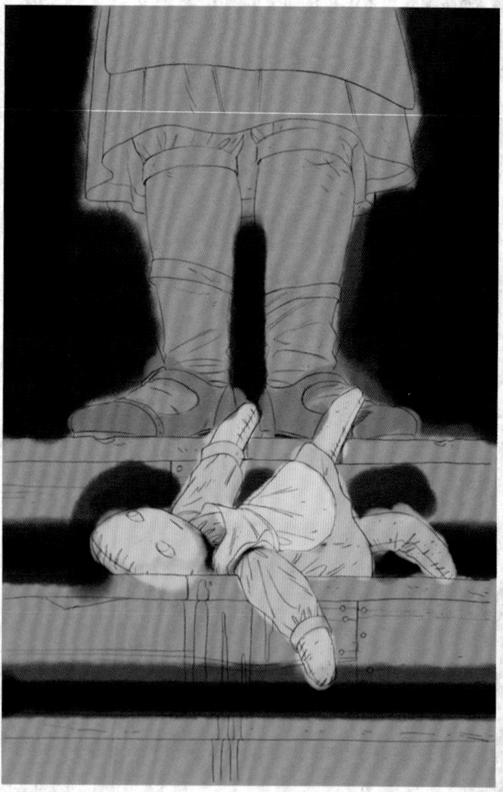

TC: Here's another instance where the simpler, more concise image was the winner. The green color was an attempt to further simplify the image and give it a tight conceptual focus.

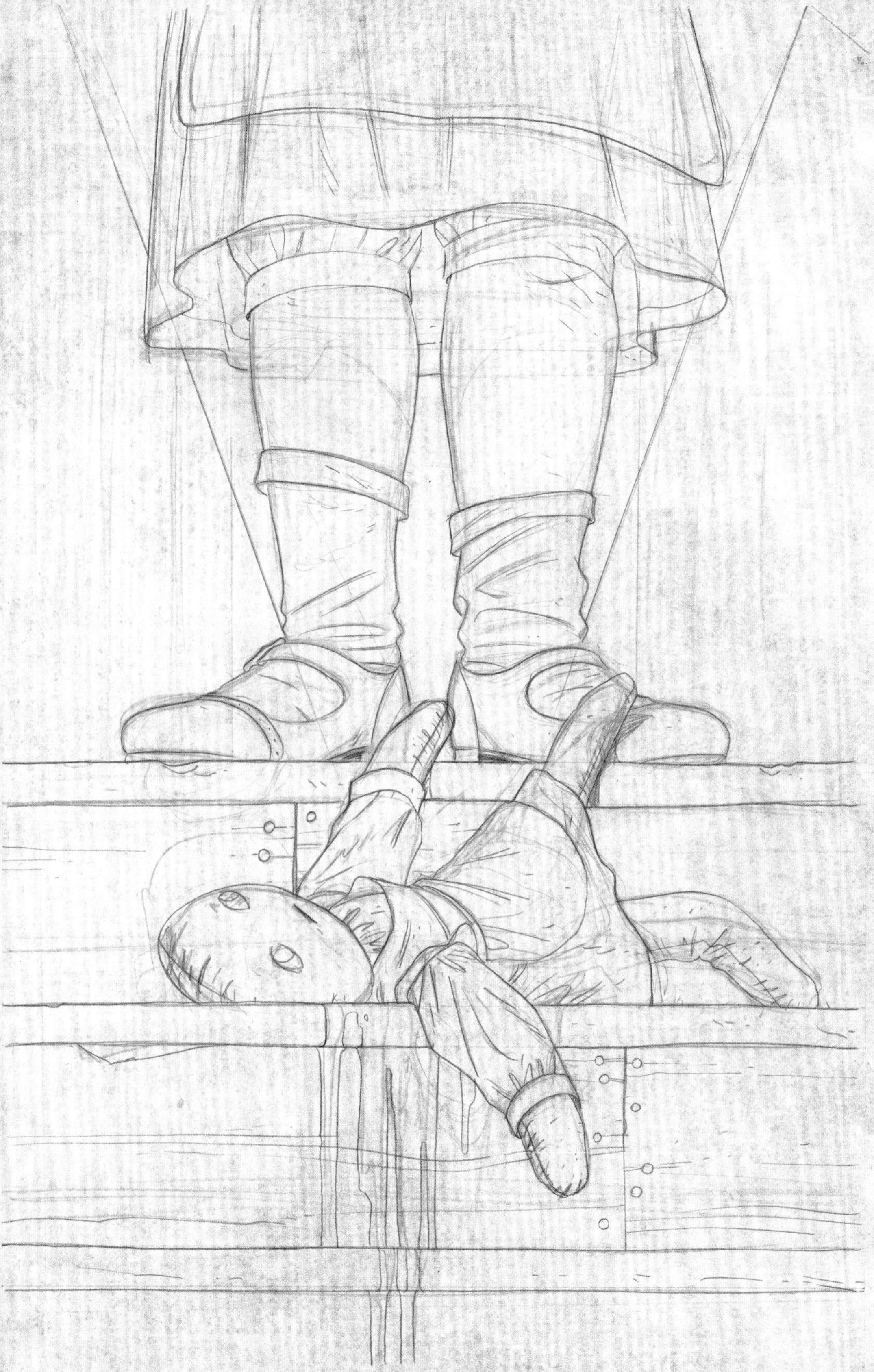

TC: . . . And more pencils! I think it's interesting to compare the way I'm penciling now to the way I penciled earlier in the series (seen on the following pages).

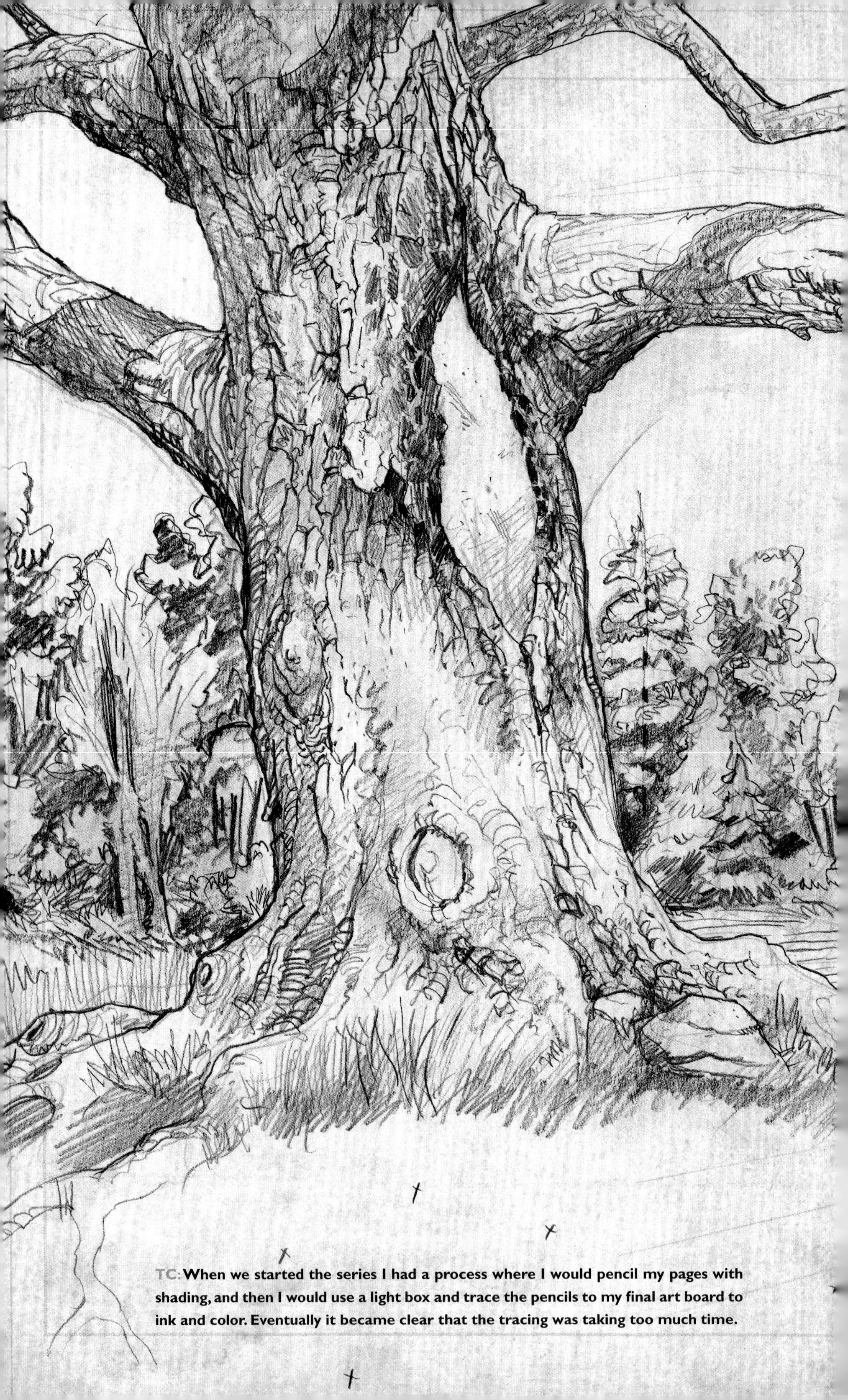

TC: When we started the series I had a process where I would pencil my pages with shading, and then I would use a light box and trace the pencils to my final art board to ink and color. Eventually it became clear that the tracing was taking too much time.

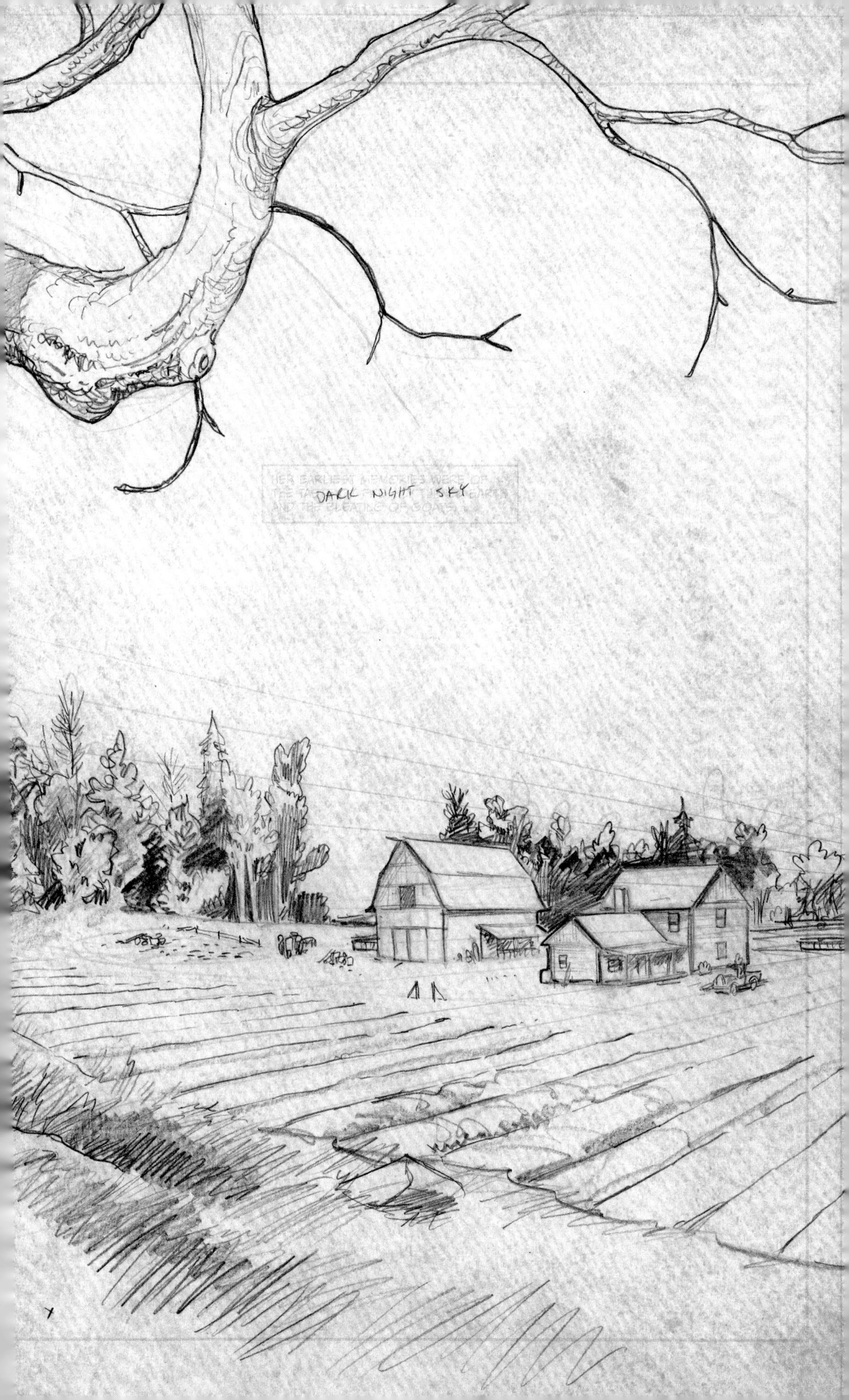
HER EARLIEST MEMORIES WERE OF
DARK NIGHT SKY
AND THE BLEATING OF GOATS

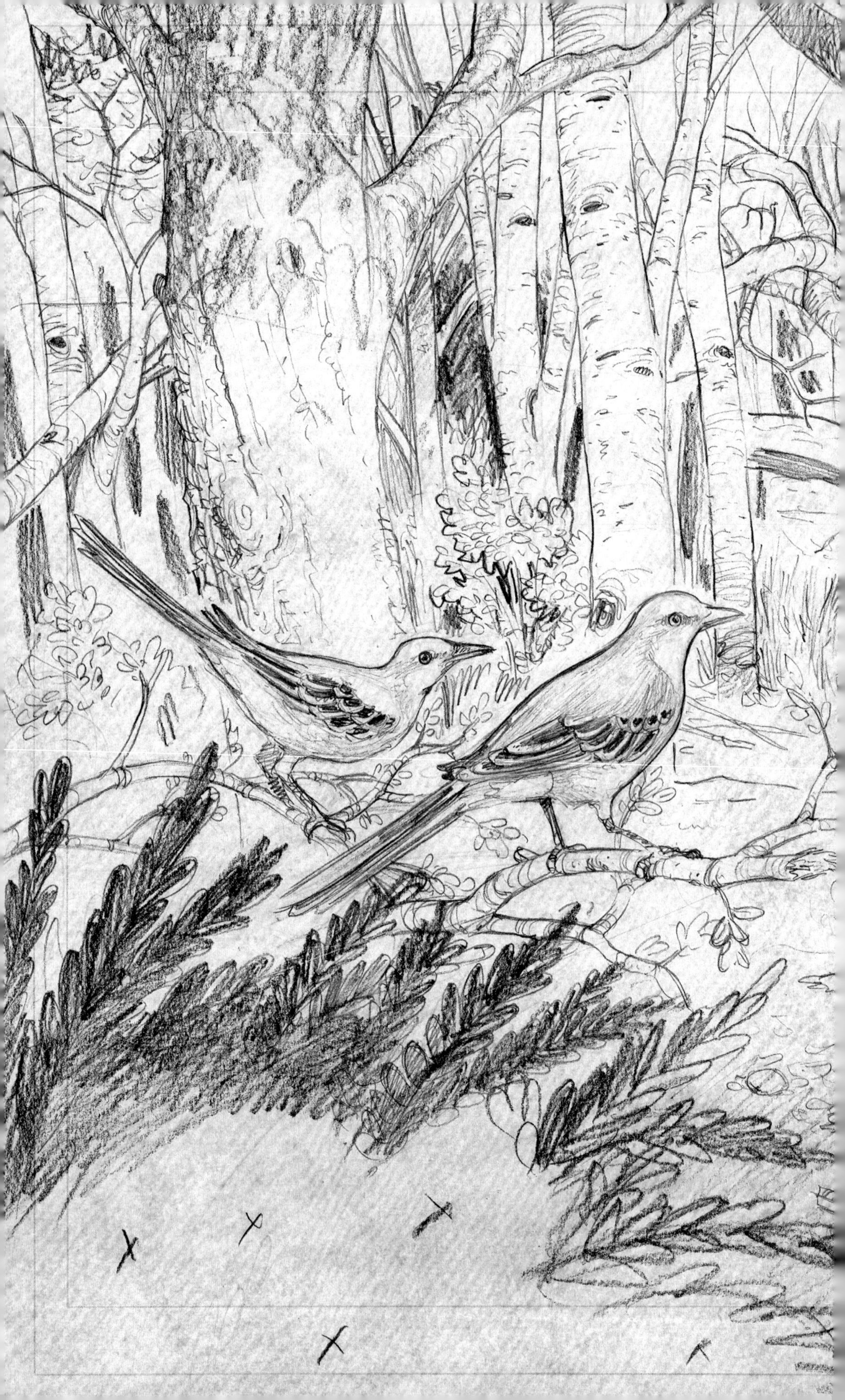

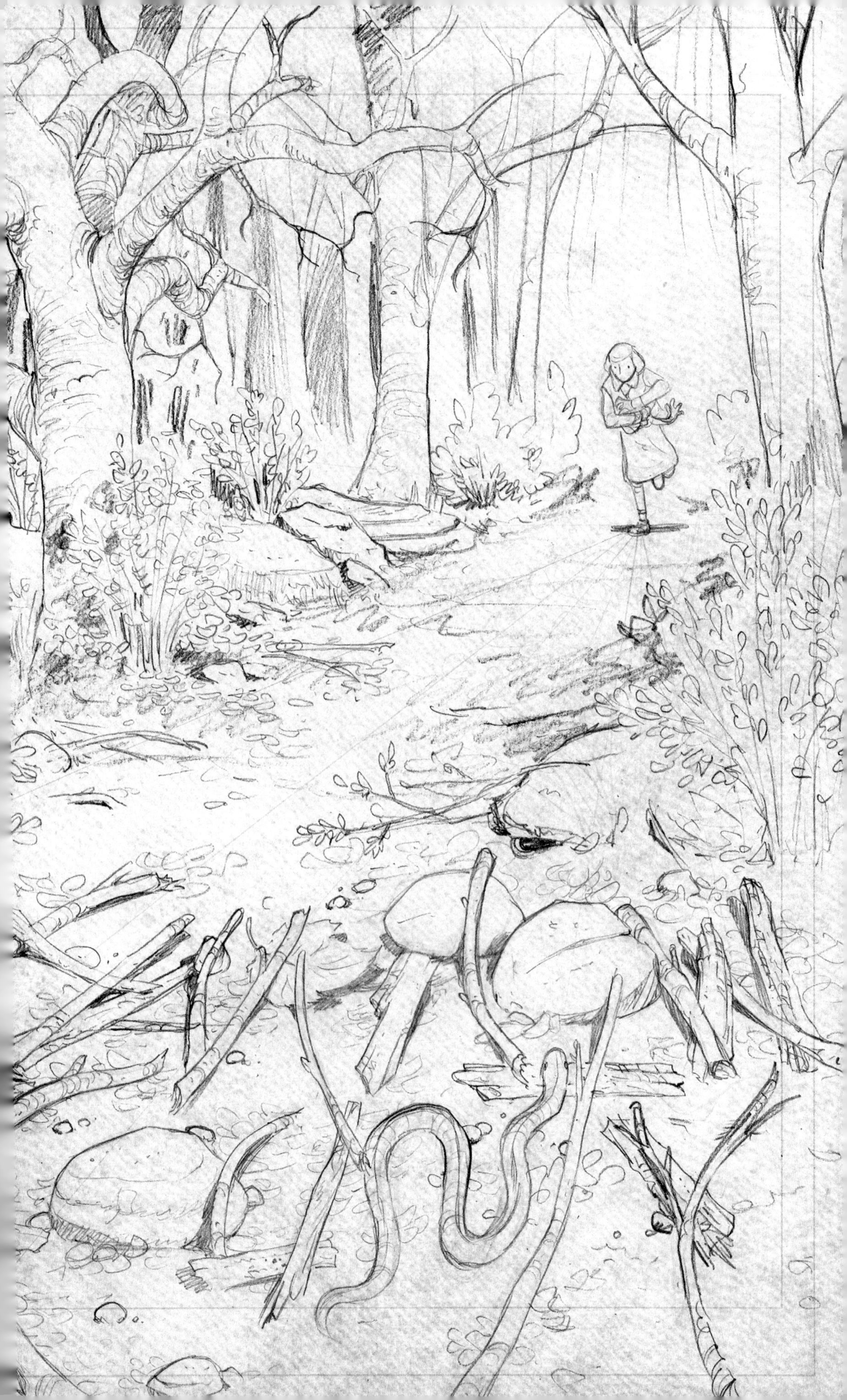

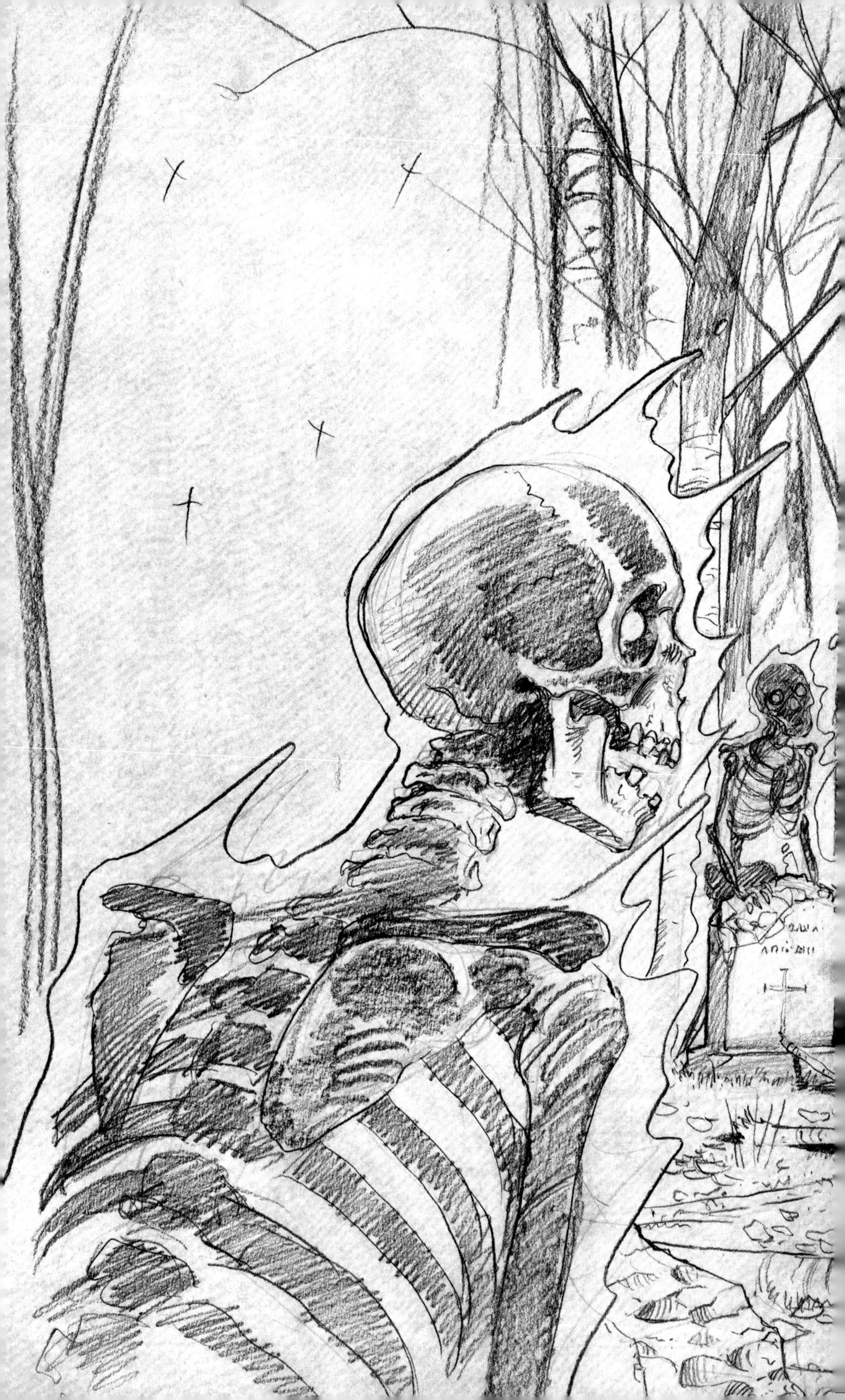

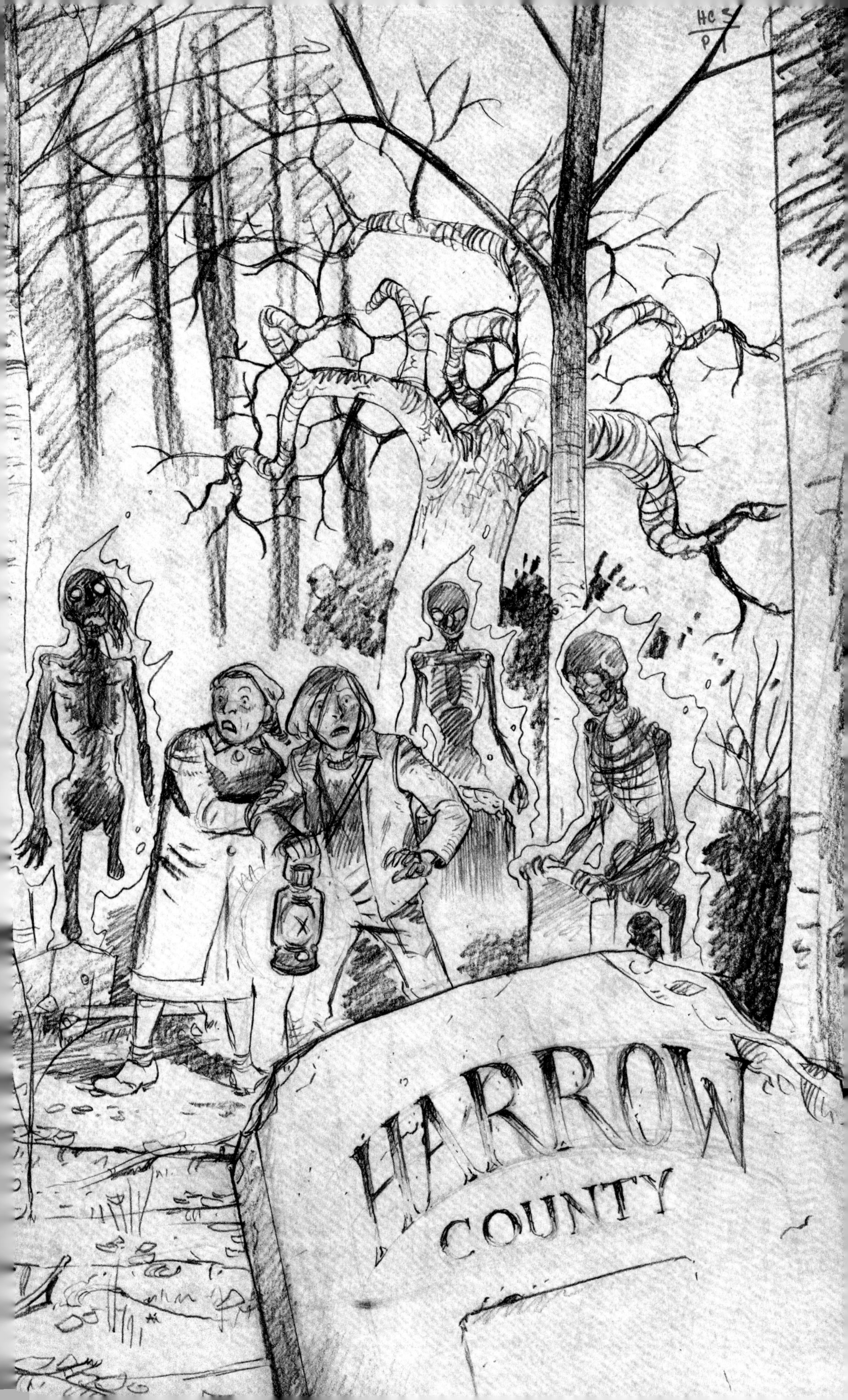
HARROW
COUNTY

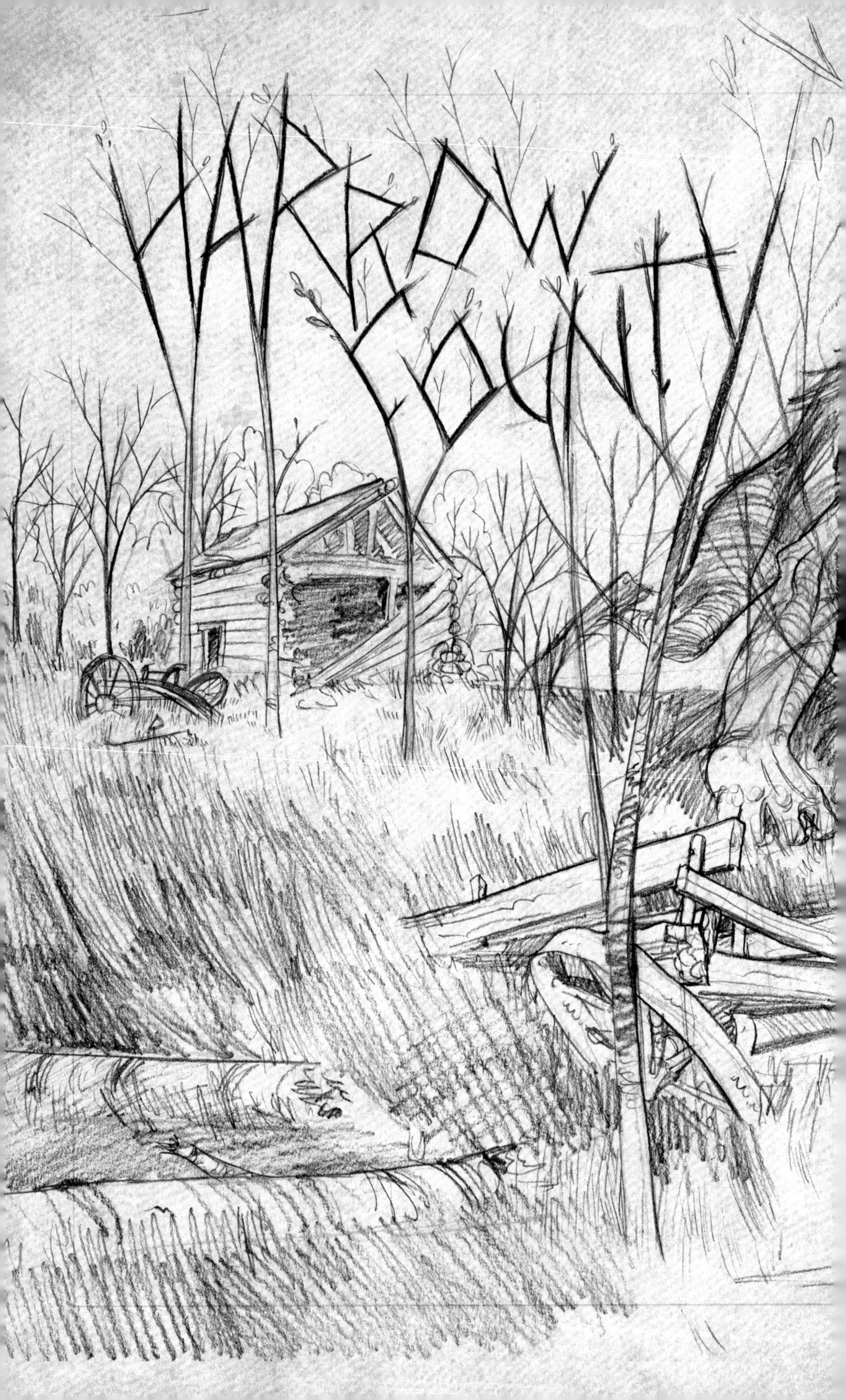
HARROW COUNTY

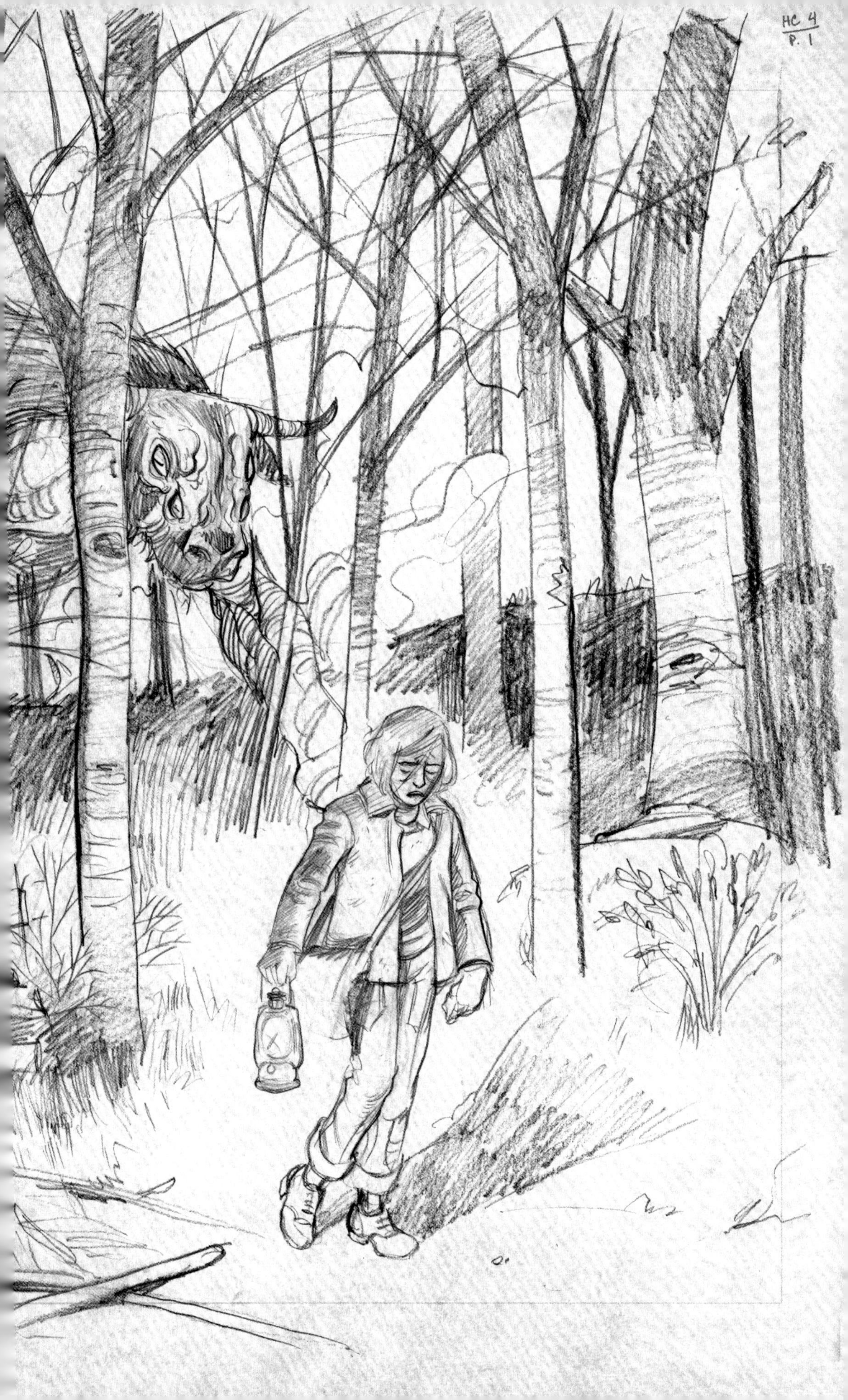
HC 4
P. 1

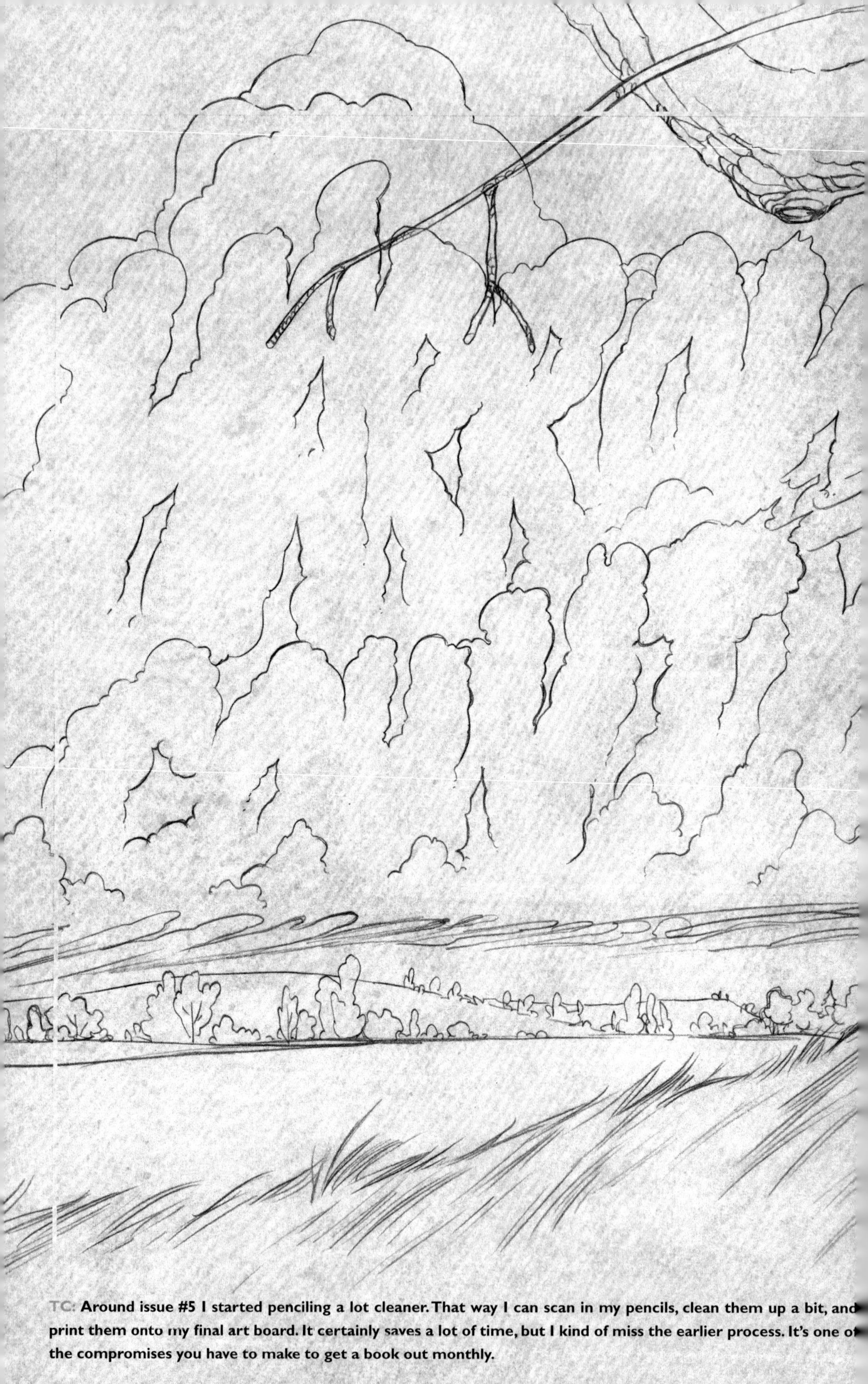

TC: **Around issue #5 I started penciling a lot cleaner. That way I can scan in my pencils, clean them up a bit, and print them onto my final art board. It certainly saves a lot of time, but I kind of miss the earlier process. It's one of the compromises you have to make to get a book out monthly.**

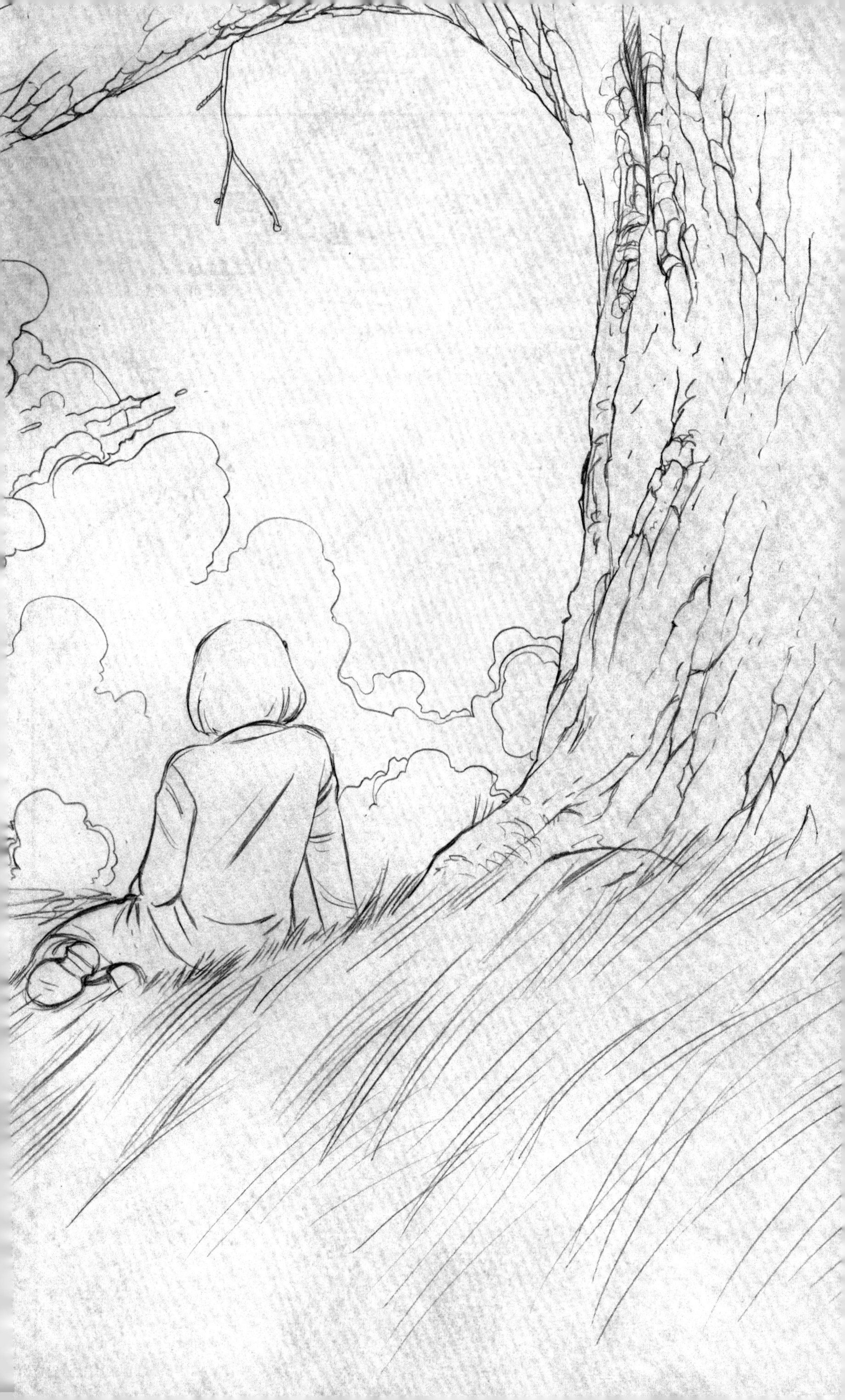

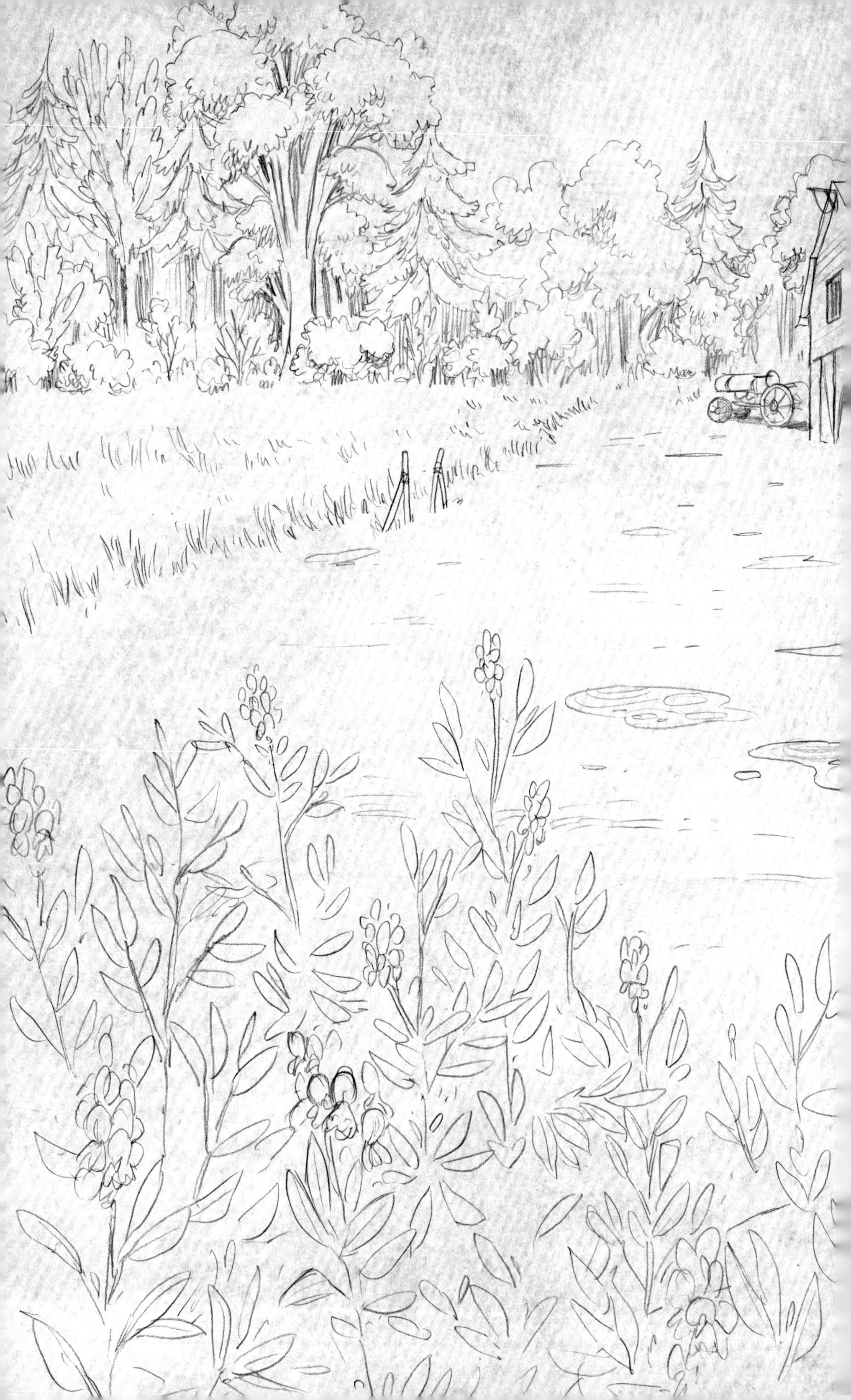

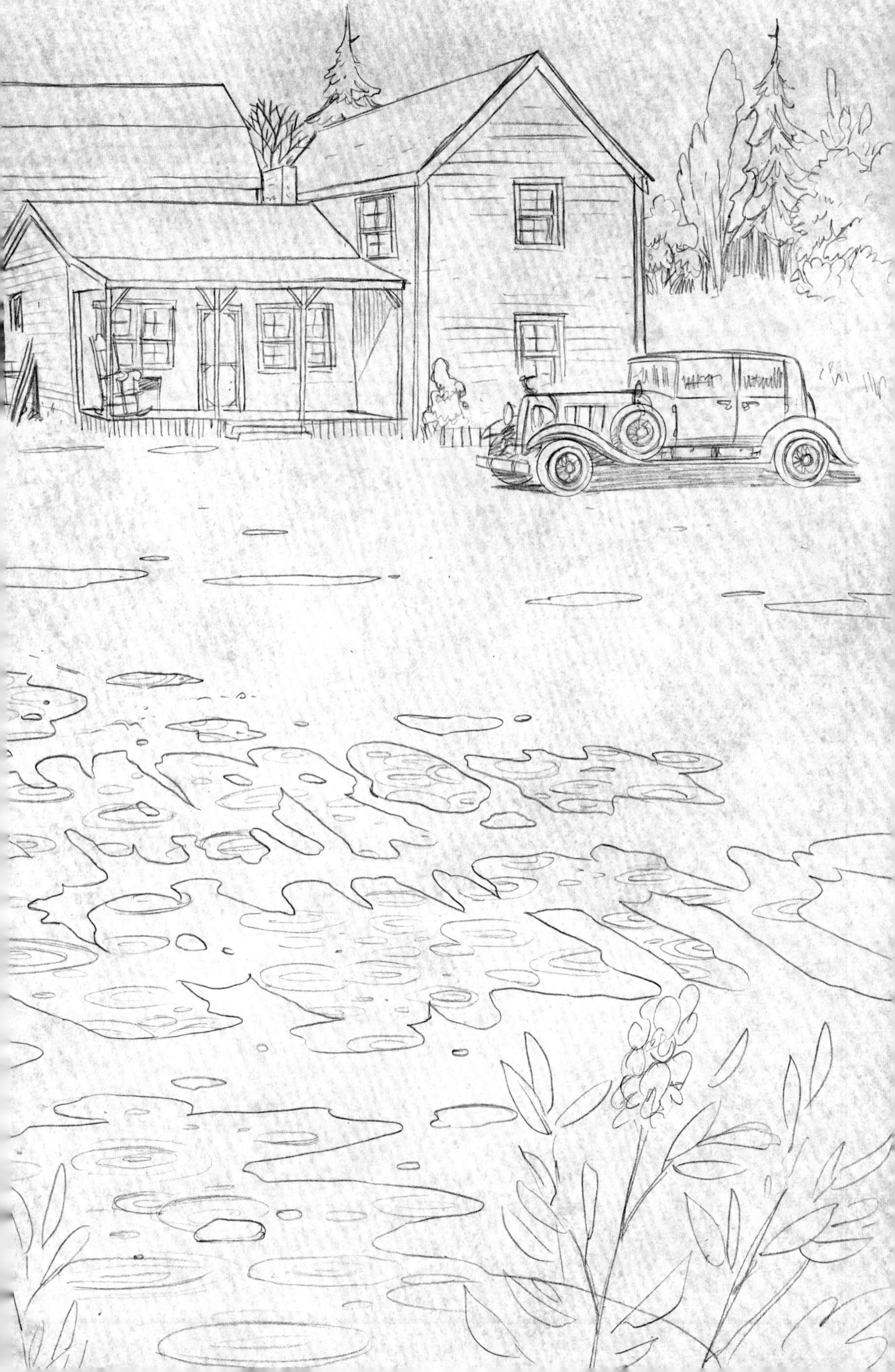

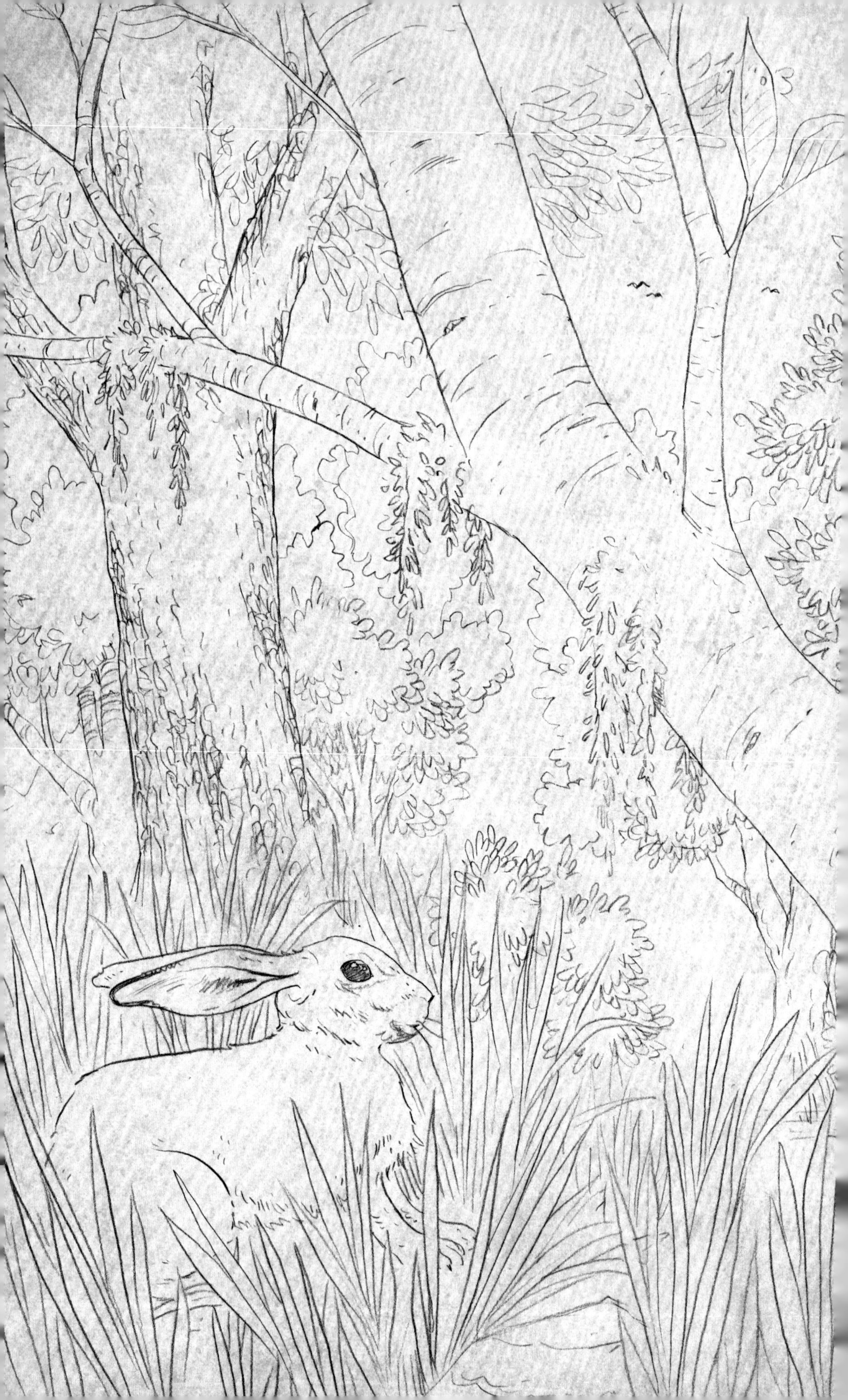

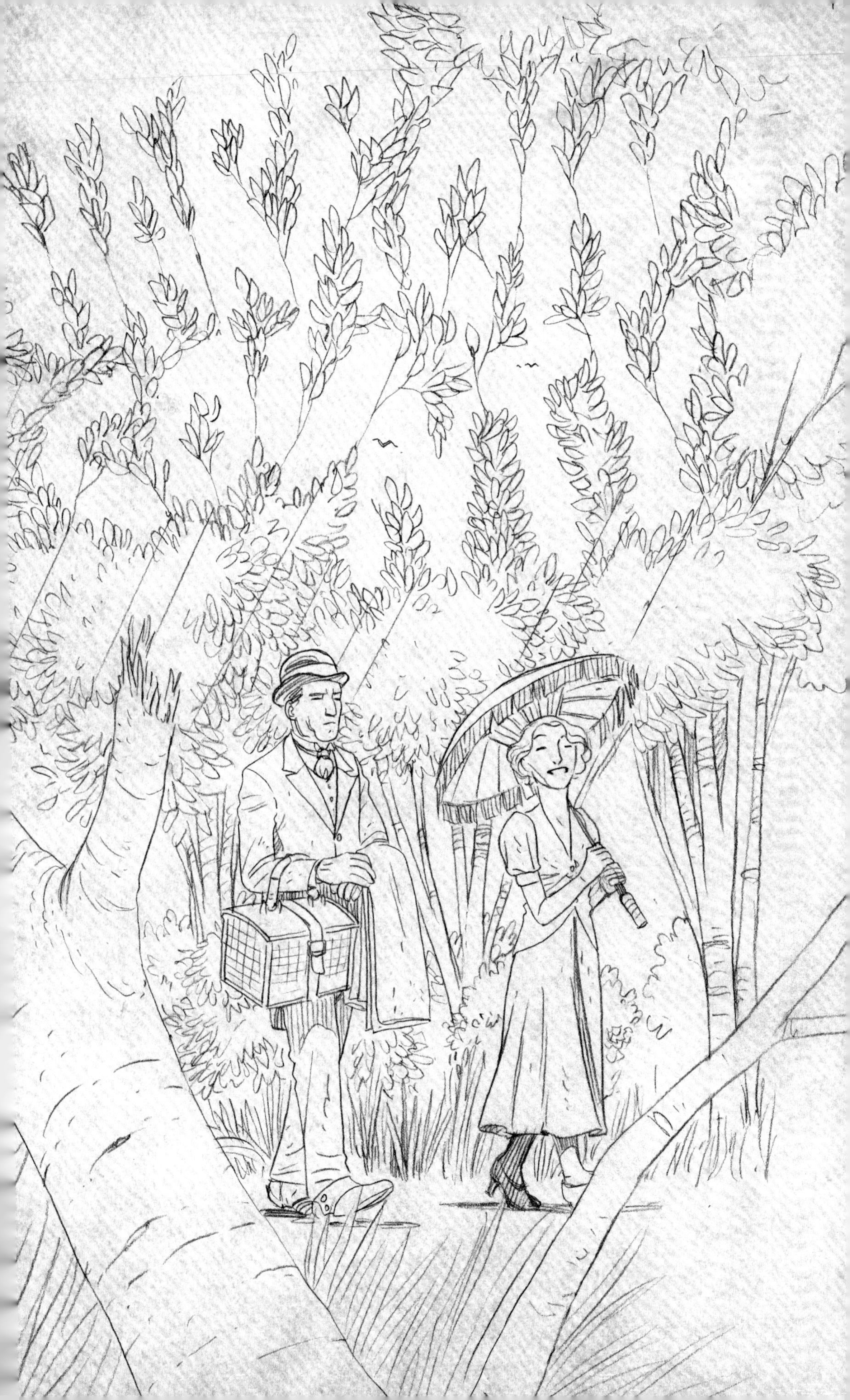

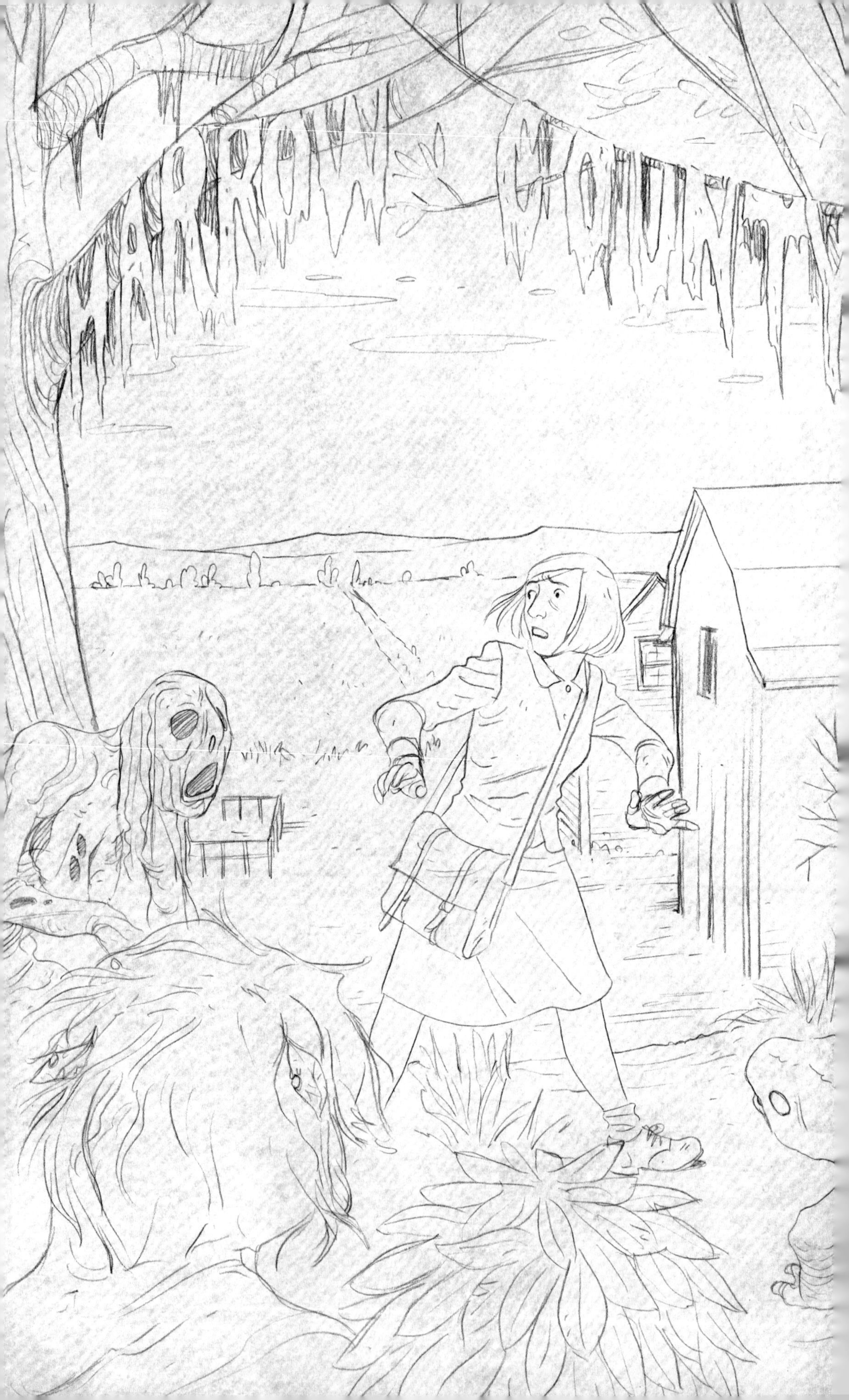
HARROW COUNTY

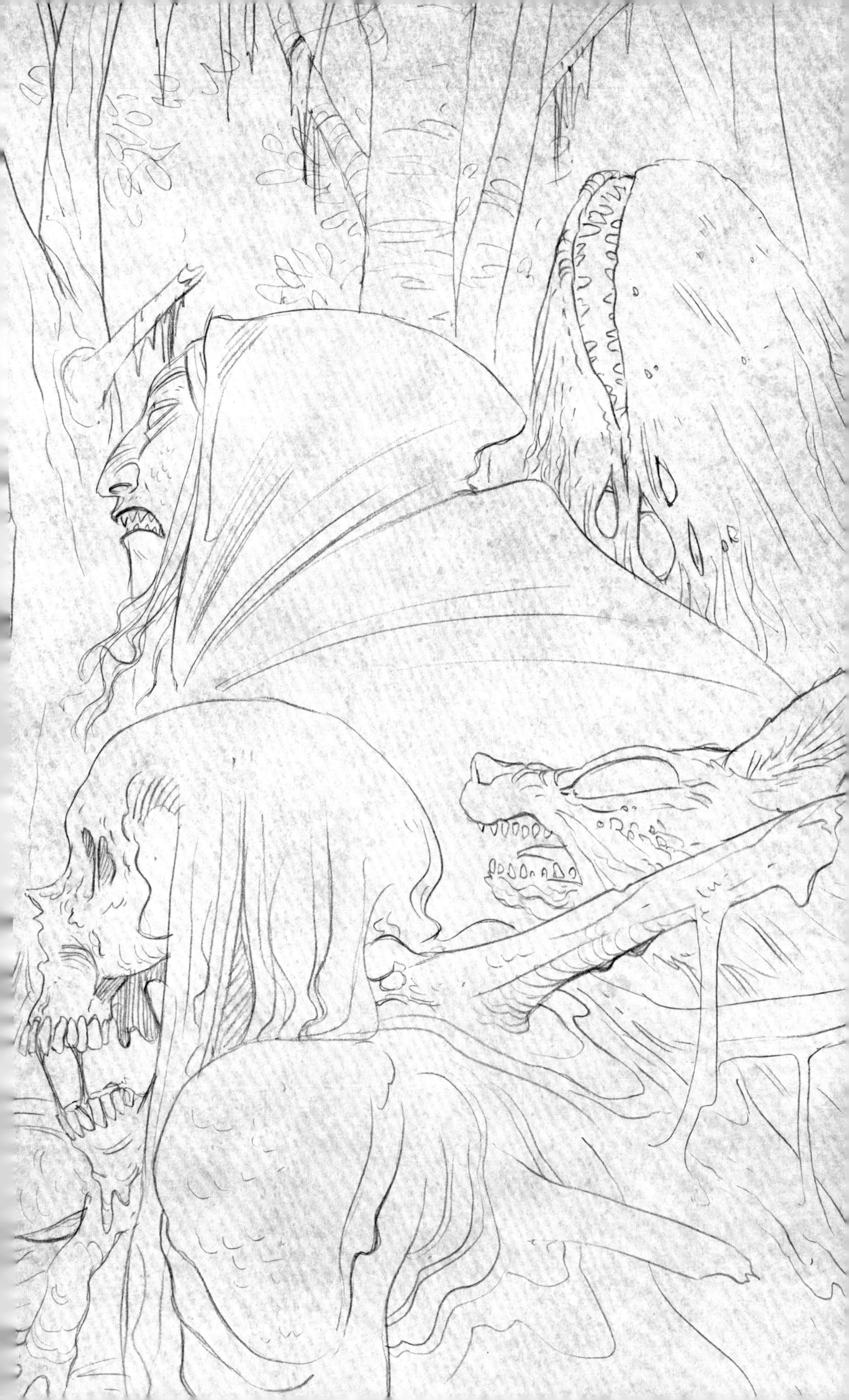

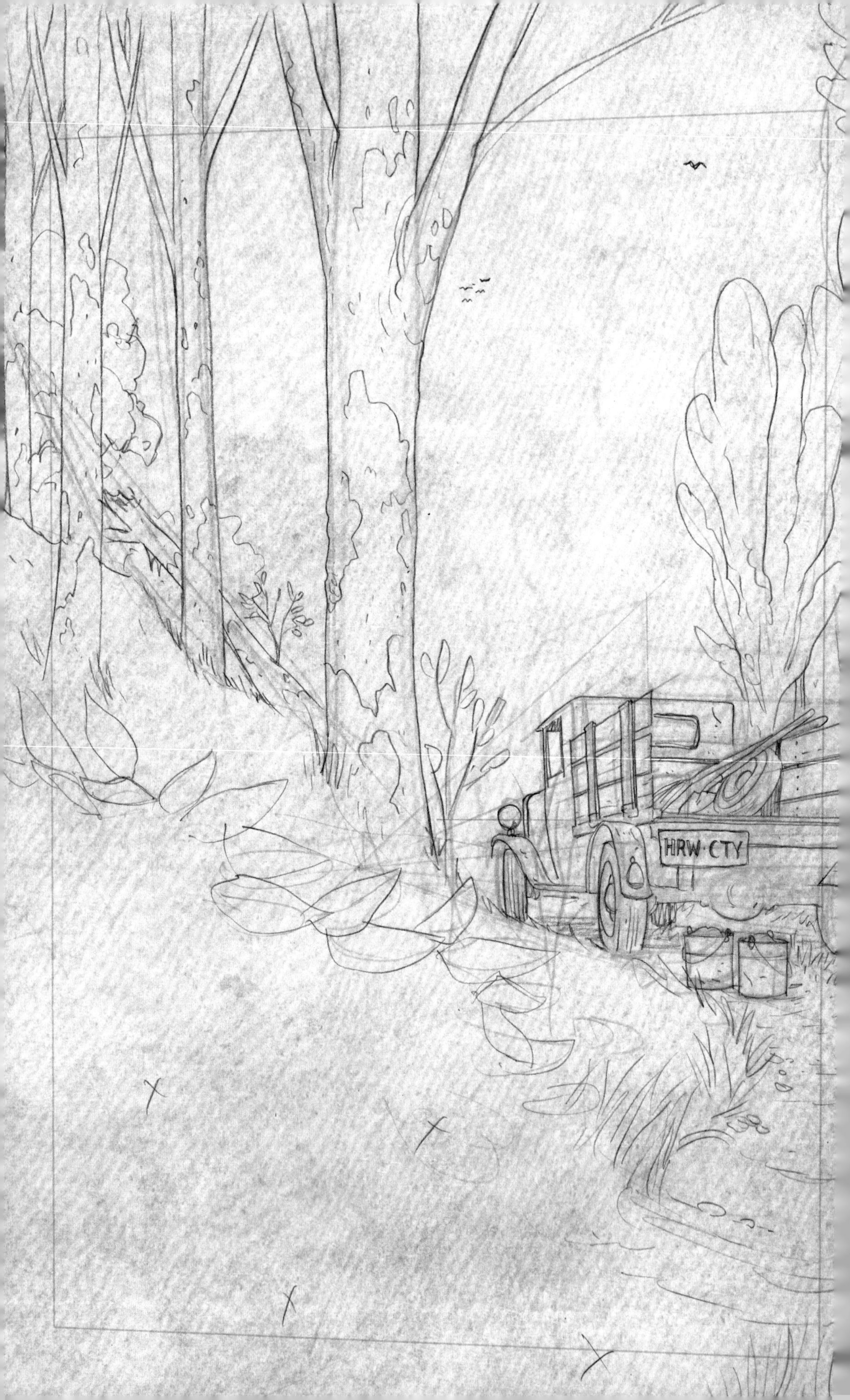
HRW·CTY

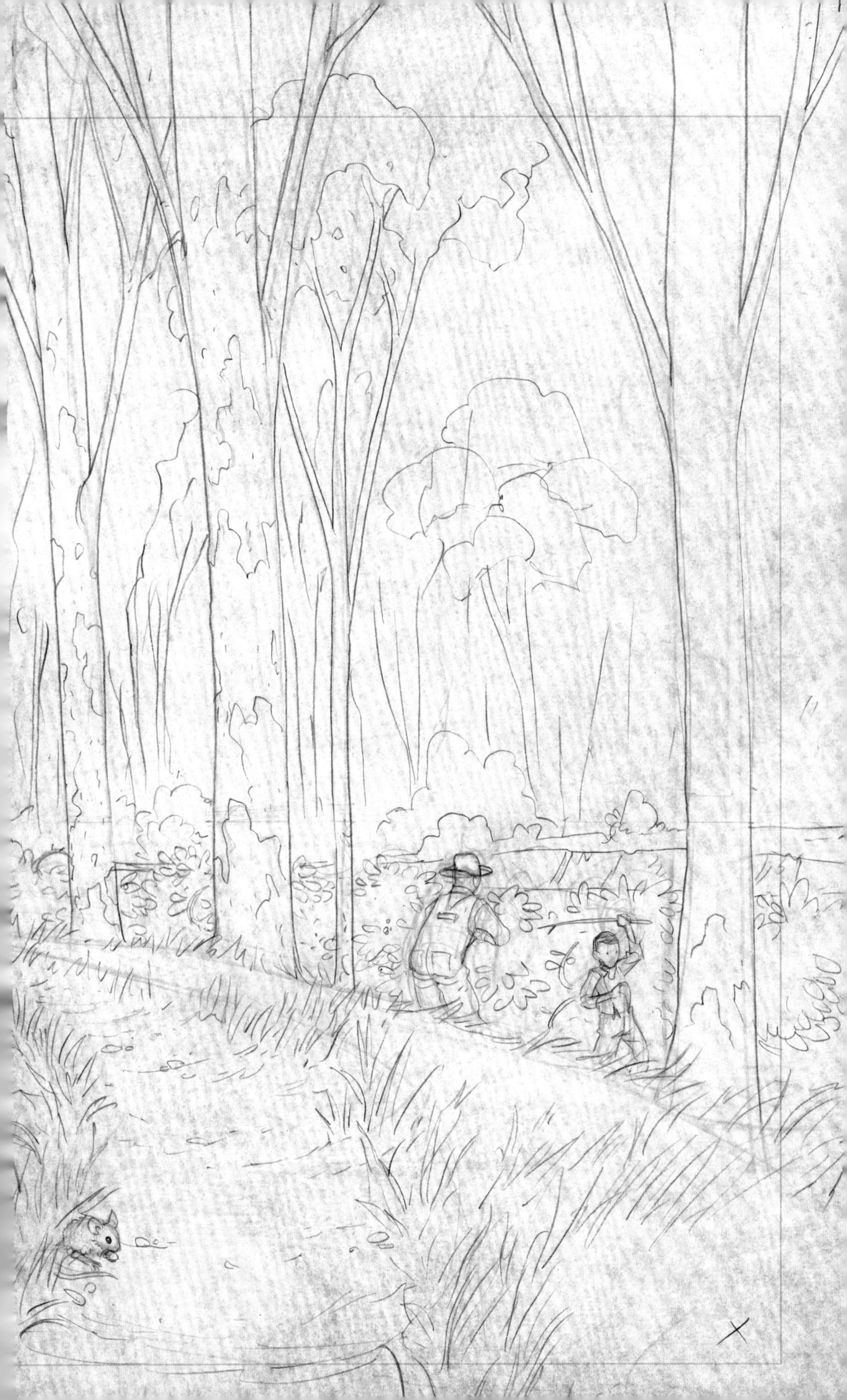

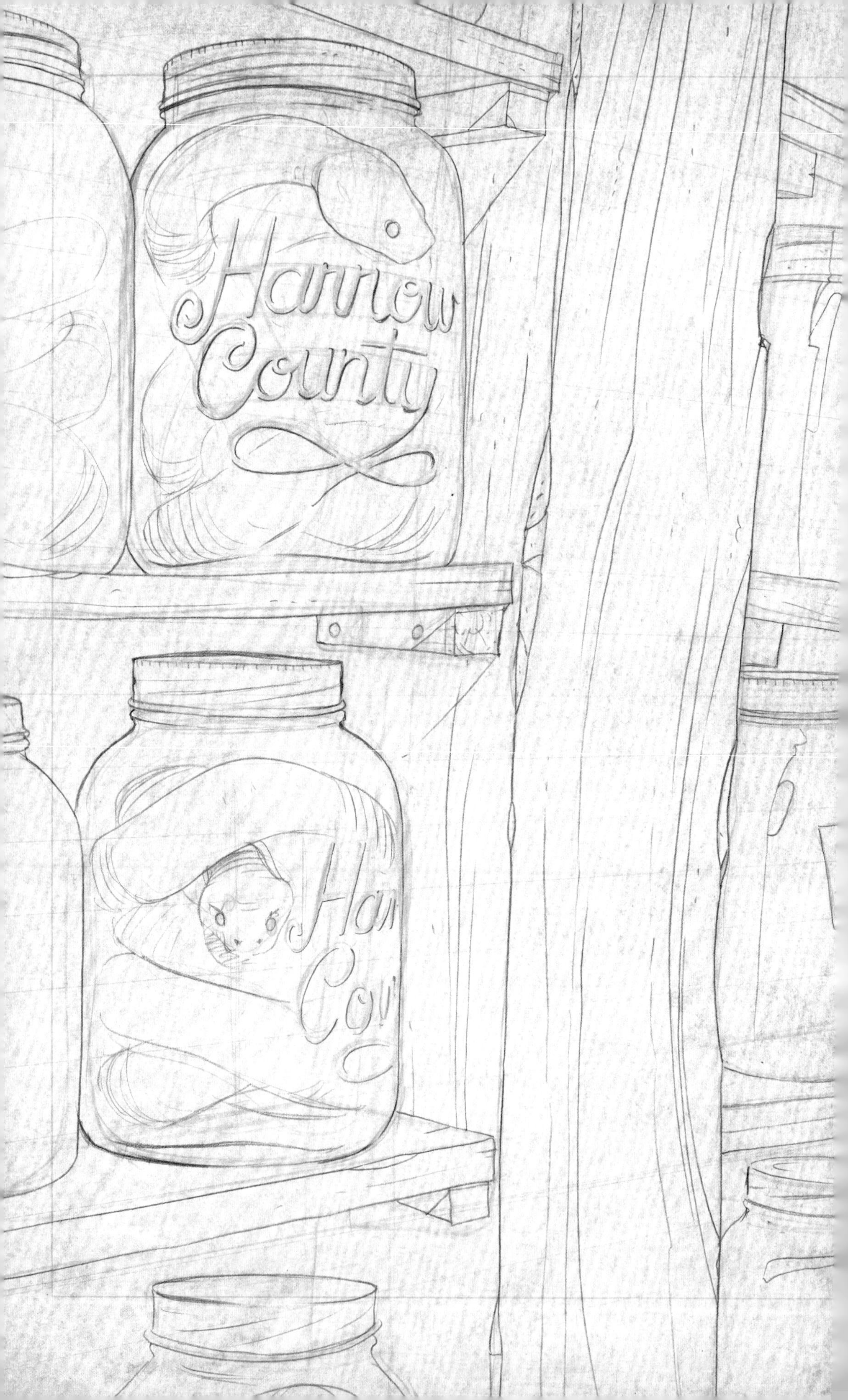
Harrow County

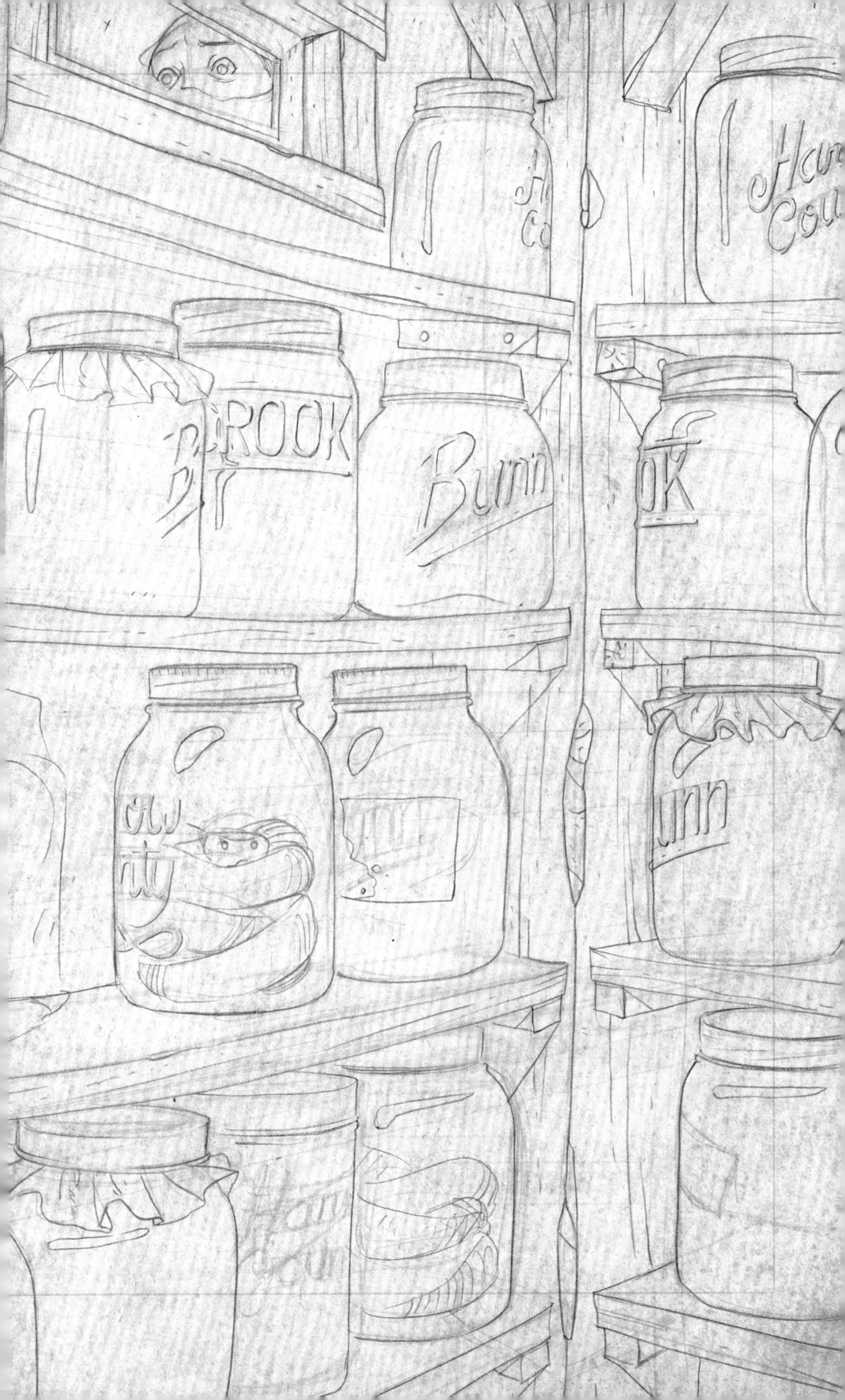
ROOK

PAINTING PROCESS

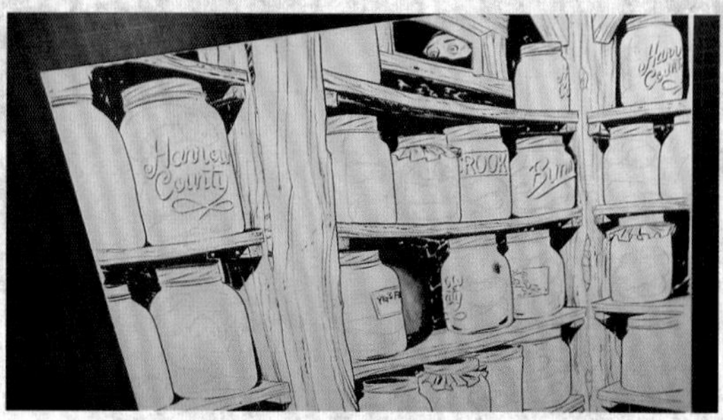

TC: This is the splash page for issue #11. You can see I didn't ink the snakes, because I wanted them to feel like they were behind glass.

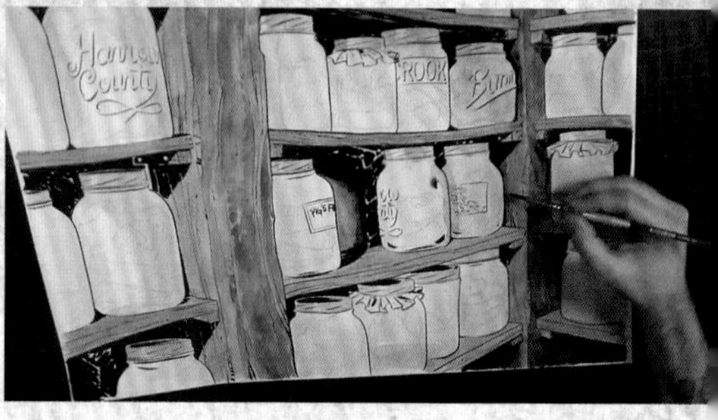

For the wood, I laid down a brown texture and ther went back in with blacks and blues to add shadows.

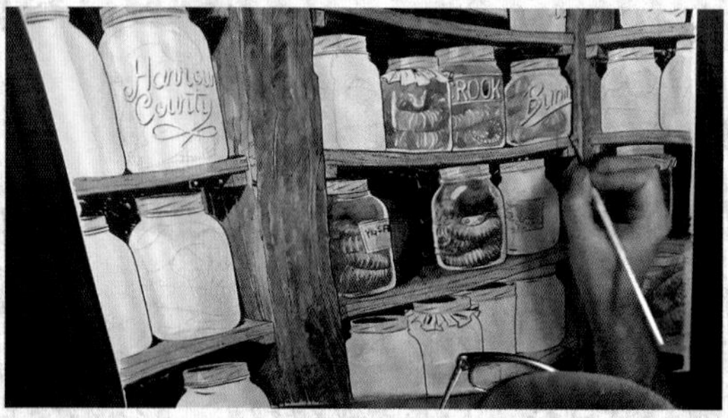

I painted the snakes by building up layers of blue and black paint. I left areas of white showing through for the highlights on the glass.

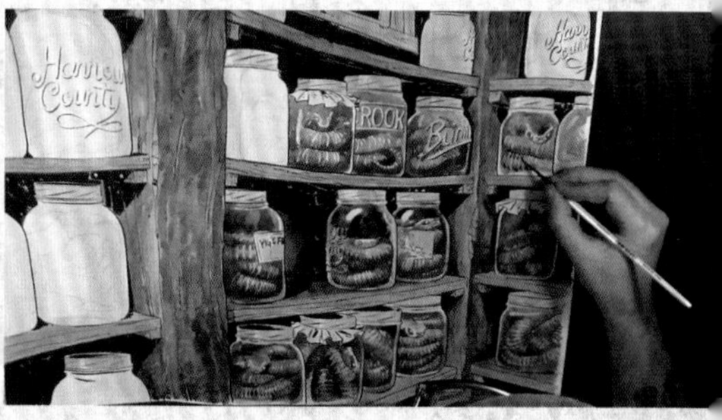

I tried to give each snake a unique pose. And for som weird reason I worked on them in a random order.

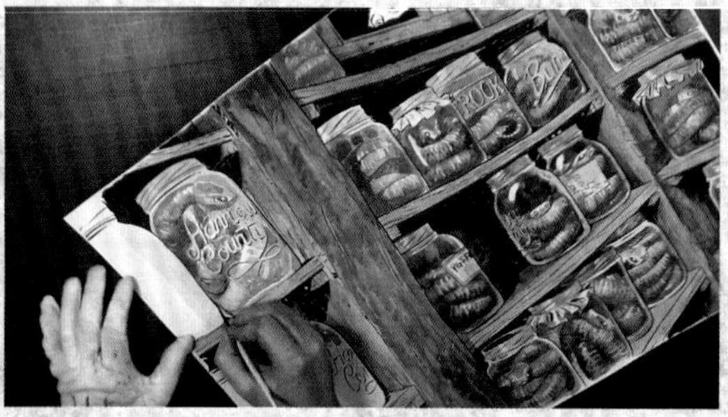

Watercolor paint doesn't like to adhere to oil, so I use that white cotton glove to prevent leaving oily fingerprints on the paper as I work.

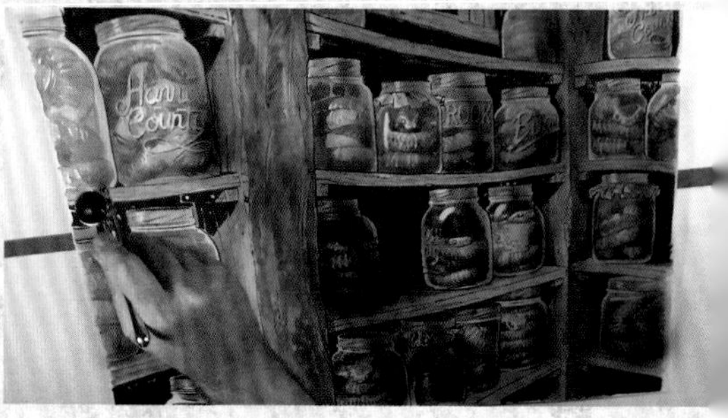

I used an airbrush to add soft shadows to the jars.

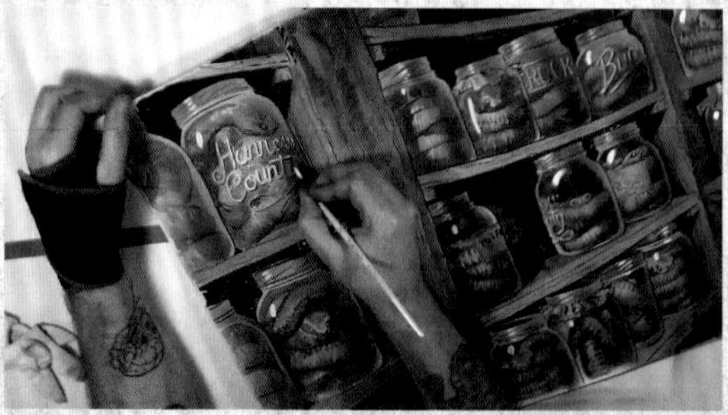

The last steps were to go in with colored pencil and opaque gouache to tighten up the highlights and some of the shadows.

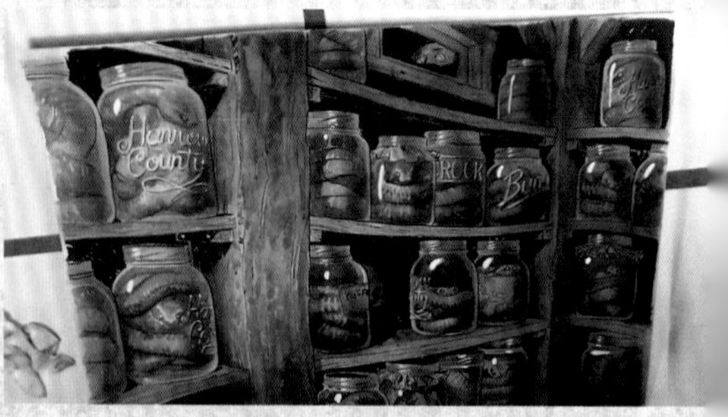

Finally I was all done, so I went to bed or something

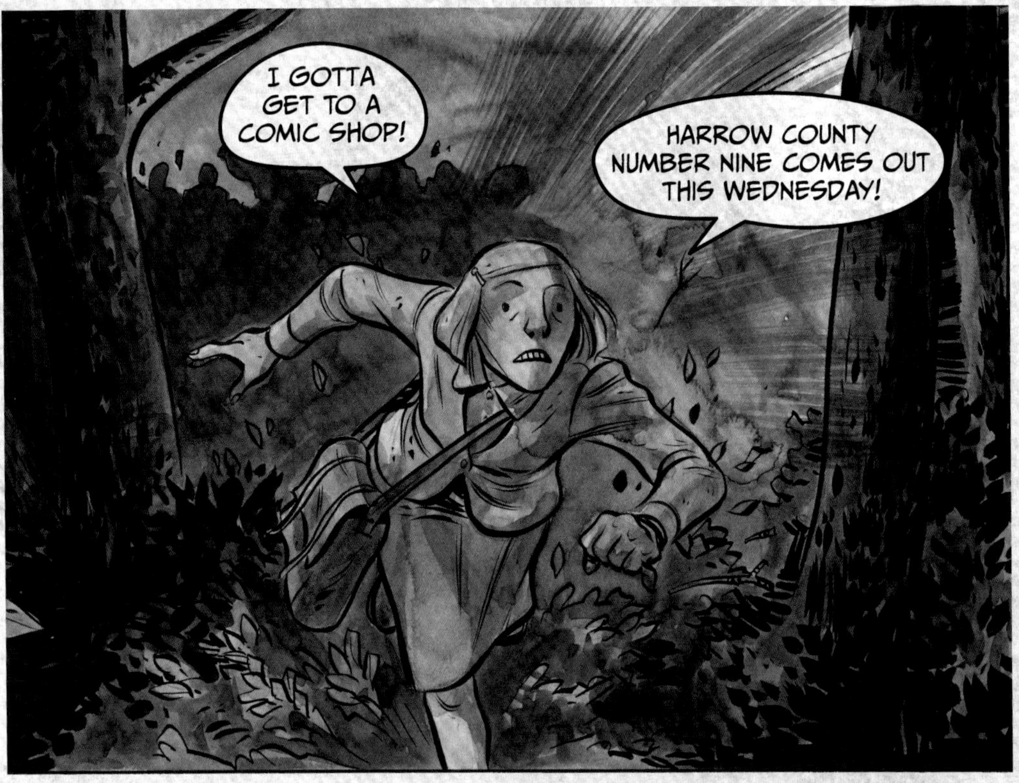
I GOTTA GET TO A COMIC SHOP!
HARROW COUNTY NUMBER NINE COMES OUT THIS WEDNESDAY!

FEB. 10, 2016

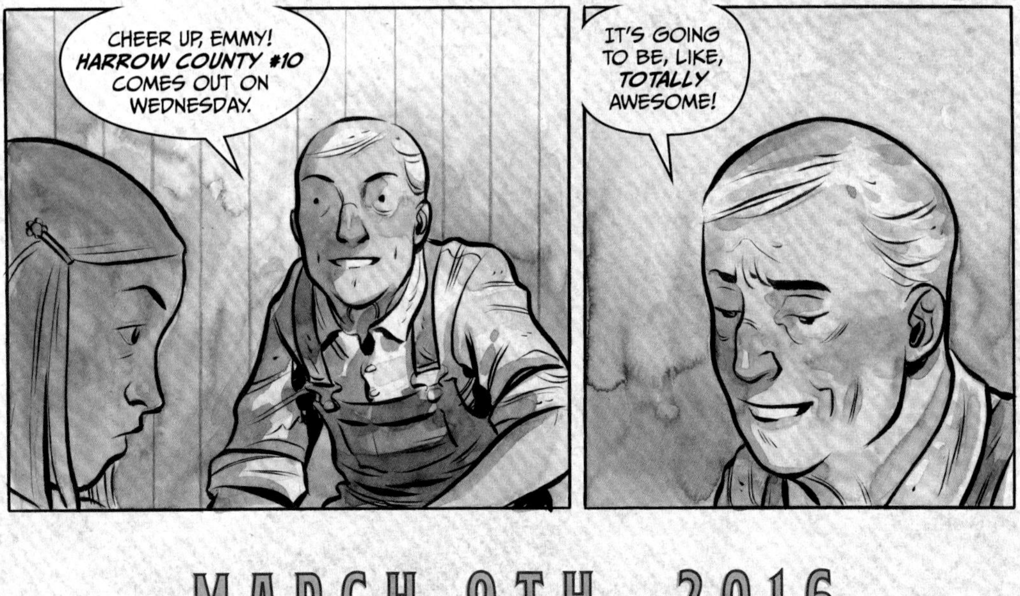
CHEER UP, EMMY! *HARROW COUNTY #10* COMES OUT ON WEDNESDAY.
IT'S GOING TO BE, LIKE, *TOTALLY* AWESOME!

MARCH 9TH, 2016

TC: One of my favorite things is doing these little images to promote the newest issue. It's fun to find silly ways for the people of Harrow County to discuss going to the comic shop.

CULLEN BUNN   A. C. ZAMUDIO   CARLOS NICOLAS ZAMUDIO   SIMON BISLEY

DEATH FOLLOWS ™

Birdie, her sister, their pregnant mother, and their sickly father all live together on a struggling farm. When an itinerant farmhand named Cole comes to their aid, the children should be relieved. Instead, they find their lives spiraling into nightmare, as Cole regards Birdie's sister with menacing desire. To make matters much worse, wherever he goes, the dead grow restless. As the horror threatens to consume her home and her family, Birdie is haunted by a chilling warning: some secrets are meant only for the dead.

AVAILABLE AT YOUR LOCAL COMICS SHOP OR BOOKSTORE

TO FIND A COMICS SHOP IN YOUR AREA, CALL 1-888-266-4226.

DARKHORSE.COM